Flunking Grades:
Research and Policies on Retention

Education Policy Perspectives

General Editor: **Professor Ivor Goodson,** Faculty of Education, University of Western Ontario, London, Canada N6G 1G7

Education and policy analysis has long been a neglected area in the United Kingdom and to an extent in the USA and Australia. The result has been a profound gap between the study of education and the formulation of education policy. For practitioners such a lack of analysis of the new policy initiatives has worrying implications particularly at such a time of policy flux and change. Education policy has, in recent years, been a matter of intense political debate — the political and public interest in the working of the system has come at the same time as the consensus on educational policy has been broken by the advent of the 'New Right'. As never before the political parties and pressure groups differ in their articulated policies and prescriptions for the education sector. Critical thinking about these developments is clearly necessary.

This series aims to fill the academic gap, to reflect the politicization of education, and to provide practitioners with the analysis for informed implementation of policies that they need. It will offer studies in broad areas of policy studies. Besides the general section it will offer a particular focus in the following areas: Schools organization and improvement (David Reynolds, *University College, Cardiff, UK*); Social analysis (Professor Philip Wexler, *University of Rochester, USA*); and Policy studies and evaluation (Professor Ernest House, *University of Colorado-Boulder, USA*).

Policy Studies and Evaluation Series
Editor: Professor Ernest House, Laboratory for Policy Studies, University of Colorado-Boulder, USA

FLUNKING GRADES: RESEARCH AND
POLICIES ON RETENTION
Edited by Lorrie A. Shepard and Mary Lee Smith

Education Policy Perspectives

Flunking Grades: Research and Policies on Retention

Edited by
Lorrie A. Shepard
and
Mary Lee Smith

LB
3063
.F57
1989
West

 The Falmer Press

(A member of the Taylor & Francis Group)
London • New York • Philadelphia

UK	The Falmer Press, Falmer House, Barcombe, Lewes, East Sussex, BN8 5DL
USA	The Falmer Press, Taylor & Francis Inc., 242 Cherry Street, Philadelphia, PA 19106-1906

© Lorrie A. Shepard and Mary Lee Smith 1989

All rights reserved. No part of this publication may be reproduced, stored in a retrieval system, or transmitted in any form or by any means, electronic, mechanical, photocopying, recording or otherwise, without permission in writing from the Publisher.

First published 1989

Library of Congress Cataloging-in-Publication Data
Flunking grades.
  (Education policy perspectives. Policy studies and evaluation series)
  Includes bibliographies and index.
  1. Promotion (School)—United States. 2. Grade repetition—United States. 3. Academic achievement.
I. Shepard, Lorrie A. II. Smith, Mary Lee. III. Series
LB3063.F57 1989   371.2′8′0973   88-33611
ISBN 1-85000-338-6
ISBN 1-85000-339-4 (pbk.)

Typeset in 11/13 Bembo by
Mathematical Composition Setters Ltd, Salisbury, Wiltshire

Jacket design by Caroline Archer

Printed in Great Britain by Taylor & Francis (Printers) Ltd, Basingstoke

Contents

Notes on Contributors		vii
Chapter 1	Introduction and Overview L. A. Shepard and M. L. Smith	1
Chapter 2	Grade Level Retention Effects: A Meta-Analysis of Research Studies C. T. Holmes	16
Chapter 3	Repeating and Dropping Out of School J. B. Grissom and L. A. Shepard	34
Chapter 4	A Review of Research on Kindergarten Retention L. A. Shepard	64
Chapter 5	Academic and Emotional Effects of Kindergarten Retention in One School District L. A. Shepard and M. L. Smith	79
Chapter 6	Attitudes of Students, Parents and Educators toward Repeating a Grade D. A. Byrnes	108
Chapter 7	Teachers' Beliefs about Retention M. L. Smith	132
Chapter 8	Ending Social Promotion in Waterford: Appearances and Reality M. C. Ellwein and G. V Glass	151

Contents

Chapter 9	Alternatives to Student Retention: New Images of the Learner, the Teacher and Classroom Learning *P. L. Peterson*	174
Chapter 10	Policy Implications of Retention Research *E. R. House*	202
Chapter 11	Flunking Grades: A Recapitulation ✓ *M. L. Smith and L. A. Shepard*	214
Index		237

Notes on Contributors

Deborah A. Byrnes is Associate Professor of Elementary Education in the College of Education at Utah State University. Her research interests are the social and emotional well-being of children, especially regarding social isolation, discrimination and school practices such as retention.

Mary Catherine Ellwein is Assistant Professor of Educational Studies in the Curry School of Education at the University of Virginia. She specializes in both qualitative and quantitative research methods and policy analysis. She won the 1987 outstanding dissertation award from the American Education Research Association for her study, *Standards of Competence: A Multi-site Case Study of School Reform*.

Gene V Glass is Professor of Leadership and Policy Studies in the College of Education at Arizona State University. He is past president of the American Educational Research Association and past editor of the *Review of Educational Research* and the *American Educational Research Journal*. He is noted for his contributions in social science methodology, statistics and educational policy research.

James B. Grissom is Research Psychologist in the Basic Research Department at CTB/McGraw Hill. He specializes in large-scale data analysis and psychometrics.

C. Thomas Holmes is Associate Professor of Educational Administration and Associate Director of the Bureau of Educational Services at the University of Georgia. His expertise includes policy analysis pertaining to grade level retention and teacher salary determination.

Ernest R. House is Director of the Laboratory for Policy Studies and Professor of Education at the University of Colorado at Boulder. His research focuses on educational evaluation and educational policy

Notes on Contributors

analysis. He has authored numerous books including *School Evaluation: The Politics and Process* and *Evaluating with Validity*.

Penelope L. Peterson is Co-Director of the Institute for Research on Teaching and Professor of Educational Psychology and Teacher Education at Michigan State University. She is vice-president of the American Educational Research Association and editor of the *Review of Educational Research*. Her research addresses classroom teaching and learning and policy issues pertaining to the reform of teacher education.

Lorrie A. Shepard is Professor of Research and Evaluation Methodology in the School of Education at the University of Colorado at Boulder. Her research focuses on psychometrics and the use of tests in educational settings. Topics of various journal publications include test bias, standard setting, the influence of testing on instruction, teacher testing, the identification of mild handicaps, and early childhood assessment. Dr Shepard has been president of the National Council on Measurement in Education, vice-president of the American Educational Research Association, and editor of the *Journal of Educational Measurement* and the *American Educational Research Journal*. She received her PhD in Research Methods from the University of Colorado at Boulder.

Mary Lee Smith is Professor of Educational Psychology in the College of Education at Arizona State University. She specializes in qualitative research methods and studies of diversions in pupils' careers. She is co-author of *Research and Evaluation in Education and the Social Sciences, School Class Size, Benefits of Psychotherapy* and *Meta-Analysis in Social Research,* and author of *How Educators Decide Who Is Learning Disabled: Challenge to Psychology and Public Policy in the Schools*. Dr Smith is president of the Qualitative Research Group of the American Educational Research Association and past editor of the *American Educational Research Journal*. She received her PhD in Counseling from the University of Colorado at Boulder.

Chapter 1:
Introduction and Overview

Lorrie A. Shepard and Mary Lee Smith

This book is about research on the topic of flunking. A pejorative term avoided by adults, flunking is used by children to describe the experience of repeating a grade in school. Although research on 'grade retention' has a long history, it is of particular importance today when strict grade-to-grade promotion standards are being imposed as part of educational reform.

The End of Social Promotion

The highly visible reforms of public education in the 1980s reject the soft-headed, open education, child-centred curriculum of the late 1960s and 1970s. Characterized by the label 'educational excellence', these most recent correctives are a more demanding version of the back-to-basics and minimum competency testing movements of the late 1970s. Get-tough reformers share an abhorrence for lowered educational standards leading to test score declines and incompetent high school graduates.

Improving education in the 1980s has commanded extraordinary popular attention because it has been linked to economic crisis and the future of US competitiveness in world markets. *A Nation at Risk* (National Commission on Excellence in Education, 1983), the most visible of the reform reports, described the loss of US pre-eminence in 'commerce, industry, science, and technological innovation' as a consequence of inattention to the purposes of schooling. We are falling behind the Japanese in production of both automobiles and student math scores, creating a danger keenly felt by the public. Although some reformers have provided sophisticated, future-oriented analyses of the complex educational preparation needed to preserve Americans' standard of living in a changing world economy (Carnegie Forum's Task Force, 1986), the most common understanding of the crisis is the urgent need to reinstate the standards of the past.

Ending social promotion is seen as one of the most obvious and direct means to redress lax standards. The widespread practice of promoting students with their age-peers regardless of achievement is in disrepute. Blatant disregard for standards out of tenderness for students' self-esteem is blamed for the current educational disarray. The National Commission on Excellence in Education (1983) specifically recommended that, 'placement and grouping of students, as well as promotion and graduation policies, should be guided by academic progress of students and their instructional needs, rather than by rigid adherence to age' (p. 30). If students are not passed to the next grade until they have mastered grade-level subject matter, then students would not arrive in high school incapable of reading and doing basic math.

A precursor to the present reforms was the famous educational malpractice case, where Peter W. (1976), a high school graduate, sued the San Francisco Unified School District because of his inability to read. His complaint held that the school district (i) failed to apprehend his reading disabilities; (ii) assigned him to classes in which he could not read 'the books and other materials'; (iii) allowed him 'to pass and advance from a course or grade level' with knowledge that he had not achieved either its completion or the skills 'necessary for him to succeed or benefit from subsequent courses'; (iv) assigned him to classes in which the instructors were unqualified or which were not 'geared' to his reading level; and (v) permitted him to graduate from high school although he was 'unable to read above the eighth grade level, as required by the Education Code. ...' (Yudof, Kirp, van Geel and Levin, 1982). Although the courts found in favour of the school district, the case of Peter W. is remembered with trepidation by educators as a symbol of their potential liability in promoting students without basic skills.

Employers have complained that the high school diploma can no longer be trusted as a certificate of basic competence. Apparently there are many graduates who cannot read or compute. Beginning in the late 1970s, nineteen states enacted legislation requiring that students pass a minimum competence examination before being awarded a diploma (Education Commission of the States, 1985). A National Academy of Education panel warned, however, that high school graduation tests were unworkable because of limitations in the measurement art and the harmful effect on individuals with 'accumulated educational deficits' (1978, p. 9). The NAE panel approved, instead, of 'critical competency points' at selected lower grade levels for 'diagnosing individual student weaknesses and pinpointing remediation needs' (p. 9). Likewise in the courts, it appeared that high school competency tests would only be upheld if there was an adequate phase-in period, giving students sufficient warning and time to acquire necessary skills (Debra P. v. Turlington, 1981).

What began as an attempt to enforce standards at the exit from public education was translated downward into 'promotional gates' at earlier grade levels. As expressed by Owen and Ranick (1977) in explaining the Greensville, Virginia achievement-based promotion system: 'If a student doesn't know that 4 times 9 equals 36, there's no point in passing him to the next grade where he will have to deal with 329 times 436' (p. 532). According to policy analysts, the institution of New York City's promotional gates at fourth and seventh grades was partly in response to anticipated failure rates on state competency tests (Association for Supervision and Curriculum Development, 1984). 'Few believe that the solution lies at the high school level. One of education's incontrovertible propositions is the high premium returned on early teaching.... If high school diplomas are to have meaning (and if children are to have advance warning and a reasonable chance to meet standards) then the process leading there has to be strengthened as well' (Mann, 1984). The rhetoric of Superintendent Macchiarola's (1981) 'Promotional policy for students in grades kindergarten through grade 9', was almost identical to statements in Philadelphia (Toch, 1984) and other cities:

> Student promotion will be determined by the degree to which the student has mastered the basic skills required in each grade. Automatic advancement from grade to grade without evidence of achieving required performance standards in basic skills places an unfair burden on students in succeeding grades. The early mastery of basic skills will help to ensure that today's elementary school student is not tomorrow's high school dropout. The current dropout rate is intolerable and a program to attack this problem must be mounted immediately.

According to the rationale of Macchiarola (1981) and others, rigorous adherence to grade-level promotion standards is expected to improve the achievement of individual students in two ways. First, students will be more diligent in their efforts to learn if they perceive some genuinely negative consequence for failing to learn. Second, students who fail will not be passed on unnoticed but will have another opportunity to acquire necessary skills. Furthermore, at a time when the nation's future is in peril, removing those who lag behind is also expected to facilitate the pace of learning for students who merit promotion.

The end of social promotion is enthusiastically endorsed by the public. In the 1983 Gallup Poll, 75 per cent of US citizens agreed with the statement 'children should be promoted from grade to grade only if they can pass examinations' (p. 38). In the 1986 Gallup survey, Americans strongly favored making requirements stricter for both grade to grade promotion and high school graduation, with endorsements of 72 per cent and 70 per cent respectively. Sixty-eight per cent favored 'stricter requirements for high school graduation even if it meant that significantly fewer students would graduate than is now the case' (pp. 52-3).

Many educators agree with the general public that retention in grade is essential to assuring student achievement. Teachers and principals dispute negative findings from research on retention, hearkening instead to common sense and their own personal experience in retaining students (letters to the editor, *Phi Delta Kappan*, 1988a, 1988b). When teachers are surveyed regarding the effects of repeating a grade or an extra year of kindergarten, they report benefits for nearly all pupils (Brevard County Public Schools, 1987; Schuyler, 1985).

'Public opinion' and the rhetoric of reform, therefore, are in agreement that promotion from grade to grade must be based on merit. Retention in grade is seen as the logical means to correct inadequate learning and to ensure greater subsequent achievement both individually and collectively.

History of Graded Education

The commonsense view that students should repeat a grade to repair deficient skills implies a particular conception of education. According to this view, subject matter can be broken down into sequential units that are presented in a linear fashion. Furthermore, it is presumed that fixed subject matter must be mastered in a particular grade and that uniform progress can be standardized in all subject areas so that, for example, all fourth graders are ready for fourth grade reading, long division in math, local history, and so forth, the same for everyone.

Anderson (1969) provided a short history of graded education which serves as background to the conflict between retention and social promotion policies. What Americans presume to be the natural form of schooling is a product of the industrial revolution and mass education beginning in the mid-nineteenth century. Earlier, when only a few students were educated, each could proceed at his own pace through increasingly difficult material. A graded system of education was developed to handle large numbers of students efficiently, in a mode that Labaree (1984) referred to as large-scale batch production. Advocates for grade uniformity believed that equal accomplishment could be achieved by diligent effort and recommended discipline of both retarded and precocious children (Wells, 1867). From the beginning of graded schools, however, there has been an inherent conflict between meritocratic values, i.e., that promotion should be based on merit, and the need to treat all pupils the same for purposes of organizational efficiency (Labaree, 1984). In the nineteenth century merit prevailed. Grade retention was widely practiced, affecting more than 70 per cent of all students (Anderson, 1969). Very few students were expected to pass the necessary exams to be admitted to high school.

Although social promotion is often thought to be a phenomenon of the liberal 60s, a broader purview shows it to be the pervasive educational practice of the twentieth century. Concern over the negative consequences of so many misfitting overage students was voiced as early as 1909 (Ayers). As the purpose of education changed, intended for all students instead of the elite few, 'continuous progress' policies served the purpose of keeping students in school rather than forcing them out. Holding students in school and out of the work force was especially important during the depression of the 1930s (Medway and Rose, 1986). A steady decline in the proportion of overage students was observed from 1918 to 1952 (Lennon and Mitchell, 1955). The inevitable tension created by students functioning at vastly different levels of achievement was solved by ability groupings or tracking within grades (Anderson, 1969). Ironically nostalgic yearnings for standards are based on a distorted vision of the past. There never was a time when students were held to strict promotion standards without there also being segregation of pupils by ability or massive school leaving by eighth grade.

What has been the effect of minimum competency testing and reforms in the 1980s on the incidence of non-promotion? Is it possible to detect in current practices a reinstatement of standards and reversal of social promotion trends?

Retention Rates

There are no national data on the number of children retained in grade each year. A widely shared perception exists that the number of retentions has increased substantially as schools in many jurisdictions, especially large cities, have installed achievement-based promotion policies.

Despite its salience, rates of promotion and retention are not kept by governmental agencies. Instead retention rates must be inferred from the proportion of pupils of a given age who are not in the appropriate (or modal) grade. For example, third grade is the normal grade for eight-year-olds. Therefore, most eight-year-olds enrolled in second or first grade are likely to have been retained. This indicator has been used since the turn of the century (Thorndike, 1908). Table 1 is a summary of enrollment data from the US Bureau of the Census (1971, 1978, 1979a, 1979b, 1981, 1983 and 1985). Consistent with popular conceptions, retentions in grade were at an all-time low in the early 1970s. The percentage of overage students began to climb, however, in the late 1970s in response to minimum competency testing. Compared to practices in the 1950s, more recent data also show a very large increase in the number of students who are overage by third grade, in keeping with the belief that students should be retained early in their school careers. Aggregate data in table 1 obscure differential rates by sex and race. In 1982, for example, at age 13 29.9 per cent of males were below modal grade as compared to 21.9 per cent of females. At age 13, 23.4

Table 1: Percentages of Children Enrolled Below the Modal Grade from 1950 to 1984

Age	1950	1960	1970	1976	1978	1980	1982	1984
5			(3.0)	(2.7)	(3.8)	(3.3)	(3.6)	(4.7)
6			(4.4)	(6.5)	(7.2)	(9.4)	(11.1)	(11.1)
7			(13.1)	(11.0)	(13.6)	(16.1)	(18.4)	(18.5)
8	6.6	4.0	3.4 (15.1)	3.8 (14.7)	(16.5)	(19.5)	(20.8)	(20.7)
9	11.2	6.5	5.1 (18.6)	4.9 (16.5)	(18.3)	(19.6)	(20.9)	(22.0)
10	15.7	8.1	6.7 (21.2)	5.7 (18.6)	(20.4)	(19.6)	(24.4)	(24.0)
11	18.0	9.2	7.4 (23.0)	6.7 (19.5)	(20.4)	(22.1)	(23.5)	(26.1)
12	21.6	10.5	8.4 (22.4)	7.6 (20.5)	(19.5)	(22.9)	(24.7)	(29.1)
13	23.6	11.7	9.0 (23.6)	8.0 (19.9)	(19.5)	(22.4)	(26.0)	(26.8)
14	25.0	13.9	10.2 (23.1)	8.5 (19.5)	(19.2)	(23.1)	(21.9)	(26.3)
15	26.4	15.2	10.7 (24.3)	9.6 (23.8)	(23.0)	(25.5)	(25.1)	(26.7)
16	24.6	15.0	10.8 (25.5)	11.0 (24.5)	(25.5)	(24.1)	(25.7)	(27.5)
17	22.0	14.9	11.0 (22.1)	11.2 (24.0)	(22.4)	(23.9)	(23.4)	(24.6)

Note: Data from 1950 through 1976 were collected in the spring of the school year. Data reported in parentheses from 1970 onwards were collected in October.

Introduction and Overview

per cent of whites were enrolled below modal grade compared to 38 per cent of blacks. The discrepancies between spring and fall statistics in 1970 and 1976 also reveal the limitations in using overage to infer retention. To account for a range of school entry cutoffs, the spring census used a two-year span for modal grade thus undercounting retentions; conversely the October census slightly overcounts students as below modal grade in states with early cutoffs. These indices serve only as rough barometers of trends in retention practices nationally.

Rose, Medway, Cantrell and Marus (1983) made an effort to gather retention data from fifty states and the District of Columbia. Only fifteen states had collected retention information for the 1979-80 school year or immediately preceding years. For comparative purposes the same fifteen states were contacted for retention rates from 1979 to the present.[1] Tables 2 and 3 report data for the 1979-80 school year, based on state documents or Rose *et al.* (1983) data, and for the 1985-86 school year. Although these figures were collected to document the impact of educational reform on retentions, the increase from 1980 is quite modest, less than one percentage point on average. In a few states the annual rates have grown more substantially, for example, in Arizona from 3.5 per cent to 7.2 per cent retained. Although the change data do not reveal dramatic trends, percentages of repeaters in these states are considerably higher than in other developed countries. For example,

Table 2: Percentages of Students Retained in Each Grade at the Conclusion of the 1979-80 School Year

State or Region	K	1	2	3	4	5	6	7	8	9	10	11	12	Total (K-12)
Arizona	5.2	7.7	4.0	2.4	1.9	1.4	1.3	3.1	2.3	4.4	2.4	2.5	6.9	3.5
Delaware*	NA	11.4	5.1	2.9	2.4	3.1	2.4	7.9	8.1	13.1	12.6	7.7	6.6	7.0
District of Columbia*	NA	15.3	10.0	7.2	7.2	6.3	3.1	NA	NA	20.5	NA	NA	16.6	NA
Florida	6.1	13.7	7.4	7.0	5.9	4.6	5.5	10.4	8.3	10.2	11.5	7.5	4.4	8.0
Georgia		11.0	4.7	3.8	2.8	2.5	2.6	5.3	7.4	13.3	10.8	7.9	4.0	6.5
Hawaii*	NA	1.1	0.7	0.5	0.4	0.4	0.4	0.2	2.3	13.1	10.1	8.5	5.2	3.8
Kentucky	2.3	12.6	5.7	3.4	2.2	1.8	1.9	4.2	3.6	5.8	4.2	2.8	3.2	4.4
Maryland*		7.6	3.5	3.3	2.5	2.5	1.8	8.5	7.6	8.6	11.3	6.2	4.4	5.8
Mississippi*		15.1	6.9	4.8	5.0	5.6	5.1	13.5	11.1	12.4	11.7	8.1	6.0	8.9
New Hampshire		8.6	3.3	2.0	1.3	1.1	0.9	2.5	2.8	7.7	4.9	3.6	3.6	3.6
North Carolina	4.5	9.8	6.0	4.5	3.2	2.8	3.4	6.8	7.1	14.1	14.8	8.6	4.2	6.9
South Carolina*		8.3	4.4	3.5	2.7	2.6	3.5	3.8	2.6	NA	NA	NA	NA	2.6
Tennessee	2.4	10.7	5.6	3.9	3.1	3.3	2.8	7.3	5.6	8.5	6.3	4.1	6.1	5.4
Virginia	6.2	11.0	6.3	5.3	4.4	4.2	4.2	7.7	12.6	11.5	8.3	6.3	7.4	7.4
West Virginia	1.7	10.8	3.4	2.2	1.9	1.8	1.4	3.5	2.5	NA	NA	NA	NA	3.4

Note: NA = data not available.
* Data from Delaware, District of Columbia, Hawaii, Maryland, Mississippi, South Carolina are as reported in Rose, Cantrell and Marus (1983). South Carolina data were from the 1977-78 school year.

Table 3: Percentages of Students Retained in Each Grade at the Conclusion of the 1985-86 School Year

State or Region	K	1	2	3	4	5	6	7	8	9	10	11	12	Total (K-12)
Arizona	8.0	20.0	8.0	5.0	4.0	4.0	4.0	8.0	7.0	6.0	3.0	2.0	14.0	7.2
Delaware	5.4	17.2	4.9	2.8	2.3	3.0	3.2	9.6	7.7	15.6	16.8	8.7	7.5	8.1
District of Columbia		12.7	8.4	7.4	5.4	4.6	2.8	10.6	6.6	NA	NA	NA	NA	7.3
Florida	10.5	11.2	4.7	4.5	3.8	2.6	3.5	7.9	5.8	12.1	11.9	8.9	3.5	7.2
Georgia	8.0	12.4	6.7	7.8	5.2	3.9	5.3	6.7	7.5	18.1	12.2	8.7	4.5	8.5
Hawaii	2.0	1.6	1.0	0.7	0.5	0.4	0.5	2.1	2.8	8.9	6.9	5.5	0.8	2.6
Kentucky	4.0	5.3	4.9	3.0	2.3	1.9	2.7	5.4	3.8	9.6	6.3	4.6	3.4	5.3
Maryland	NA	NA	NA	NA	NA	NA	NA	NA	NA	NA	NA	NA	NA	5.5
Mississippi	1.4	16.1	7.0	5.3	5.7	6.0	5.6	11.2	9.3	12.9	12.6	9.0	5.7	8.9
New Hampshire	4.4	9.1	3.7	1.5	1.1	1.0	7.0	3.3	3.2	10.5	5.5	4.2	4.9	4.2
North Carolina	6.0	9.3	5.0	5.7	2.7	2.1	8.1	7.9	11.0	13.9	13.2	9.3	3.9	7.7
South Carolina	NA	NA	NA	NA	NA	NA	NA	NA	NA	NA	NA	NA	NA	NA
Tennessee	3.9	10.9	5.1	3.9	3.3	3.2	3.2	8.1	6.1	9.6	8.6	7.0	5.9	6.2
Virginia	8.3	10.2	4.8	4.2	3.7	2.9	3.4	8.1	9.7	13.9	8.8	6.1	7.0	7.2
West Virginia	4.4	7.5	3.3	2.7	2.3	2.2	1.8	4.6	2.5	NA	NA	NA	NA	3.5

Note. NA = data not available.

the annual percentage repeating in primary education is 0 per cent in Japan, 0 per cent in the United Kingdom, and 1.9 per cent in the Federal Republic of Germany. Available data in the US more closely resemble retention practices in Kenya or Cuba (Office of UNESCO Statistics, 1984).

Furthermore, annual retention rates give a misleading picture of the impact of non-promotion policies. Consider the first line of table 3. In 1985-86, only 7.2 per cent of all students in Arizona were retained. To form a more accurate impression of the number of students affected by retention, however, it is more realistic to sum the rates across grades. For example, 8 per cent of kindergartens and 20 per cent of first graders in Arizona repeated that year. If there were no double retentions and annual rates followed the same pattern each year, then by third grade 41 per cent of Arizona children (8 + 20 + 8 + 5) would have been held back. Of course, to obtain the cumulative retention rate for a specific entering class of kindergartners it is more correct to add kindergarten retentions in 1979, first grade retentions in 1980, and so forth. However, when these sums were computed they differed in most states by only a few percentage points from the cumulative totals that can be calculated from table 3. (Arizona is an exception because its annual rates jumped substantially from 1980 to 1986.) Many school districts have policies against double retentions within the same level of education, thus it is reasonable to consider these rates additive. More-

Introduction and Overview

over, from census data and the large-city data sets analyzed by Grissom and Shepard in chapter 3, it is possible to estimate that double retentions account for roughly 15 per cent of all retained students by grade 8.

A simple sum of the recent retention data in Arizona through grade 8, before students have begun to drop out, is 68 per cent. If this rate is adjusted to allow for double retentions, then 9 per cent of Arizona students will have been retained twice before leaving eighth grade and 50 per cent will have been retained once. These cumulative rates are surprisingly high but are based on actual retention data. The only way that these cumulative effects would not occur is if the annual rates in the early grades dropped drastically in the next few years. Instead the rates have been rising steadily. The 50 per cent estimate can be adjusted by altering the proportion of double retentions but with a corresponding increase in the percentage of students made to repeat two years.

Arizona is not alone in the high proportion of students affected by retention at some time in their school career. Cumulative rates over 50 per cent pertain in all of the states with annual rates of 7 per cent or 8 per cent. Florida actually reported a decrease in annual retention rates from 1970-80 to 1985-86. Yet according to the more recent figures, 55 per cent total retentions have occurred by eighth grade, meaning that approximately 7 per cent of eighth graders have repeated two grades and an additional 41 per cent of eighth graders have repeated one grade. Thus the data do show dramatic results of rigorously enforced grade level standards in response to educational reform. States with higher, but seemingly modest annual retention rates (7 per cent, 8 per cent, 9 per cent), have established cumulative rates of non-promotion greater than 50 per cent, which characterized nineteenth century schools before the days of social promotion.

Overview of this Volume

In spite of reform rhetoric and non-promotion practices affecting substantial numbers of school children, there is little reason to expect that the increase in retentions will result in an overall rise in accomplishment with the long term promise of national economic revival. In fact, the evidence to be presented in this book suggests the opposite. What is the evidential basis for evaluating these claims and counter claims? Does retaining pupils in grade have a salutary effect? Will strict achievement-based promotion policies improve student learning and increase the life chances of students who would otherwise drop out? Research in this volume is addressed to these questions.

The purpose of this book is to present both the research evidence on the effects of grade retention and research on school policies and practices regarding retention. The book is organized to illuminate the discrepancy between what research says and widely held beliefs about the efficacy of retention.

Chapters 2 through 5 are structured to provide a comprehensive treatment of research findings on retention. Until 1984 the definitive review of the retention literature was by Jackson, published in 1975 in the *Review of Educational Research*. In 1984 also in the *Review of Educational Research*, Holmes and Matthews produced a more up to date review of non-promotion studies using quantitative methods of research synthesis. These two articles are generally cited as the authoritative references on the topic because of their visibility and completeness and because these authors critically examined how the quality of study controls affects research conclusions. Thomas Holmes was invited to update the previous synthesis to incorporate the recent spate of comparative studies. Chapter 2 is a summary wherein he presents the results of sixty-three controlled studies. Selected contrasts allow the reader to see plainly what the average effect of retention is on student achievement and self-concept from all available studies, to compare retention in first grade with retention in fourth grade, to consider the effect of initial matching on study outcomes, and so forth. Common understandings about retention usually acknowledge some potential harm to a child's self-esteem but hold that achievement gains are more important than this potential risk. Contrary to popular belief, however, the negative effect of retention is greater for achievement measures than for personal adjustment, self-concept, or attitude toward school.

Holmes' chapter is definitive in the sense that it omits none of the available research on grade retention. The entire literature on retention is limited, however, by the lack of systematic investigation of long term effects. Chapter 3 by James Grissom and Lorrie Shepard is the report of work undertaken to investigate more long term consequences of grade retention. Previous studies from the school dropout literature and new large scale analyses address the effect of repeating a grade on dropping out of school. Even with the necessary caveats for interpreting quasi-experimental data, the results starkly contradict the rhetoric of reform, that retention will make students less at risk for dropping out.

Chapter 4 is a separate review of research focused exclusively on kindergarten retention. Compared to grade failure which has its origins in the previous century, repeating kindergarten is a very recent phenomenon. An extra year to mature or acquire readiness skills is seen by some as a way to prevent subsequent stress and failure. Research-based conclusions about kindergarten retention have not been rehashed exhaustively by reviewers. Here Shepard analyzes the results of fifteen controlled studies, mostly dissertations to evaluate the effects of extra-year programs. Then in chapter 5 Lorrie Shepard and Mary Lee Smith present the results of an additional controlled study of kindergarten retention. In this study the authors were able to institute more rigorous controls than previous studies to ensure that retained children were compared to promoted children who were equally young and unready when they first entered kindergarten. Intended program benefits were assessed by outcome measures such as attention span and learner self-concept as well as academic achievement. Narrative interview data from parents of retained children provide evidence about competing positive and negative effects of retention not available in other studies. The claim that retention works when children are selected for immaturity is not supported when studies of just this type are isolated. According to parent interviews, most kindergartners are not protected from the trauma of being held back by being too young to notice.

The second part of the book focuses on the practice of retention. Deborah Byrnes' research in chapter 6 includes both surveys of parents, teachers, and principals and interviews with retained children. Thus Byrnes addresses both the practice of retention as seen by educators and direct effects of retention, measured by the feelings and attitudes of affected children. The data available in this chapter are rare. To our knowledge there have not been systematic attempts to survey the attitudes of these groups. In Byrnes' study the opinions of educators and parents, even parents of retained children, closely match those of the general public (Gallup Poll, 1983). Children as young as first grade also accept the necessity of retention as something that happens to you for being bad or doing poor work.

Trying to assess what educators believe about retention is something more than simulating how they would vote, given a referendum on non-promotion policies. Terms such as 'teacher beliefs' or 'teacher thinking' are used by educational researchers to refer to mental constructs or working theories in the minds of teachers that determine instructional decisions. It is plain from statistical data that the number and types of children retained in grade differ profoundly from one school to the next, more so than can be explained by the biology or sociology of the children themselves. Can these differences in practice be explained by the philosophical or theoretical orientation of teachers?

Mary Lee Smith's chapter 7 is a qualitative study of teacher beliefs about retention. Based on teachers' accounts of individual children, decisions about retention are related to views about child development, to teachers' theories about instructional intervention, and to conceptions of school structure.

A book on grade retention practice in the 1980s would be incomplete without a close look at district policies to install test-based promotional gates. Chapter 8 by Mary Catherine Ellwein and Gene Glass is a case study in educational reform. Unlike implicit theories in the minds of teachers or informal policies, this study focuses on implementation of formal policies intended to end social promotion. They trace the standard-setting process and consequences of competency testing at grades K, 2, 5 and 7. Ellwein and Glass found inconsistencies between public statements about reform and actual retention practices. From the perspective of a multi-site case analysis the authors are able to see a recurring pattern, for policy makers to invest heavily in the technology of impressive standards at the outset but purposely ignore follow-up examination of consequences.

Two distinguished scholars were invited to review the research in the preceding chapters and comment on its implications for educational practice and policy. Their analyses comprise the last section of the book. Penelope Peterson, recognized for her extensive research on teaching and learning, was asked to consider instructional alternatives to retention. In chapter 9 Peterson draws on her own analysis of teacher beliefs and classroom practices to propose that greater teacher knowledge about how children learn might make teachers less ready to see retention as a remedy. Instead 'the challenge for the teacher would become one of accessing and diagnosing the knowledge and abilities of their children to solve problems and then organizing and arranging the learning environment and learning activities to facilitate children's development of that knowledge'. Ernie House is a prominent researcher in educational evaluation and policy analysis and one of the national experts called in to audit the evaluation of New York City's Promotional Gates Program. House was asked to respond to the relevance of research in this volume to policies beyond the classroom. His recapitulation of research findings is caustic, referring to retention as a pernicious educational practice. House suggests alternatives in the form of legal and legislative interventions but ultimately ideological beliefs are not likely to change unless educators themselves collect evidence on the consequences of their own retention practices.

In the concluding chapter we reconsider research findings and attempt to reconcile them with teachers' beliefs about the necessity and benefit of retention. We also propose explanations for current beliefs; school structure, standardized curriculum, graded education, and the need of some teachers to establish homogeneous classrooms by removing children who are difficult to teach.

In sum, the book is intended to extend research-based knowledge on grade retention by considering effects heretofore unexamined, by systematically examining retention practices, and by addressing directly the discord between perceptions about grade-level standards and measured effects of non-promotion.

Note

1 We are grateful to M. Elizabeth Graue for conducting the telephone survey and for the subsequent analysis of documents.

References

ANDERSON, R. H. (1969) 'Pupil progress' in EBEL, R. L. (Ed.), *Encyclopedia of Educational Research*, 4th edn, Toronto, Macmillan.
ASSOCIATION FOR SUPERVISION AND CURRICULUM DEVELOPMENT (1984) *Retention Policy Analysis*, Alexandria, VA, ASCD.
AYERS, L. P. (1909) *Laggards in our Schools*, New York, Russell Sage.
BREVARD COUNTY PUBLIC SCHOOLS (c 1987) *Developmental Placement Program Evaluation: 1986-87*, Rockledge, FL, Brevard County Public Schools.
CARNEGIE FORUM'S TASK FORCE ON TEACHING AS A PROFESSION (1986) *A Nation Prepared: Teachers for the 21st Century*, excerpts in *The Chronicle of Higher Education*, 21 May, pp. 43–54.
DEBRA, P. v. TURLINGTON (1981) 474 F. Supp. 244, 252 (M. D. Fla. 1979) affd in part, 644 F. 2d 397 (5th Cir. 1981).
EDUCATION COMMISSION OF THE STATES (1985) *State Activity-Minimum Competency Testing*, Denver, CO, ECS, November.
GALLUP, A. M. (1986) 'The 18th annual Gallup Poll of the public's attitudes toward the public schools', *Phi Delta Kappan*, 68, pp. 43–59.
GALLUP, G. H. (1983) 'The 15th annual Gallup Poll of the public's attitudes toward the public schools', *Phi Delta Kappan*, 65, pp. 33–47.
LABAREE, D. F. (1984) 'Setting the standard: Alternative policies for student promotion', *Harvard Educational Review*, 54, pp. 67–87.
LENNON, R. T. and MITCHELL, B. C. (1955) 'Trends in age-grade relationships, *School and Society*, 82, pp. 123–5.
LETTERS TO THE EDITOR (1988a) *Phi Delta Kappan*, 70, pp. 389–91.
LETTERS TO THE EDITOR (1988b) *Phi Delta Kappan*, 70, pp. 460–4.

MACCHIAROLA, F. J. (1981) *Promotional Policy for Students in Grades Kindergarten Through Grade 9*. Brooklyn, NY, New York City Board of Education.

MANN, D. (1984) 'Education in New York City: Public schools for whom?' in GRACE, G. (Ed.) *Education and the City*, London, Routledge and Kegan Paul.

MEDWAY, F. J. and ROSE, J. S. (1986) 'Grade retention', in KRATOCHWILL, T. R. (Ed.), *Advances in School Psychology*, Hillsdale, NJ, Lawrence Erlbaum.

NATIONAL ACADEMY OF EDUCATION (1978), *Improving Educational Achievement*, Washington, DC, NAE.

NATIONAL COMMISSION ON EXCELLENCE IN EDUCATION (1983) *A Nation at Risk: The Imperative for Educational Reform*, Washington, DC, U.S. Department of Education.

OFFICE OF UNESCO STATISTICS (1984) 'Wastage in primary education from 1970-1980', *Prospects*, 14, pp. 347–68.

OWEN, S. A. and RANICK, D. L. (1977) 'The Greensville program: A commonsense approach to basics', *Phi Delta Kappan*, 58, pp. 531–3 and 539.

PETER, W. v. SAN FRANCISCO UNIFIED SCHOOL DISTRICT (1976) 60 Cal. App. 3d 814, 131 Cal. Rptr. 854.

ROSE, J. S., MEDWAY, F. J., CANTRELL, V. L. and MARUS, S. H. (1983) 'A fresh look at the retention-promotion controversy', *Journal of School Psychology*, 21, pp. 201–11.

SCHUYLER, N. B. (1985) 'Does retention help?', paper presented at the annual meeting of the American Educational Research Association, Chicago, April.

THORNDIKE, E. L. (1908) *Elimination of Pupils from School*, U.S. Bureau of Education Bulletin, No. 4. Washington D.C., Government Printing Office.

TOCH, T. (1984) 'The dark side of the excellence movement', *Phi Delta Kappan*, 66, pp. 173–6.

U.S. BUREAU OF THE CENSUS (1971) Current Population Reports, Series P-20, No. 222. 'School Enrollment: October 1970.' Washington, DC, U.S. Government Printing Office.

U.S. BUREAU OF THE CENSUS (1978) Current Population Reports, Series P-20, No. 319. 'School Enrollment — Social and Economic Characteristics of Students: October 1976.' Washington, DC, U.S. Government Printing Office.

U.S. BUREAU OF THE CENSUS (1979a) Current Population Reports, Series P-20, No. 337. 'Relative Progress of Children in School: 1976'. Washington, DC, U.S. Government Printing Office.

U.S. BUREAU OF THE CENSUS (1979b) Current Population Reports, Series P-20, No. 346. 'School Enrollment — Social and Economic Characteristics of Students: October 1978'. Washington, DC, U.S. Government Printing Office.

U.S. BUREAU OF THE CENSUS (1981) Current Population Reports, Series P-20, No. 400. 'School Enrollment — Social and Economic Characteristics of Students: October 1980.' Washington, DC, U.S. Government Printing Office.

U.S. BUREAU OF THE CENSUS (1983) *Current Population Reports*, Series P-20, No. 408. 'School Enrollment — Social and Economic Characteristics of Students: October 1982.' Washington, DC, U.S. Government Printing Office.

U.S. BUREAU OF THE CENSUS (1985) *Current Population Reports*, Series P-20, unpublished. 'School Enrollment — Social and Economic Characteristics of Students: October 1984.' Washington, DC, U.S. Government Printing Office.

WELLS, W. H. (1867) *The Graded School: A Course of Instruction for Public Schools; With Copious Practical Directions to Teachers, and Observations on Primary Schools, School Discipline, School Records, etc..* Barnes.

YUDOF, M. G., KIRP, D. L., VAN GEEL, T. and LEVIN, B. (1982) *Educational Policy and the Law*, 2nd edn, Berkeley, CA, McCutcheon Publishing.

Chapter 2:
Grade Level Retention Effects:
A Meta-Analysis of Research Studies

C. Thomas Holmes

Editors' Introduction

Because of the high visibility of grade retention policies more than twenty reviews of retention research have been authored since 1980. The most distinguished of these was by C. Thomas Holmes and Kenneth M. Matthews using meta-analytic techniques and published in the Review of Educational Research *in 1984. In this chapter, Holmes provides an update of their earlier synthesis. In the few ensuing years, nineteen new controlled studies were conducted, more than in the previous decade, again indicating the salience of the topic.*

Meta-analysis is a relatively recent and sophisticated method for integrating the findings of multiple research studies. It has several important features that recommend it over traditional narrative reviews. First, meta-analytic summaries are more comprehensible to the reader than lengthy recounting of each individual study's methods and results. Second, the quantification of effects is based on the actual difference between treated and control groups averaged across studies rather than tests of statistical significance. Traditional vote counting methods that tally statistically significant differences can alternately obscure or exaggerate practically important differences because of their dependence on sample size. Finally, meta-analysis permits systematic examination of study attributes that might influence study results. In the case of retention research, for example, do studies where promoted and retained children are well matched on initial characteristics lead to the same conclusions as studies with poorer controls? Although there is always more to be learned from future research, these features of meta-analysis enable a definitive statement about what research says on a topic.

Holmes answers the question as to whether retention works better than promotion. What are its effects on student achievement and personal adjustment? Are results different depending on whether students repeat in first grade or fourth grade? Do initial effects persist over time? What are the characteristics of the few positive studies that were found? Did these studies involve special students or special treatments or were anomalous results attributable to features of research design?

The grade organization of schools has traditionally required that teachers make promotional decisions concerning low-achieving students. As early as 1904, Superintendent W. H. Maxwell of the New York schools sounded the alarm over the use of retention as a means of improving the achievement of low-achieving students (Coffield and Blommers, 1954). By the beginning of the twentieth century, millions of poor performing students nationwide were being retained (Ayres, 1909).

Although there have been periods since the early 1900s when strict retention policies were not employed, retention remains the major strategy used by educators as a remedy for academic failure. This practice of retention persists despite reviews of the literature that show little or no academic achievement benefits from retention (Bocks, 1977; Holmes, 1983 and 1986; Holmes and Matthews, 1984; Jackson, 1975). The perpetuation of retention is fueled by advocates who assert that competency based education and 'back to basics' cannot be accomplished without grade-level standards.

Does adherence to grade-level requirements improve student achievement? Are there definitive conclusions from research on non-promotion? The current study is an integration of the extant body of research; especially, it is intended to extend the synthesis provided by Holmes and Matthews (1984).

Light and Smith (1971) concluded that 'progress will only come when we are able to pool, in a systematic manner, the original data from...studies' (p. 443). The purpose of this chapter is to summarize the empirical studies on the effects of grade retention and to examine study characteristics which account for differences in research conclusions. A meta-analytic technique, such as the one pioneered by Glass (1978), was chosen as suitable for examining the effects of grade level retention on pupils. This technique allows for systematic synthesis of study results and permits testing of the extent to which study results vary as a function of study characteristics. For example, does the efficacy of a treatment, such as non-promotion, vary as a function of a pupil's grade level? Do well-controlled studies lead to different conclusions from those with poor research designs?

Sources of Data

A systematic search of the literature was conducted to identify studies that were potentially relevant. Descriptors such as grade retention, grade repetition, non-promotion, grade failure, and suggested synonyms were used across reference data bases. In the initial phase, *Current Index to Journals in Education* (ERIC), *Research in Education* (ERIC), and *Dissertation Abstracts International* were computer searched. In addition, a manual search was conducted of *Education Index* and *Master's Thesis in Education*. In the second phase, each report located in phase one was consulted, when possible, for additional citations. The search produced a bibliography of approximately 850 entries.

The following selection criteria were used to reduce the completed bibliography to the list of sixty-three studies included in the meta-analysis. To have been included in the final list, the reported study must have (a) presented the results of original research of the effects on pupils of retention in kindergarten, elementary, or junior high school grades; (b) contained sufficient data to allow for the calculation or estimation of an effect size; and (c) described an investigation with an identifiable comparison group. The sixty-three studies consisted of twenty published studies, twenty-two dissertations, eighteen master's theses, and three unpublished papers. Forty-four of these studies had been included in the 1984 meta-analysis (Holmes and Matthews). Discarded references were largely reviews or essay discussions without empirical data. Approximately 1 per cent of the 850 references could not be included because they failed to report means and standard deviations.

Calculation of Effect Sizes

Meta-analysis, as defined by Glass (1978), is based on the concept of effect size (ES), which represents the benefit (or harm) of an educational intervention. In this study, effect size was defined as the difference between the mean of the retained group, $\overline{X}_r$, and the mean of the control (promoted) group, $\overline{X}_p$, divided by the standard deviation of the control group, s_p.

$$ES = (\overline{X}_r - \overline{X}_p)/s_p$$

This procedure results in a measure of the difference between groups expressed in quantitative units which are comparable across studies. Because each effect is standardized with respect to the control group standard deviation, it then becomes possible to combine the results from many different outcome measures including different tests at different grade levels, as well as personality rating scales. A negative ES means that the treatment, in this case retention, had a negative or deleterious effect compared to promotion.

If the research reports being reviewed had always contained the means of the groups and the standard deviation of the control group, effect sizes could have been calculated directly from the definitional formula. In those cases where the necessary data were not provided, estimates of the ES's were obtained by working backwards from the reported significance tests (as described in Holmes, 1984).

Results of the Initial Integration

In all, 861 individual effect sizes were calculated. Although this represents a mean of almost fourteen effect sizes per study, as many as 160 ES's and as few as one ES were obtained from individual studies. As indicated in table 1 the mean effect size, based on 861 effects, was −.15. This value indicates that on the average retention produced a negative result. The groups of non-promoted pupils scored .15 standard deviation unit lower than the promoted comparison groups on the various outcome measures.

Because some of the studies yielded many effect sizes and others produced only one, the data were reexamined to see if individual studies had created substantial distortions in the mean effect sizes. All individual effect sizes within a study were averaged, then the mean of these averages was computed across studies. This second method of combining effects, weighted by study rather than individual effect sizes, gave each study equal weight in determining the overall result. From this perspective, the overall findings are slightly more negative, with an ES of −.26. Later, when studies were classified as either positive or negative based on the sign of their average effect, fifty-four were classified as negative and only nine as positive. However, the nine positive studies averaged twenty-one individual effects per study, while the negative studies averaged only twelve. Therefore, the few positive studies had had a disproportionately large influence on the computations of the overall result.

The overall effect sizes were calculated for data measuring several different kinds of dependent variables and represent the overall effect of non-promotion on pupils retained in kindergarten, elementary, or

Table 1: Mean Effect Sizes

	# of ES's	# of Studies	ES (Weighted by Effect)	ES (Weighted by Study)
Overall effect size	861	63	-.15	-.26
Academic achievement	536	47	-.19	-.31
Language arts	106	18	-.16	-.33
Reading	144	34	-.08	-.30
Mathematics	137	31	-.11	-.25
Social studies	7	3	-.35	-.37
Grade point average	4	3	-.58	-.78
Personal adjustment	234	27	-.09	-.21
Social	101	27	-.09	-.21
Emotional	33	10	+.03	-.12
Behavioral	24	10	-.13	-.23
Self-concept	45	11	-.13	+.06
Attitude toward school	39	10	-.05	-.18
Attendance	7	5	-.18	-.22

junior high grades. These 861 ES's were then grouped for further study into five major categories of the dependent variables, (a) academic achievement; (b) personal adjustment; (c) self-concept; (d) attitude toward school; and (e) attendance.

Academic Achievement

The majority of all effect sizes (62 per cent) were measurements of academic achievement. This is particularly true of measures obtained from more recent studies. The 536 achievement ES's were obtained from forty-seven individual studies and indicated that the retained groups scored .19 of a standard deviation unit lower than the promoted comparison groups. With each study given equal weight, the mean ES was -.31. When academic achievement was further subdivided into language arts, reading, mathematics, and social studies measures, the promoted comparison groups outscored the retained groups in each subarea. When the effects of retention on achievement were explored by grade of retention (see table 2), ES's in the upper elementary grades were more strongly negative. On average, children who repeated fourth grade were later found to be .37 standard deviation behind promoted control children. The negative effects of retention were not so great in the earlier grades but nonetheless showed harm rather than

Table 2: Mean Effect Sizes for Academic Achievement

By grade of retention	K	1	2	3	4	5–7
TOTAL						
weighted by effect (# effects)	−.08(41)	+.06(75)	+.29(29)	−.20(123)	−.37(81)	−.37(108)
weighted by study (# studies)	−.28(8)	−.28(12)	−.10(4)	−.15(7)	−.36(6)	−.38(5)
NEGATIVE STUDIES	−.32(25)	−.52(35)	−.45(11)	−.39(105)	−.37(81)	−.37(108)
	−.37(7)	−.54(9)	−.38(3)	−.33(6)	−.36(6)	−.38(5)
POSITIVE STUDIES	+.29(16)	+.57(40)	+.74(18)	+.95(18)	0	0
	+.29(1)	+.53(3)	+.74(1)	+.95(1)		

Equal years (same age, different grades)	1 Yr	2 Yrs	3 Yrs	3+ Yrs
TOTAL	−.45(178)	−.51(32)	−.67(22)	−.83(18)
	−.41(28)	−.64(5)	−.74(3)	−.88(3)
NEGATIVE STUDIES	−.46(174)	−.51(32)	−.67(22)	−.88(18)
	−.46(26)	−.64(5)	−.74(3)	−.88(3)
POSITIVE STUDIES	+.24(4)	0	0	0
	+.27(2)			

Equal grades (different ages, same grade)	1 Yr	2 Yrs	3 Yrs	3+ Yrs
TOTAL	+.25(107)	+.19(61)	+.09(33)	.00(41)
	.00(10)	+.02(7)	−.12(5)	+.04(6)
NEGATIVE STUDIES	−.03(77)	−.19(25)	−.28(15)	−.34(28)
	−.22(8)	−.28(4)	−.25(4)	−.31(4)
POSITIVE STUDIES	+.96(30)	+.46(36)	+.40(18)	+.73(13)
	+.88(2)	+.42(3)	+.40(1)	+.74(2)

benefit from retention. Based on eight studies in kindergarten and twelve studies in first grade, the average effects were −.28 and −.28, respectively.

By the nature of the phenomenon under study, all ES's could be divided into one of two categories based on the time at which the achievement measures were compared: (a) after the retained groups and the comparison groups had spent an equal number of years in school; and (b) after the retained groups and the comparison groups had completed the same grade in school. Thus, if children had been retained in first grade, type (a) comparisons would evaluate their performance at the end of a second year of first grade as compared to the performance of promoted controls who were completing second grade. Type (b) comparisons would involve waiting a year until the repeating children had also finished second grade and then comparing same-grade performance. In both same-age and same-grade studies, the retention year itself was considered year one. This is the year when retained children should have been at their best because they were repeating familiar material and taking for a second time normative tests designed for their younger classmates. Note that when same-grade, year one comparisons were made, the control children's scores were the original low test scores possibly used to select them as controls, whereas the retained children's scores were from a second year's retesting on the same test. Regression to the mean could affect the retained group's scores but not the control scores. In all other comparisons, regression artifacts could influence both sets of scores equally.

When a mean ES was calculated for those measurements taken one year after retention on same-age children, a value of −.45 was obtained. After one year the retained groups were scoring .45 standard deviation unit lower than the comparison groups who had gone on to the next grade and in many cases were being tested on more advanced material. Each subsequent year this difference became larger with the difference reaching .83 standard deviation unit for measures taken four or more years after the time of retention. Because this type of comparison produced so few positive studies, two out of twenty-eight in year one and none thereafter, the result weighted by study was very similar to the result weighted by individual effects, −.41.

When those measures taken after the completion of the same grade were used to calculate a mean ES, the retained groups outperformed the promoted comparison groups. This advantage, however, steadily decreased with the completion of subsequent grades. After three grades there was no longer a difference between the groups, although the retained children were a year older.

Personal Adjustment

Of the total 861 effect sizes calculated, 234 were grouped as measures of personal adjustment. These 234 ES's were obtained from 27 individual studies and had a mean of −.09. Following retention the retained groups scored .09 standard deviation units lower than the comparison groups on measures of personal adjustment. Three sub-categories (social adjustment, emotional adjustment, and behavior) were separated for further analysis. In each of these sub-areas the mean ES weighted by effect was not appreciably different from 0. However, this finding of 'no negative' effect is created in large part by the large number and size of positive effects from only three positive studies. If studies were weighted equally, the overall ES for personal adjustment would be −.21, and ranges from −.23 to −.12 in the subareas. Unique characteristics of the few positive studies are considered in a later section.

Self-Concept, Attitude toward School and Attendance

Eleven of the studies measured the effects of retention on the self-concepts of pupils, with a mean ES of −.13. Ten studies yielded thirty-nine ES's with measures of attitude toward school indicating that the two sets of groups were essentially not different with respect to measures of attitude. The mean ES for attendance of −.18 indicated that on average retained groups were absent from school at a greater rate.

Secondary Analysis

Because the overall effect was somewhat less negative than that reported in an earlier meta-analysis (Holmes and Matthews, 1984), where a mean ES of −.37 was obtained from an analysis of forty-four studies, an attempt was made to pinpoint what had changed. Based on an analysis of the nineteen additional studies (Holmes, 1986), a set of seven studies was separated as those which were reporting results somewhat in favor of retention. The frequency distribution of effect sizes for all studies was constructed and examined. As seen in figure 1, a slight bulge or positive skew was noted in the upper end of the distribution.

In the secondary analysis, a great deal hinged on the hint of bimodality. By chance, one would have expected some positive results from studies looking at a negative treatment. Had the curve been smooth, there would have been no justification in selecting the positive studies to analyze separately. The bulge, however, hints that there may be two populations of studies.

To represent the 'two populations of studies' all sixty-three studies were classified as either positive or negative studies based on their average effects. In addition to the seven new positive studies, two positive studies were found among the pre-1984 studies. Mean effect sizes were then calculated for the two types of studies as shown in table 2. The implication is that two different kinds or conditions of retention are being investigated in these studies: (a) one in which the retained pupils suffer negative consequences from being retained and (b) one in which some positive benefits are obtained.

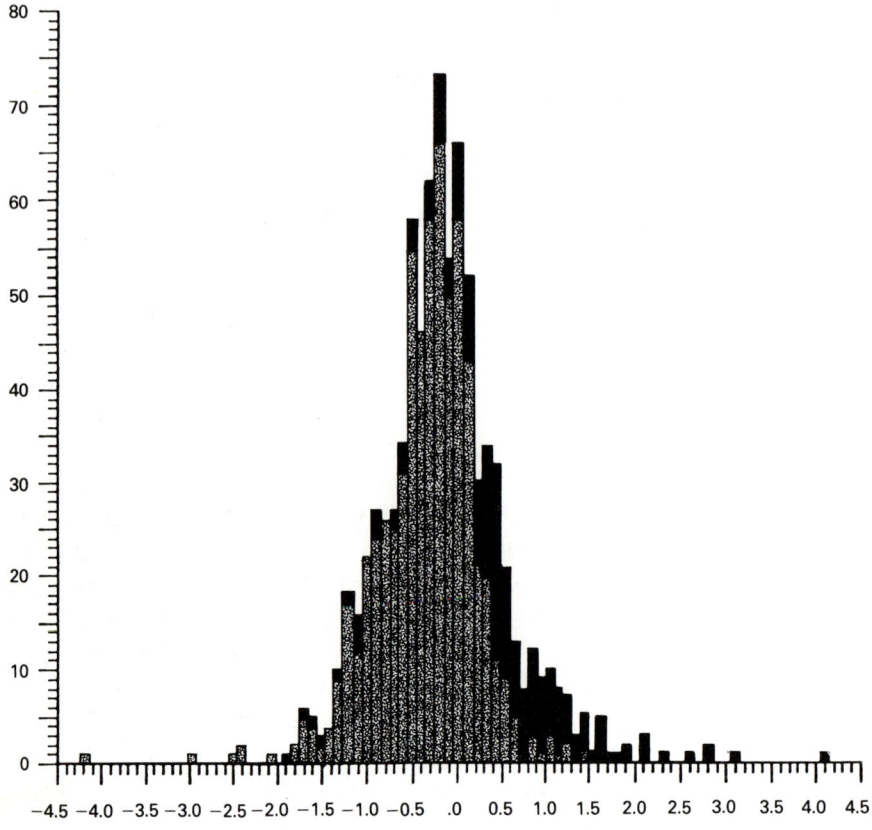

Figure 1: Distribution of Effect Sizes from Positive (■) and Negative (□) Studies

The Negative Studies

Of the total of sixty-three studies, fifty-four resulted in overall negative effects. When the effects in table 1 were reanalyzed using only data from the negative studies, the mean effect sizes were substantially more negative for all areas and subareas. Academic achievement was the area with the largest negative mean ES. Retained groups scored .4 of a standard deviation below the comparison groups. Table 2 reveals that for the majority of studies with negative average effects, early retention is not less harmful than when it occurs during higher grades. In addition, the data suggest that the negative effect not only remains, but continues to grow during subsequent years.

The Positive Studies

The set of positive studies consisted of nine investigations, most of which have been published during the 1980s. These studies have generally focused on academic achievement as the outcome measure. Seven of these nine studies were conducted as dissertation or masters theses studies. Although the samples and conditions of retention were not always reported in detail, an attempt was made to provide a description of these retentions which appear to be at least somewhat effective.

Sample characteristics

It appears that all of these studies were conducted in settings described as suburban and included few if any black subjects. The populations were described as ranging from lower middle to upper middle class. In most cases some form of IQ score was reported for the retained pupils. These children tended to all have IQ scores at or about 100. In addition these children tended to be scoring less than .75 of a standard deviation below norm on standardized achievement tests. In fact, although they were reading well below norm, in one study the retained children were scoring at national average in mathematics and language arts. Thus, children in the few studies where retention 'worked', were systematically more able than the traditional population of retainees who were more likely slower learners with below average IQ and achievement. In some cases, a more able population may have been obtained simply because the local school district was more affluent. In other cases the constraints of data collection may have produced results for only the retained children with the best attendance records and least mobility. In one study (Hains, 1981), students were systematically excluded from the analysis if they had a 'high rate of mobility', which resulted in a greatly disproportionate reduction in the retained sample.

Program characteristics

The following is a composite description of the retention plans of the positive studies. Potential failures were identified early and were given special help. When the decision to retain was made, the parents were first consulted for permission. An individualized and detailed educational plan was prepared for remediation purposes. The children were not recycled through the same curriculum but were instead placed in special classes with low student-teacher ratios. One of the plans, described in the greatest detail, placed all retainees in classes of twelve to fifteen students with a teacher and a full-time aide (Dolan, 1982). In addition, many of the children were mainstreamed into the regular program with their age peers for part of the day. Pupil-personnel-services teams consulted on a regular basis and a continuous evaluation was made. The results of this continuing evaluation could at any time allow for the child to rejoin his or her age cohort.

While most of the successful retention comparisons involved extra help for the retained children, none of the positive studies provided extra help to the at-risk control children. In cases where such a comparison was made (for example, Leinhardt, 1980), the promoted children with extra help did better than the retained children with extra help, causing the study to be classified as a negative outcome.

Academic achievement

From the seven positive studies which measured academic achievement, 112 ES's were obtained which yielded a mean effect size of +.60. Large positive ES's were obtained for language arts, reading and mathematics. All but four of these effect sizes were obtained from comparisons made after an equal number of grades had been completed (the retained groups had been in school an additional year and were therefore one year older). The positive effects of retention observed after the repeat year tended to diminish over the subsequent grades.

Matched Studies

In summarizing research on retention, there was particular concern that findings might depend on the degree of statistical control. Would markedly different findings result when the retained and promoted subjects were matched on various relevant criteria? Twenty-five of the sixty-three studies had matched subjects. All but one of these had included IQ and/or achievement test scores among the matching criteria. Table 3 summarizes the matching criteria employed by each of the studies and its respective mean effect size. A mean ES of −.28 was calculated. When just those studies matching on prior achievement test scores were used a mean ES of −.30 was obtained. Although these groups of retained students had been matched prior to retention on achievement test scores, they were scoring almost one-third of a

Table 3: Studies with Matched Subjects

Study	Matched On						ES
	IQ	Achievement test	SES	Sex	Grades	Other	
1	X		X	X		X	−.23
2	X		X	X			−.39
3		X					−.73
4	X			X		X	−.96
5				X	X	X	−.66
6		X					−.42
7	X	X	X	X		X	−.63
8	X	X				X	−.06
9		X		X		X	−.40
10	X			X		X	+.20
11	X			X		X	−.32
12		X				X	−.05
13		X					−.04
14		X		X			−.43
15	X	X		X		X	−.48
16	X		X			X	+.31
17		X	X			X	+.76
18		X					−.39
19		X	X	X		X	−.41
20		X	X	X		X	−.13
21	X	X				X	−.65
22	X			X		X	−.59
23	X						−.61
24	X	X		X		X	−.15
25	X	X	X	X			+.35
Mean	−.30	−.30					−.28

standard deviation below their matched counterparts. Thus, better controlled studies showed on average a greater negative effect for retention.

Conclusions

The meta-analysis of the sixty-three studies is consistent with previous reviews of research and an earlier meta-analysis finding largely negative effects for retention. On average, retained children are worse off than their promoted counterparts on both personal adjustment and academic outcomes.

Of the sixty-three empirical studies, fifty-four found negative results while only nine were positive. Although it appears that some success has been achieved by those plans being evaluated in the 'positive studies', two notes of caution must be emphasized. First, the few positive studies involved intensive remediation plus retention and ironically an unusually able population of retainees. These studies failed to compare retention plus remediation to promotion plus an equivalent amount of remediation. Second, positive studies tended to be based on more favorable comparisons with grade peers rather than age peers, used only academic outcome measures, and most did not follow-up past one year. When all available longitudinal studies were taken together, the same-grade apparent benefit disappeared over time so that retained children were no better off in relation to their younger at-risk controls who went immediately on to the next grade.

When only well-matched studies were examined, a greater negative effect was found for retention than in the research literature as a whole. In studies where retained children and promoted controls were matched on IQ and prior achievement, repeating a grade had an average negative effect of −.30 standard deviations. The weight of empirical evidence argues against grade retention. As Holmes and Matthews concluded in 1984, 'Those who continue to retain pupils at grade level do so despite cumulative research evidence showing that the potential for negative effects consistently outweighs positive outcomes' (p. 232).

References

Ayres, L. P. (1909) *Laggards in our Schools*, New York, Russell Sage Foundation.

Bocks, W. M. (1977) 'Non-promotion: A year to grow?', *Educational Leadership*, 34, 5, pp. 379–83.

Coffield, W. H. and Blommers, P. (1954) 'Effects of non-promotion on educational achievement in the elementary school', *Journal of Educational Psychology*, 47, 4, pp. 235–50.

Glass, G. V. (1978) 'Integrating findings: The meta-analysis of research', *Review of Research in Education*, 5, pp. 351–79.

Holmes, C. T. (1983) 'The fourth R: Retention', *Journal of Research and Development in Education*, 17, pp. 1–6.

Holmes, C. T. (1984) 'Estimating effect sizes in meta-analysis', *Journal of Experimental Education*, 52, 2, pp. 106–9.

Holmes, C. T. (1986) 'A synthesis of recent research on non-promotion: A five year follow-up', paper presented at the annual meeting of the American Educational Research Association, San Francisco, April.

Holmes, C. T. and Matthews, K. M. (1984) 'The effects of nonpromotion on elementary and junior high school pupils: A meta-analysis', *Review of Educational Research*, 54, 2, pp. 225–36.

JACKSON, G. B. (1975) 'The research evidence on the effect of grade retention', *Review of Educational Research*, 45, pp. 613–35.
LIGHT, R. J. and SMITH, P. V. (1971) 'Accumulating evidence: Procedures for resolving contradictions among different studies', *Harvard Educational Review*, 41, pp. 429–71.

Appendix: Studies Included in the Meta-analysis

ABIDIN, R. R., GOLLADAY, W. M. and HOWERTON, A. L. (1971) 'Elementary school retention: An unjustifiable discriminatory and noxious policy', *Journal of School Psychology*, 9, pp. 410–17.
ALLEN, J. W. (1971/1972) 'The retained pupil: An ex post facto investigation of school nonpromotion as it related to school grades, teacher ratings, and self-concepts', *Master's Thesis in Education*, 21, 18.
AMMONS, J. D. (1975) 'A study of the effects of nonpromotion and promotion as related to achievement and self concept of elementary school students', *Dissertation Abstracts International*, 36, 5011A (University Microfilms No. 76-46 17).
ANDERSON, H. V. (1957) 'The identification and evaluation of differences among promoted, not promoted, and considered for non-promotion but promoted pupils in the third grades', *Dissertation Abstracts International*, 18, 128 (University Microfilms No. 24 223).
ANFINSON, R. D. (1941) 'School progress and pupil adjustment', *The Elementary School Journal*, 41, 501–14.
ARCHER, M. C. (1967) 'A study of non-promotion relative to normal grade expectancy in selected Catholic elementary schools in Illinois', unpublished doctoral dissertation, Loyola University.
ARTHUR, G. A. (1936) 'A study of the achievement of sixty grade one repeaters as compared with that of nonrepeaters of the same mental age', *Journal of Experimental Education*, 5, pp. 203–5.
ASKEW, F. E. (1983) 'A causal-comparative study of achievement test scores of promoted and non-promoted elementary students with similar intellectual abilities' (master's thesis, Central Washington University), *Master's Thesis in Education*, 33, 21.
BOESEL, F. F. (1960) 'Effects of non-promotion on reading achievement and behavior tendencies in the primary grades', *Dissertation Abstracts International*, 21, 2191 (University Microfilms No. 60-839).
CAPLAN, P. J. and KINSBOURNE, M. (1973) 'The role of classroom conduct in the promotion and retention of elementary school children', *Journal of Experimental Education*, 41, 8–11.
CHANSKY, N. M. (1964) 'Progress of promoted and repeating grade 1 failures', *Journal of Experimental Education*, 32, pp. 225–37.
COFFIELD, W. H. (1954) 'A longitudinal study of the effects of nonpromotion on educational achievement in the elementary school', *Dissertation Abstracts International*, 14, 2291 (University Microfilms No. 10 200).
COOPER, A. D. (1980) 'The relationship between nonpromotion and achievement, self-concept, and overt behavior of children experiencing difficulty

in kindergarten or first grade', *Dissertation Abstracts International*, 41, 1940A (University Microfilms No. 80-26 108).
DOBBS, V. and NEVILLE, D. (1967) 'The effect of nonpromotion on the achievement of groups matched from retained first graders and promoted second graders', *Journal of Educational Research*, 60, pp. 472–5.
DOLAN, L. (1982) 'A follow-up evaluation of a transition class program for children with school and learning readiness problems', *The Exceptional Child*, 29, 2, pp. 101–10.
DOTSON, M. M. S. (1977) 'The relationship between fifth grade children's attitude toward reading and factors such as success or failure in reading, intelligence quotient, sex, grade retention, and socioeconomic status', unpublished doctoral dissertation, University of Tennessee, Knoxville.
FARLEY, E. S. (1936) 'Regarding repeaters: Sad effect of failure upon the child', *Nation's Schools*, 18, 37–39.
FINLAYSON, H. J. (1975) 'The effect of non-promotion upon the self concept of pupils in primary grades', unpublished doctoral dissertation, Temple University.
GERONIME, M. E. (1959/1960) 'An evaluation of promotion versus non-promotion in the primary grades', *Master's Thesis in Education*, 9, 17.
GERSTEL, D. J. (1981) 'An investigation of non-promotion and its effect on reading achievement and social and emotional development' (doctoral dissertation, Hofstra University), *Dissertation Abstracts International*, 42/02A, 524.
GOODLAD, J. I. (1954) 'Some effects of promotion and nonpromotion upon the social adjustment of children', *Journal of Experimental Education*, 22, pp. 301–28.
GUTIERREZ, M. L. (1983) 'The effects of nonpromotion on first through fourth grade students and intellectual maturity' (doctoral dissertation, Northern Arizona University), *Dissertation Abstracts International*, 44/04A, 984.
HAINS, A. A. (1981) 'The effect of retention on self concept of elementary students in grades three through five as compared to the self concept of elementary students who have been socially promoted', *Dissertation Abstracts International*, 42, 2398A (University Microfilms No. 81-17 518).
HASSEN, J. K. (1980) 'The effectiveness of the transition room in the Centralia, Washington School District' (master's thesis, Central Washington University), *Master's Thesis in Education*, 30, 19.
HENDERSON, E. H. and LONG, B. H. (1971) 'Personal-social correlates of academic success among disadvantaged school beginners', *Journal of School Psychology*, 9, pp. 101–13.
HIGHTOWER, A. J. (1955) 'A study of the selected differences between normally progressing and educationally retarded pupils enrolled in the Emery Street High School, Dalton, Georgia, 1954–1955', unpublished master's thesis, Atlanta University.
KAMII, C. K. and WEIKART, D. P. (1963) 'Marks, achievement, and intelligence of seventh graders who were retained (non-promoted) once in elementary school', *Journal of Educational Research*, 56, pp. 452–9.
KLAUBER, R. W. (1971) 'The effects of failure on the academic achievement

level of elementary school children', *Dissertation Abstracts International*, 31, 3959A (University Microfilms No. 71-03 276).
KOONS, C. L. (1968) 'Non-promotion of first and second grade students and subsequent reading performance', unpublished doctoral dissertation, University of Tulsa, OK.
LEINHARDT, G. (1980) 'Transition rooms: Promoting maturation or reducing education?', *Journal of Educational Psychology*, 72, 1, 55–61.
LONG, J. M. (1970/71) 'A review of the academic gains made by non-promoted and promoted pupils in the Tenino Elementary School', *Master's Thesis in Education*, 20, 17.
MAY, D. C. and WELCH, E. L. (1984) 'The effects of developmental placement and early retention on children's later scores on standardized tests', *Psychology in the Schools*, 21, pp. 381–5.
MCDANIEL, A. (1987) 'The effects of non-promotion on social adjustment in elementary students', paper presented at the annual meeting of the American Educational Research Association, Washington, DC, April.
MCELWEE, E. W. (1932) 'A comparative study of the personality traits of 300 accelerated, normal, and retarded children', *Journal of Educational Research*, 26, pp. 31–4.
MCGILL, M. E. (1965/1966) 'A comparative study of the gains made by nonpromoted and promoted students in the Snoqualmie Valley elementary schools', *Master's Thesis in Education*, 15, 24.
MENDENHALL, M. S. (1933) 'Relative effect of special promotion and repetition upon progress in achievement tests', unpublished master's thesis, University of North Carolina, Chapel Hill.
MILLER, D. R. (1942) 'A study of some factors involved in promotion practices in elementary schools', unpublished master's thesis, University of Virginia.
MILLERT, M. M. (1977/1978) 'The effects of retention and promotion in the primary grades on the academic achievement of low achieving students', *Master's Thesis in Education*, 27, 18.
MITCHELL, W. A. (1968) 'A longitudinal study of the effects of non-promotion and remedial summer school on educational achievement in the elementary schools of Rapid City', unpublished doctoral dissertation, University of Wyoming, Laramie.
NIKLASON, L. B. (1984) 'Non-promotion: A pseudoscientific solution', *Psychology in the Schools*, 21, pp. 485–99.
OGDEN, K. W. (1971) 'An evaluation of non-promotion as a method of improving academic performance', unpublished doctoral dissertation, University of Southern California.
OGILVIE, W. L. (1960/1961) 'A longitudinal study of the effects on achievement of promotion and nonpromotion at grade 3 level', *Master's Thesis in Education*, 10, 28.
OLDHAM, B. R. (1982) 'The longitudinal effects of pupil retention practices in the first three grades' (doctoral dissertation, University of Kentucky), *Dissertation Abstracts International*, 43/12A, 3772.

OTT, E. R. (1964/1965) 'A comparison of attitudes and behavior patterns between promoted and non-promoted pupils in the elementary school', *Master's Thesis in Education*, 14, 19.

PETERSON, S. E., DEGRACIE, J. S. and AYABE, C. R. (1987) 'A longitudinal study of the effects of retention/promotion on academic achievement', *American Educational Research Journal*, 24, 1, pp. 107–18.

PLUMMER, D. L. (1982) 'The impact of grade retention on the social development of elementary school children', unpublished master's thesis, University of Georgia.

PYRON, W. L. (1987) 'Effects of Chapter 1 intervention treatment on promoted and retained students', unpublished doctoral dissertation, University of Georgia.

ROGERS, M. C. and TRAINOR, D. A. (1955) 'The non-promotion policy versus the social-promotion policy in the Boston public school system', unpublished master's thesis, Boston University.

RUSSELL, D. H., ALEXANDER, R., SHELLHAMMER, T. A. and SMITTER, F. (1952) 'The influence of repetition of a grade and of regular promotion on the attitudes of parents and children toward school', *California Journal of Elementary Education*, 21, pp. 29–41.

SANDIN, A. A. (1944) *Social and Emotional Adjustments of Regularly Promoted and Non-promoted Pupils* (Child Development Monograph No. 23), New York, Bureau of Publications, Teachers College, Columbia University.

SANDOVAL, J. and FITZGERALD, P. (1985) 'A high school follow-up of children who were promoted or attended a junior first grade', *Psychology in the Schools*, 22, pp. 164–70.

SCHUYLER, N. B. and MATTER, M. K. (1983) 'To retain or not to retain: Should achievement be your guide?', paper presented at the annual meeting of the American Educational Research Association, Montreal, April.

SHEPARD, L. A. and SMITH, M. L. (1985) 'Effects of kindergarten retention at the end of first grade', paper presented at the annual meeting of the American Educational Research Association, Chicago, April.

SKELTON, E. E. (1963/1964) 'The effectiveness of promotion and nonpromotion on academic achievement of primary groups in the Plainfield Community Elementary School', *Master's Thesis in Education*, 13, 21.

SPITHILL, A. (1965/1966) 'Effects of nonpromotion on achievement and maturation in the junior high school', *Master's Thesis in Education*, 15, 24.

STILES, H. M. (1929) 'A comparative study of a semester's gain made by three groups of elementary school pupils', unpublished master's thesis, University of Oregon.

TALMADGE, S. J. (1981/1982) 'Descriptive and predictive relationships among family environments, cognitive characteristics, behavioral ratings, transition room placement, and early reading achievement' (doctoral dissertation, University of Oregon), *Dissertation Abstracts International*, 42/8A, 3520.

TAYLOR, C. C. (1964/1965) 'A study of the tested differences between promoted and non-promoted pupils enrolled in the William J. Scott School, Atlanta, Georgia', *Master's Thesis in Education*, 14, 20.

VAUGHN, R. C. (1968) 'An analysis of the relationships among factors related to the promotion and retention of pupils', unpublished doctoral dissertation, University of Virginia.
VOLLRATH, F. K. (1982) 'A comparative study of achievement and classroom behaviors of retained and non-retained kindergarten, third and sixth grade students' (doctoral dissertation, University of Kansas), *Dissertation Abstracts International*, 44/04A, 1039.
WHITE, K. and HOWARD, J. L. (1973) 'Failure to be promoted and self concept among elementary school children', *Elementary School Guidance and Counseling*, 7, pp. 182–7.
WORTH, W. H. (1959) 'The effect of promotion and non-promotion on pupil achievement and social-personal development in the elementary school', unpublished doctoral dissertation, University of Illinois.
WRIGHT, J. B. (1979) 'The measured academic achievement of two groups of first grade students matched along five variables when one group has been retained' (doctoral dissertation, Temple University), *Dissertation Abstracts International*, 41/08A, 3418.

Chapter 3:
Repeating and Dropping Out of School[1]

James B. Grissom and Lorrie A. Shepard

Editors' Introduction

In a typical end-of-school-year news story, USA Today *reported that one-quarter of the first graders in a Mississippi community would be held back because 'they can't read at a first-grade level'* (USA Today, 15–17 April 1988, p. 1). *Consistent with the view that retention will repair deficient skills and improve students' life chances, the principal explained her decision: 'In years past, those students would have been promoted to second grade. Then they might have dropped out in five, six, or seven years.'*

What are the effects of grade retention on dropout prevention? Is it true to say that holding children back will make them less at risk for dropping out? In the research literature on retention there is little mention of long term consequences. In Holmes' review (chapter 2), for example, only eighteen of sixty-three controlled studies provided any data three or more years past the retention year. None followed retained students into high school. It is in the literature on school dropouts, however, where an association between retention and dropping out is noted consistently. This correlational evidence suggests that holding children back increases rather than decreases their risk for dropping out of school.

In this chapter, Grissom and Shepard review previous studies that examined the retention-dropout relationship. Then they use causal modeling techniques to assess the direct effect of repeating on dropout behavior while accounting for relevant background factors, especially school achievement. Their findings, consistent across districts of very different socioeconomic levels, show that retained students experience a greater risk for dropping out that cannot be explained by their poor achievement. Even with appropriate caveats regarding the limitations of non-experimental analytic methods, the most defensible reading of the evidence suggests that the first graders made to repeat in Mississippi have now been placed more at risk for failing to complete high school, perhaps to a significant degree.

To the teacher deciding whether Justin should be retained in first grade, his later pupil career and its successful conclusion seem remote considerations. To the high school counselor, the concern for keeping pupils in school is only too immediate and the word 'retention' has a different meaning altogether. Recent statistics on the proportion of school dropouts have led some to declare a crisis. Policy researchers have looked for reasons and predictors. They have found for example that family background and early school achievement predict tendencies to drop out (Natriello, 1987). Pertinent to this volume on grade failure, various researchers have noted the strong relation between the tendency to dropout and the fact of having repeated a grade in school.

Often when the correlation between grade retention and dropping out has been observed, its potential importance for educational policy has been dismissed because of the obvious explanation that poor achievement very likely accounts for both retention and school leaving. For example, in a longitudinal study of dropouts in Dade County, Florida, Stephenson (1985) found that the dropout rate was 55 per cent for overage students compared to only 27 per cent for normal-age students. However, he cautioned readers, 'not to conclude that retention *per se* causes higher dropout rates. More likely is the occurrence that low achievement causes both being retained and dropping out. Even more likely is the occurrence that low interest in school, little extra-school support for school accomplishment, and a host of other factors cause low achievement, which ultimately causes "dropping out"' (p. 11). Rarely has there been a systematic attempt to account for achievement or the interrelation among antecedent variables before assessing the retention-dropout relation.

The purpose of this chapter is to examine the effect of grade retention on dropping out of school. We summarize briefly the simple correlational studies which first raised the issue that retention might exacerbate the problem of high school dropouts. Then, the few studies which provided some degree of statistical control are discussed in more detail. Next, our own analyses of three large-city data sets are presented using causal modeling. Lastly, the research findings on the reasons for dropping out are summarized in an attempt to understand why factors that pull students out of school may be more potent for those who are overage for their grade as a consequence of their retention.

Simple Descriptive and Correlational Research

Reviewers of the dropout literature are able to construct profiles of the typical school dropout by listing across studies the variables that distinguish graduates from dropouts. Dropouts consistently come from lower socioeconomic backgrounds, have little support for school from home, perform poorly on academic tasks, have poor self-esteem, a history of poor attendance and trouble with school, and so on (Rumberger, 1987; Wehlage and Rutter, 1986). It is also typical that dropouts have repeated one or more grades in school. For example, the Association of California Urban School Districts (1985) reported that in Los Angeles dropouts had been retained five times more often than graduates. 'A student who fails either of the first two grades has only a twenty percent chance of graduating' (p. 2).

It is not our intention to recount all individual studies. Rather, we present a few examples to illustrate the methods and findings of simple descriptive and correlational studies. It is not possible to make cause-and-effect interpretations with certainty from such data. But the relationships between retention and dropping out are striking and suggestive of the need for further investigation.

Table 1 is taken from a report by Randall (1966) examining the characteristics of dropouts and graduates in the Bloomington public schools of Minnesota. Two-thirds of the dropouts had repeated one or more grades compared to only 3 per cent of graduates. These data are a classic example of the results found in dozens of unpublished reports from school districts across the United States over the past twenty years. The study also provided similar cross-tabulations contrasting dropouts and graduates on standardized test results, attendance, grade point average, and participation in extra-curricular activities with differences occurring in the predictable direction in each case. The interrelationships among these factors were not examined. A more contemporary example of a similar school district study was reported by Noth and O'Neill (1981). In the Pasco School District in Wash-

Table 1: Percent of Dropouts and Graduates in the Bloomington Class of 1965 Who Repeated None, One, or Two Years of School

	Dropouts Percent	Graduates Percent
None	34.1	97.1
One year	45.9	2.9
Two years	20.0	0.0

Source: Randall (1966)

ington state, 50 per cent of the high school dropouts had repeated a grade in school. Of those dropouts who repeated, far more than half had repeated first grade.

Another older study is an example of large-scale surveys of dropouts conducted by social scientists interested in education or labor economics. Bachman, Green and Wirtanen (1971) studied a nationally representative sample of high school boys and, again, identified various variables that distinguished three groups, those who dropped out, those who graduated but did not attend college, and those who went on to college. Their conclusions about failing a grade in school (against which they caution inferring cause and effect) were as follows:

> The relationship between failing a grade and later educational attainment is quite strong. More than half of the dropouts had failed a grade by the time they reached tenth grade; the same sort of failure had occurred for 27 per cent of those who ended their education with high school graduation, and only 8 per cent of those who went on to college. (p. 54).

Bachman *et al.* (1971) also conducted multiple classification analyses to determine how well dropping out could be predicted from a combination of background, school experience, and personality measures. Similarly, multiple regression or discriminant function analyses found in most up-to-date studies are an improvement over single variable studies because they acknowledge the interrelationships among predictive factors. Multiple correlation studies have not, however, been focused on the unique effect of retention. Instead, most studies have been designed to answer an actuarial question: 'What variables are effective in predicting dropouts so that district administrators can identify students at risk and intervene?'

A recent example of a multivariate study was reported by Curtis, Doss, MacDonald and Davis (1983). Table 2 shows the differences between dropouts and graduates on each of their significant predictors. Grade level is the retention variable with students categorized according to their normal-progress grade expectation. The disproportionate number of repeaters among the dropouts is again observed. A discriminant function equation based on these variables was able to predict dropping out versus graduating with 78 per cent accuracy. Also shown in table 2 are the standardized coefficients which reflect the weight[2] of each predictor. Being behind in grade is the second strongest predictor of dropping out. Although the authors did not try to isolate the effect of retention, the fact that grade level makes a modest but significant

Table 2: Descriptive Statistics and Discriminant Analysis Results, Dropouts and Nondropouts, Austin Independent School District

	Descriptive Statistics	
	Dropouts (N = 942)	Graduates and stay-ins (N = 2965)
GPA		
Average	76.6	85.8
% in 60–69.9 gpa range	19.8%	1.5%
% in 70–79.9 gpa range	47.1%	18.9%
% in 80–89.9 gpa range	28.7%	47.5%
% in 90–99.0 gpa range	4.4%	32.1%
Grade level		
% Below grade	45.3%	15.2%
% At grade	53.1%	75.5%
% Above grade	1.6%	9.3%
Ethnicity		
% Hispanic	35.6%	20.6%
% Black	19.7%	16.4%
% Anglo/Other	44.7%	63.0%
Discipline		
Average # of Serious Discipline Incidents	.5	.1
Sex		
% Male	52.3%	50.4%
% Female	47.7%	49.6%

	Stepwise Discriminant Analysis Results		
Step	Variable	Wilk's Lambda	Standardized Coefficients
1	GPA	.770	.85
2	Grade Level	.752	.32
3	Black	.744	.24
4	Discipline	.742	–.13
5	Sex	.739	–.13

Source: Curtis, Doss, MacDonald and Davis (1983)

contribution to the prediction after considering grade point average suggests that the effect of retention cannot be explained as merely the effect of poor achievement.

Two other multiple correlational studies deserve brief mention because they are often cited in the dropout literature. In a 1972 study of black males in St. Louis, Stroup and Robins found that repeating grades in elementary school was the single strongest predictor of dropping out of high school. The study included numerous family background measures and IQ but no measure of school achievement. Lloyd (1978) could predict dropping out with 75 per cent accuracy using IQ, reading scores, retention, gpa, and family background. The surprising feature of Lloyd's study was that all these variables were measured in the third grade. Being overage in third grade or having been retained by that time correlated .31 and .27, respectively, with dropping out of high school.

Accounting for Achievement

Repeating a grade might directly increase the risk of dropping out. The competing hypothesis is that poor achievement explains both retention and dropping out. Is it possible to disentangle the effects of poor achievement and grade failure? Here we focus on a series of studies (Hess and Lauber, 1985; Rice, Toles, Schulz, Harvey and Foster, 1987; Schulz, Toles, Rice, Brauer and Harvey, 1986) conducted in the Chicago public schools that in various ways adjusted for student achievement before examining the effect of retention on dropping out. The Chicago studies are also exemplary in that extensive effort was made to improve the validity of the dropout information. All categories of school leaving were included, follow-ups were made of delayed graduations, and cohorts of students were studied over time so that the true attrition from an entering freshman class could be examined.

Hess and Lauber (1985) first controlled for achievement simply by comparing normal-age and overage dropout rates within achievement strata. Table 3 is reproduced from their report. Students with low reading achievement scores are more likely to drop out. At each level of achievement, however, the dropout rate is appreciably higher for overage students. The authors also noted, as indicated by the diagonal arrows in table 3, that the dropout rate for overage students in the next-higher stanine is worse than for that of lower-reading normal-age

Table 3: Dropout Rates by Achievement Level for Normal-Age and Overage Students, Chicago Class of 1982

	Normal-Age	Overage
Stanine 1	62.1%	73.2%
Stanines 2 and 3	46.1%	57.5%
Stanine 4	36.3%	52.5%
Stanine 5	27.0%	43.8%
Stanine 6 up	18.3%	37.9%

Source: Hess and Lauber (1985)

students. Even if the retention could have served to raise reading scores by a stanine, the chances of students dropping out were increased.

The Hess and Lauber report was based on 30,000 students in the 1978 entering cohort. Schulz, Toles, Rice, Brauer and Harvey (1986) combined these data with successive cohorts entering through 1980 which resulted in a sample of 77,000. They predicted dropout status using both log-linear and multiple regression analyses. When eighth-grade reading scores and entry age were entered first, they (and their interaction) accounted for 80 per cent of the modeled variance (excluding error variance) or 38 per cent of the total variance. Figure 1, reproduced from their report, illustrates the relation between achievement and dropping out for normal-age and overage students. On average, the dropout rate of overage students is 13 per cent higher than the dropout rate of normal-age students with equivalent reading achievement scores. Read the other way, overage students must have reading scores approximately 2.25 grade levels higher than normal-age students to have the same chance of graduating. Schulz *et al.* (1986) concluded that a year of remedial study could not possibly boost achievement enough to offset the negative effect of being overage.

Another Chicago study, reported by Rice, Toles, Schulz, Harvey and Foster (1987), provided a direct measure of the consequences of deciding to retain more children. In the spring of 1980, a more stringent eighth-grade promotion policy was imposed. Therefore, Rice *et al.* were able to examine directly what happened to dropout rates when retentions were increased. Their data for three cohorts are presented in table 4. The freshman class entering in 1979 was the last class unaffected by stricter eighth-grade promotion standards. The 1980 class was unique because it was the only class to go through with a substantial number of low achievers removed. Low-scoring students from the class of 1980 subsequently joined the 1981 cohort after repeating the eighth grade. Notice the appreciable decline in the total number of 1980 students. Predictably, because students were being retained in eighth grade, the attrition was greatest in the normal-age and lowest achievement stratum. With so many at-risk students removed, the 1980 cohort had a substantially reduced dropout rate, 36 per cent overall compared to 42 per cent the two preceding years (see Hess and Lauber, 1985).

The intervention effect of the retention policy is seen in the 1981 data. Here the overall dropout rate climbed to an all-time high of 45 per cent. Furthermore, the *rate* of dropping out for overage students actually increased, especially for those in the middle and above-average achievement categories. Rice *et al.* (1987) used logistic regression

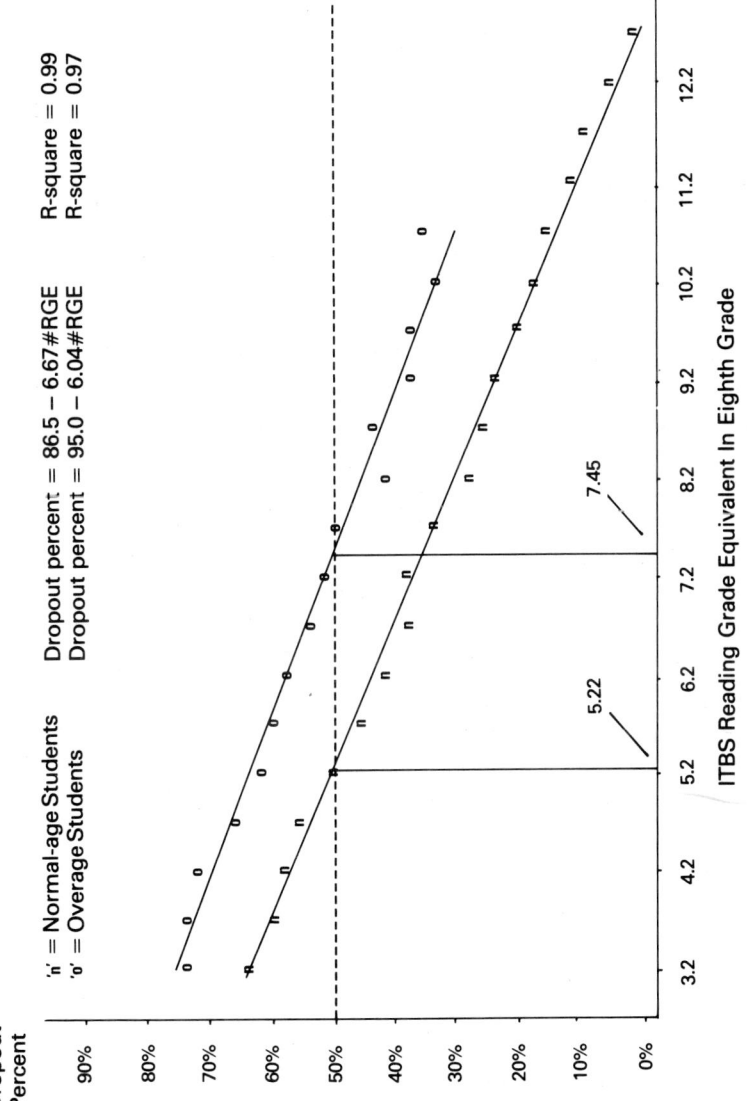

Figure 1: Plot of Dropout Rate against Reading Achievement for Normal-age and Overage Entering Freshmen, 1978–1980, Chicago Public Schools
Source: Schulz, Toles and Rice (1986)

Table 4: Enrollment and Dropout Rates 1979 to 1981, Chicago Public Schools

	Entering			Dropout Rate		
	1979	1980	1981	1979	1980	1981
Total	29,023	24,867	25,959	41.6	36.1	44.9
Age						
Normal-Age	21,495	17,959	16,769	34.2	29.0	33.9
Over-Age	7,528	6,908	9,190	62.5	54.8	64.9
Achievement[a]						
0.5 to 7.0	11,753	9,069	8,867	53.8	48.7	55.0
7.1 to 8.0	4,482	4,251	4,422	38.1	33.4	42.1
8.1+	7,881	7,448	7,389	23.2	20.6	25.9
Missing	4,547	4,099	5,281	45.2	39.5	56.7
Achievement and Age						
<7.1 & Normal-Age	7,334	5,157	4,440	46.5	40.9	44.8
7.1 – 8.0 & Normal-Age	4,071	3,440	3,282	35.8	30.6	37.4
8.1+ & Normal-Age	7,358	6,913	6,636	22.0	19.3	23.4
Missing & Normal-Age	2,732	2,449	2,411	31.5	28.8	37.8
<7.1 & Over-Age	4,419	3,912	4,427	65.9	58.9	65.2
7.1 – 8.0 & Over-Age	771	811	1,140	49.8	45.4	55.6
8.1+ & Over-Age	523	535	753	40.3	36.8	48.2
Missing & Over-Age	1,815	1,650	2,870	65.9	55.3	72.7

(a) Achievement expressed as reading grade equivalents from Iowa Test of Basic Skills.
Source: Rice, Toles, Schulz, Harvey and Foster (1987)

weights based on the 1979 class to predict dropping out in the 1981 cohort; predictors included race and sex as well as reading achievement and entry age. According to the authors, 'The 1979 parameters were unable to predict the general rise in dropout rates for the 1981 class. More importantly the 1979 model was unable to predict the dropout rate for 1981 overage students. As a result of better achievement scores, the 1979 model parameters predicted a reduction in the overage 1981 dropout rate. However, the observed dropout rate for the 1981 overage group did not decrease (it increased) which generated an under-prediction of the 1981 overage dropout rate' (p. 4). Rice concluded that being overage was more of a handicap than poor achievement.

Lastly, it should be noted that the full consequences of the non-promotion policy are very likely underestimated in the Rice et al. (1987) paper because some students may never have entered high school after being retained in eighth grade. Even after the large number of children removed from the 1980 class had had the opportunity to rejoin the 1981 group, the enrollment figures show a sharp decline compared to the entering class of 1979. A long-term decline in enrollments in Chicago makes it impossible to attribute the entire 1979 to 1981 decrease to early dropouts; nonetheless, it is plausible that some portion of the attrition is due to dropouts that occurred before high school and thus outside the boundaries of the study.

Causal-model Analyses

In this section we present our own analyses of three large-city-school data sets using causal modeling. Our purposes are to provide a conceptual framework as well as statistical controls and to test the similarity of findings across communities of quite different socioeconomic status.

Conceptual Model

For policy purposes it is important to understand whether the practice of grade retention contributes directly to the dropout problem. A structural model was developed to represent the hypothesized relations among factors leading to dropping out of high school. Causal modeling or structural equation models are the preferred statistical procedures for attempting to make causal inferences from non-experimental data.

The rationale is given here for the conceptual model used in figure 3 with data from the Austin Independent School District. The same model, with slight changes in variable definitions which we describe later, was then used to reanalyze the Chicago public schools data and data from a high socioeconomic school system.

In the model, the exogenous variables (those that exist before the schooling process begins) are student sex, ethnic group and socioeconomic status (SES). There are sex differences in early learning and behavior which account for differences in measured achievement and retention. Although the relation between sex and dropping out is modeled, it remains an open question whether gender differences in dropping out will be so strong once achievement and differential retention are accounted for. SES is expected to have an effect on both retention and dropping out but ethnicity is not thought to influence these variables once other factors are controlled. Rumberger (1983) has provided compelling evidence that apparent race differences in dropping out can be explained by group differences in family background. Rumberger's measures of SES were quite complete, however, involving the number of parents in the home, both parental education and earnings, and a cultural index counting reading materials in the home and so forth. In the school systems' data, the only indicator of SES is whether each child is eligible for reduced-price or free lunch. To the extent that family differences in educational level are not reflected by a weak index of SES, these differences are likely to be seen as ethnic effects instead. Thus, SES and ethnicity should be considered together as measures of family background which affect achievement, retention and dropping out.

Achievement precedes retention and in many cases leads directly to the decision to fail a child. (The only exceptions occur when above-average children are retained in kindergarten and first grade for reasons of immaturity [chapter 4 in this volume]). Achievement is expected to be causally related to dropping out either because poor achievers are unable to complete work required for graduation or because low achievement causes poor self-esteem and disaffection with school.

Many researchers who study the dropout problem have tended to treat grade retention as one of several measures of school achievement (for example, Rumberger, 1987). A distinctive feature of the model and perspective advanced in this chapter is that retention is *not* synonymous with very low achievement, either in terms of who is selected for retention or its subsequent effect. There are dramatic school and teacher differences that determine whether a poorly performing student will be retained. For equally poor achievement, children are more likely to be retained if they are boys, small for their age, relatively young for their grade, seem immature, or are members of a school culture that practices retention at greater rates than other schools (Shepard and Smith, 1985). As to its consequence, retention is distinctly different from poor performance in a child's regular class. Repeating a grade is a highly visible act which separates a student from his age peers. Therefore, having been retained is expected to have a direct effect on dropping out, over and above the effect of achievement.

Each of the endogenous variables in the model has errors or disturbance terms associated with it, indicating the effect of fallibly measured variables and unpredicted variance on the estimation of parameters. Exogenous variables are assumed to be measured without error. As we have discussed, this assumption is clearly not satisfied for the measure of socioeconomic status.

Conclusions based on causal modeling depend on correct specification of the model. If all of the relevant variables are included and measured without error and if the location and direction of all causal linkages have been correctly specified, then the parameter estimates clearly represent causal connections between independent and dependent variables. If important variables are omitted from the analysis, however, the results may be biased to a greater or lesser degree. As is usually the case when causal inferences are attempted from non-randomized data, it is not possible to claim that all factors contributing to dropping out have been represented in the model. Therefore, it is important to assess the adequacy of the model and consider how serious the distortions might be from missing variables. Technically, the results of structural equation modeling will not be spurious so long as missing variables are uncorrelated with the other predictors. Biases are introduced to the extent that the effects of missing variables add to or subtract from the effects of included variables with which they are correlated.

The obvious omissions from the present model are student attitudes and expectations about school, discipline problems and truancy or absenteeism. These types of variables are not usually available in large-city school data sets and, for purposes of a larger study (Grissom, 1988), we wished to test a common model across very different school systems. Based on prior multiple-prediction studies, it can be argued that these factors provide only a slight improvement to predictive accuracy once achievement and family background are considered. For example, in the large-scale High School and Beyond national survey Ekstrom, Goertz, Pollack and Rock (1986) found that self-esteem measures did not correlate with dropping out. We have already seen from the Austin data in table 2 that serious disciplinary incidents add only slightly to the predicted variance.

Considering the weak contribution of attitude, attendance and discipline variables in previous research, it is unlikely that their omission here could seriously distort conclusions about the effect of retention. To understand fully the process of dropping out, however, these variables should surely be included in a more elaborated model. Moreover, better explanatory models would require longitudinal data. Studies that wait until the high-school years to measure self-concept, educational aspirations, or truancy very likely confuse symptoms with causes. A complete model would include self-concept measured in the early grades before the influence of achievement and retention and measured again in high school prior to dropping out, and so forth.

Sample 1: Austin Schools

Austin is a large urban school district in Texas with an enrollment of

60,000. It serves a population that is approximately 26 per cent Hispanic and 18 per cent black; its dropout rate computed longitudinally is from 20–24 per cent. Data were provided by the Office of Research and Evaluation in Austin Independent School District for 29,399 students who comprise a representative sample from the 1984/85 school year in grades 7–12. Each student's completion status was updated through 1987. A student who was a tenth, eleventh or twelfth grader in 1984/85 would have had time to graduate; such students were classified as dropouts, graduates, or as currently enrolled depending on their 1987 status. Graduates and stay-ins were combined for purposes of the analysis. Obviously, because sufficient time had not elapsed to allow seventh and eighth graders to graduate, these students are not as accurately categorized as dropouts or non-dropouts. Including these latter students has a conservative effect on the analysis in that misclassification will tend to minimize the effect of retention on dropping out.

Variables for Sample 1

Student information on sex, ethnic group and eligibility for subsidized lunch was supplied by schools to the district office. To create a dichotomous variable, ethnic group membership was recategorized as minority and non-minority with Asians omitted from the analysis. Free and reduced-price lunch is used as an indicator of family socio-economic status, but is clearly more limited than if measures of parental education had been available. The inclusion of both ethnic group and achievement help compensate for the limited measure of SES. The model is therefore slightly misspecified in that the relative contribution of these three variables would shift somewhat if SES could be more accurately represented. Dichotomous variables were coded 0 and 1 with female, minority group member, and subsidized lunch receiving the higher codes.

Data were available from two separate achievement test batteries, the Iowa Test of Basic Skills (ITBS) and the Tests of Achievement and Proficiency (TAP). Within-grade percentiles permitted joint analysis using students who were in different grades; percentiles were converted to normal-curve equivalents (NCEs). Most student records included test results for more than one school year. Scores were standardized and averaged for each student on each sub-test. It is desirable to include as much information for each student as possible and hence improve the reliability of the achievement measure, because any underestimate of achievement in the analysis will act to inflate the apparent effect of retention. Lastly, confirmatory factor analysis was used to estimate a global latent achievement variable from performance on several sub-tests.

In the Austin data centralized records of grade retentions were kept from the 1980/81 school year onward. Therefore, accurate data were available on retentions over a seven-year period. For a student who was a tenth grader in 1984/85 this would mean explicit evidence of having repeated in grades 6–12. We refer to these as known instances of grade failure or verified retentions.

Retentions prior to 1980/81, largely in the students' elementary grades, had to be inferred from age. It is essential to try to capture earlier retentions because in virtually all school systems a disproportionate share of retentions occur in the early elementary years, especially in first grade. Normal age for grade was determined by historic entrance-age policies and was confirmed empirically. The cutoff date for entrance to Texas schools has been 1 September for over fifteen years. Figure 2 is an example of the month-by-month birthdate, within-grade histograms that were constructed to confirm normal-age for grade. Beginning in September 1970, there is clearly a twelve-month span with greater frequency representing normal-age eighth graders. The earlier twelve-month span from September 1969 to August 1970 are students who are one year too old for their grade. An additional twelve-month span far to the left are the few students who are two years too old. To the right of the graph is the small number of students who are too young for their grade. Most of the too young eighth graders have birthdays very near the normal age cutoff consistent with later entrance-age policies in other states.

The question arises, of course, as to how good overage is as an indicator or proxy for retention. Because Texas has had one of the earliest entrance ages in the nation, it is not likely that students could be too old for their grade by moving to Texas from another state. Overage would be less accurate as a sign of retention in California, for example, where the entrance age is 31 December; children with fall birthdates who started school in a state like Texas and then moved to California would be classified as overage. Children could also be too old without having repeated, if their parents held them out of school for an extra year. Based on kindergarten entrance practices elsewhere, it is most likely that parents would elect to hold their children out when their birthdays are within three months of the cutoff (Shepard and

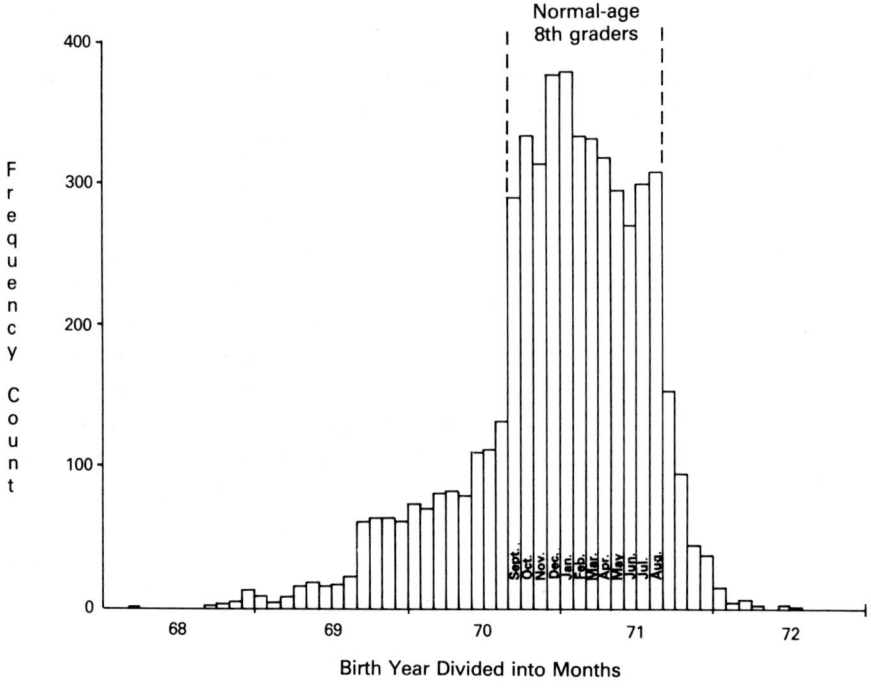

Figure 2: Austin ISD Students in Grade 8 Grouped by Birth Year and Month.

Smith, 1985). Therefore, analyses were conducted using both an exact September definition of overage and an exaggerated or stricter definition of overage with the ambiguous 3-months students removed. In addition, separate analyses were conducted using verified retentions only, verified plus inferred retentions and overage only with known retentions removed.

Ultimately the fidelity of overage as a proxy for retention is not so serious a question if overage itself becomes the variable of interest and is believed to be the aspect of retention that most influences dropout behavior. Although retention is the variable which can be manipulated by school policy, it may have its effect, in part, simply by making students older when they enter high school. These interpretations are discussed further in the final section of the chapter.

Model Estimation and Results for Austin ISD

This section provides only a brief summary of the more extensive analyses reported in Grissom (1988). Structural equations were specified on the basis of the conceptual model and parameters were estimated using multiple regression.[3]

Path coefficients for the Austin data are presented in figure 3 separately for the two different achievement composites using the exact definition of overage as the measure of retention plus know retentions. This joint definition of retention was selected for purposes of illustration because it provides the most logically defensible indicator of retention; note also that using the exact cutoff produces a more conservative measure of the retention effect on dropping out than would the exaggerated cutoff. For dichotomous variables, unstandardized regression coefficients are reported in parentheses and can be interpreted as probability statements. For example, all other things being equal, having been retained increases a student's chances of dropping out by 27 percentage points compared to those not retained. The effect of retention on dropping out is substantially greater than the direct effect of achievement on dropping out. Even when the total effect of achievement is considered (that is, its effect through retention plus its direct effect) the effect of retention is still considerably larger.[4] Consistent with Rumberger's (1983) findings, minority status does not account much for dropping out except through achievement.

The more complete ITBS data were also analyzed separately by grade, by sex, by ethnic group, within each sex and ethnic group combination, and using the various definitions of retention and overage. The greatest variation in results occurred for the separate grade analyses. Therefore, the grade-by-grade path coefficients are provided in table 5, again using the exact overage cutoff to infer retention plus verified retentions. In our view, there is little difference between the overall results and the results for grades 9, 10 and 11. As expected there is lower predictive accuracy for grades 7 and 8 because of the misclassification of some stayers and leavers. In grade 12 there was also a reduction in predictability most likely because by this time the dropout sample was quite small, n = 73, and the remaining number of repeaters had diminished to 333 in a class of 2132. In contrast there were 2659 repeaters and 1421 dropouts in the ninth grade cohort of 5214. Thus nearly all repeaters and would-be dropouts had already left school by the twelfth grade.

Retention, as defined above, explained dropping out virtually the

J. B. Grissom and L. A. Shepard

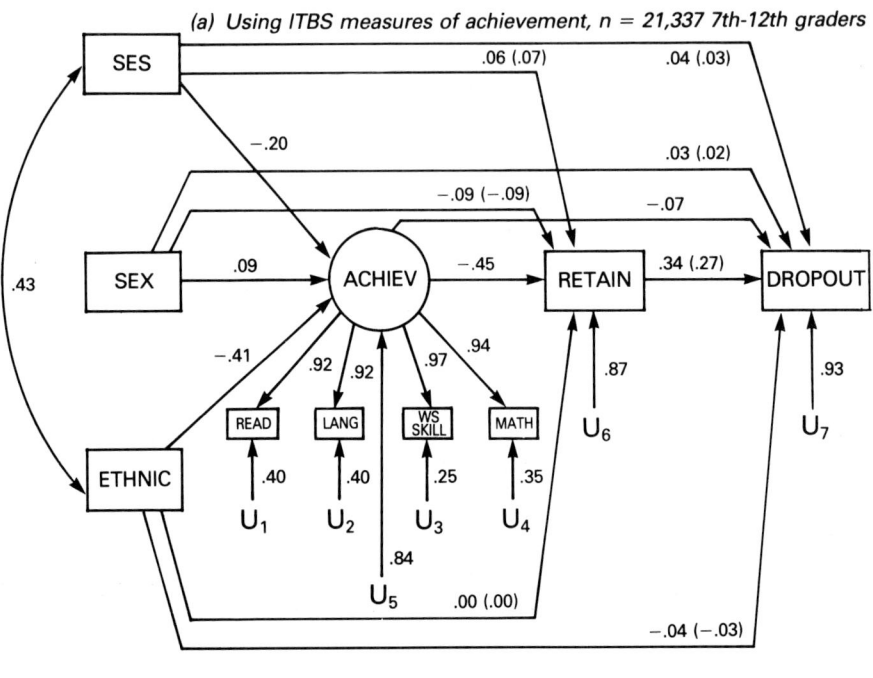

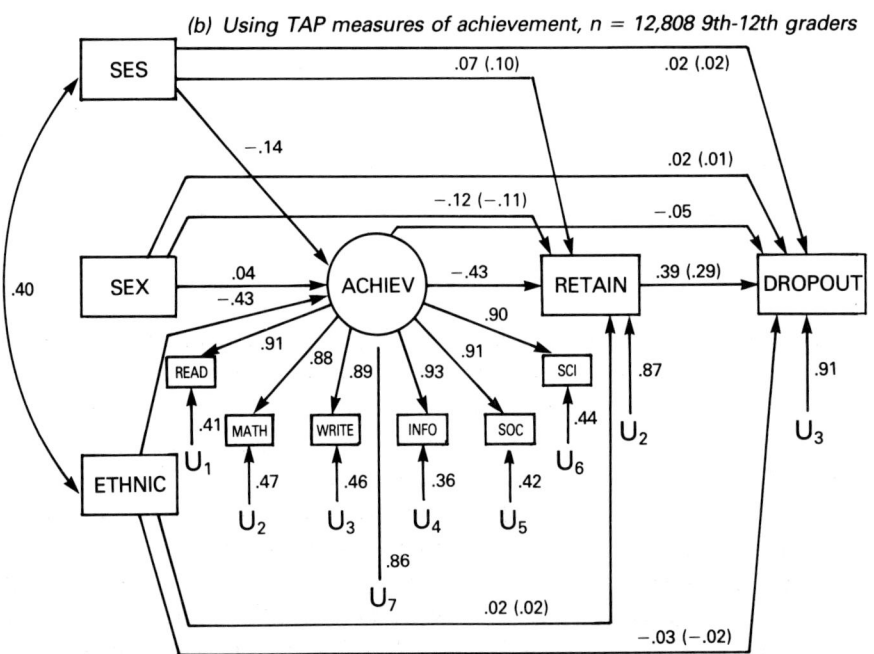

Figure 3: Causal Model of Dropping Out: Estimated from Austin ISD Data
(a) Using ITBS measures of achievement, n = 21,337 7th–12th graders
(b) Using TAP measures of achievement, n = 12,808 9th–12th graders

Table 5: Path Coefficients and R^2's for Each Grade, 7 through 12, for Students in Austin ISD Using ITB Achievement

	Achievement					
	Grade 7	Grade 8	Grade 9	Grade 10	Grade 11	Grade 12
R^2 –	.277	.286	.309	.275	.260	.267
SES	–.248	–.244	–.199	–.164	–.139	–.142
Sex	.115	.087	.086	.105	.062	.061
Ethnicity	–.359	–.375	–.439	–.426	–.435	–.445

	Retention					
	Grade 7	Grade 8	Grade 9	Grade 10	Grade 11	Grade 12
R^2 –	.249	.246	.292	.250	.212	.126
SES	.071	.078	.049	.031	.035	.064
Sex	–.122	–.075	–.071	–.103	–.152	–.037
Ethnicity	–.046	–.004	–.031	.036	–.029	–.016
Achievement	–.461	–.452	–.494	–.450	–.428	–.337

	Dropping Out					
	Grade 7	Grade 8	Grade 9	Grade 10	Grade 11	Grade 12
R^2 –	.057	.082	.191	.221	.203	.009
SES	.066	.058	.044	.020	–.002	–.015
Sex	–.001	.075	.037	.042	–.000	.005
Ethnicity	–.113	–.055	–.006	–.036	–.046	–.032
Achievement	–.104	–.155	–.085	–.014	.019	.006
Retention	.164	.170	.376	.474	.467	.109
n =	4039	4227	5214	3342	2383	2132

same for males as for females, with path coefficients of .33(.26) and .35(.29), respectively. Unstandardized regression weights are reported in parentheses. Analyzed separately by race and sex, these same coefficients were .35(.27) and .35(.26) for black males and females, .30(.27) and .35(.30) for Hispanic males and females, and .31(.24) and .32(.28) for Anglo males and females. Apparent differences by race and sex are diminished when unstandardized regression weights (probabilities) are considered. For example, both Anglo females and black males had weights of nearly .30 meaning that, other things being equal, the chances of dropping out increased by 27 or 28 percentage points for repeaters in these groups compared to non-repeaters. When a more stringent or exaggerated definition of overage was imposed the overall effect of retention on dropping out was increased to .35(.34). Known grade retentions alone (i.e., junior-high and high school retentions) had a path to retention of .34, with an increase in the probability of dropping out of 29 percentage points. When verified retentions were combined with the exaggerated definition of overage, producing the most inclusive and certain measure of retention, the effect on dropping out was .34 with a probability increase of 27 percentage points. Thus the conclusion that repeating a grade increases the likelihood of dropping out was robust for different subpopulations and for the direct and inferred indicators of retention. Although Anglo males appear to have escaped slightly from the negative effect of being overage with an unstandardized coefficient of only .24, even for them the influence of retention on dropping out was substantially greater than the effect of achievement on dropping out.

Sample 2: Chicago Public Schools

The data provided by the Department of Research and Evaluation for the Chicago Public Schools are the same data analyzed by Rice, Toles, Schulz, Harvey and Foster (1987) and summarized in table 4 (n = 79,849). However, for purposes of this research, we omitted Asians and students who were missing achievement test scores. The resulting sample size was 63,872. Chicago is a very large urban school system. Its population is 80 per cent minority with longitudinal dropout rates of 40–45 per cent.

Variables for Sample 2

Sex was coded 0 for males and 1 for females. Blacks, Native Americans, and Hispanics were called minority group members with a code of 1, Anglos were coded 0. Achievement on the ITBs administered in eighth grade had been categorized by the district as below grade level (<7.1), at grade level (7.1–8.0), and above grade level (8.1+). Retention was also represented by Rice *et al.* as overage for grade. Because Chicago has traditionally had a 1 December entrance age we would expect there to be slightly greater ambiguity (compared to the Austin study) in using overage as a proxy for retention. For example, children with September and October birthdates moving to Chicago from Texas would be erroneously classified as retained. Because we did not have actual birthdate information, we could not experiment with more stringent definitions of overage.

Model Estimation and Results for Chicago Public Schools

Structural equations were specified for a model with SES removed and using the categorical measure of achievement. Path coefficients were estimated using multiple regression again because all but one variable was dichotomous. Given that Rice *et al.* had observed a change in the predictability of dropping out after the institution of more stringent eighth grade promotion policies, the Chicago data were analyzed separately by entering class cohort.

Results are portrayed in figure 4 for the 1979 and 1981 high-school entering classes. The 1979 class was the last to be unaffected by the stricter enforcement of eighth grade promotion standards. The 1981 class includes approximately 2000 students who had been held back from the 1980 class.

In the Chicago data achievement and retention are the two most important predictors of dropping out (in standardized units or percent of variance accounted for). Prior to the increase in non-promotions, however and in contrast to the Austin findings, achievement was the stronger predictor. The 1981 estimates show the increased effect for retention and diminished effect for achievement discussed previously by Rice *et al.* In the 1981 model, all other things being equal, a retained student's chances of dropping out of school are increased by 18 percentage points.

The effect of retention on dropping out in Chicago is represented by a coefficient of only .18 compared to effects on the order of .30 in the Austin data.[5] Yet the smaller values occur in a situation where the retention policy was directly manipulated and a perceptible increase in the dropout rate was experienced. Therefore, the more potent Austin values take on even greater practical significance. Differences between the two cities may well reflect differences in populations and the processes being modeled. It is also true that the weaker path from retention to dropout in the Chicago data is consistent with the more ambiguous definition of overage in that sample.

Sample 3: High Socioeconomic District

Sample 3 is from a large suburban school system in the North-east. The

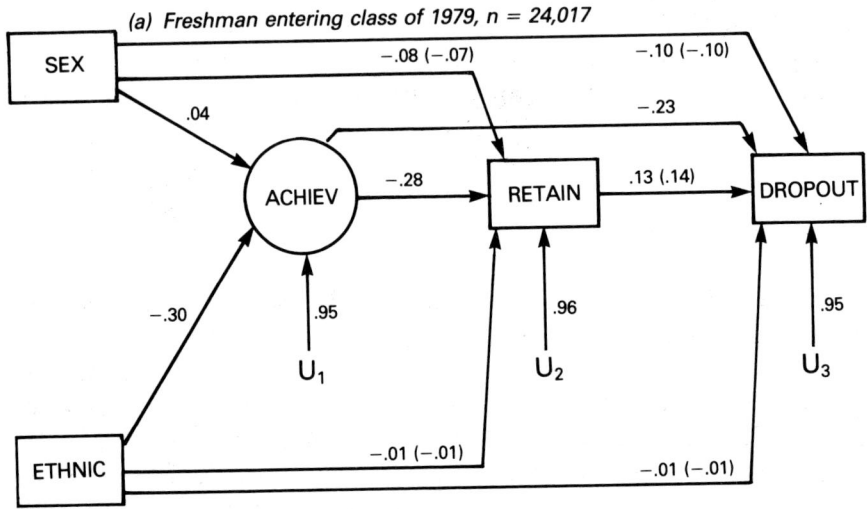

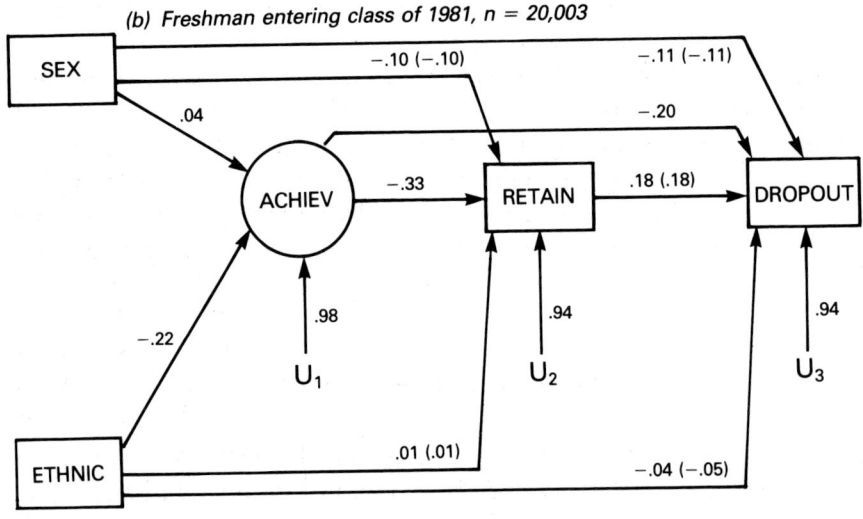

Figure 4: Causal Model of Dropping Out: Estimated from Chicago Public Schools Data
(a) Freshman entering class of 1979, n = 24,017
(b) Freshman entering class of 1981, n = 20,003

district was selected because of its high average socioeconomic level to test the effect of retention on dropping out in quite different circumstances. District 3 has a minority population of 21 per cent and a dropout rate of 4 per cent. Data were provided by the Research and Testing Office for a 1985/86 sample of 38,364 seventh–twelfth graders. Subsequent grade retentions and school leaving status were then updated over the next two school years. It was agreed that the district would not be identified by name.

Variables for District 3

Sex was coded 0 for males and 1 for females. Blacks and Hispanics were coded 1 as members of minority groups, Anglos were coded 0. Achievement was estimated by composite score on the California Achievement Test (CAT). Using normal curve units, test scores were averaged for each student across the years of available data.

Records of actual grades repeated were available for the most recent three years. In addition retention was inferred from overage using the procedures described previously. However, District 3, like many other districts in the North-eastern region of the country, has a late entrance age of 31 December. Therefore, when overage is defined precisely as this boundary, there will be many students with September to December birthdays who appear to be too old but were never retained. Instead, if they had started school in a state like Texas, they would have been made to wait an extra year to enter. Given the potential for misclassifying students who have moved between regions of the country, the exaggerated definition of overage is more interpretable in District 3. In this case, students with birthdates from the four months at the boundary were removed to create the exaggerated definition of overage.

Model Estimation and Results for District 3

Multiple regression was used to estimate model parameters. The results for two versions of the analysis are shown in figure 5. With all grades combined, the path coefficient from retention to dropping out was .29 when verified retentions were added to retentions inferred from an exaggerated definition of overage. Known retentions in the past three years alone produced a coefficient of .27. The unstandardized

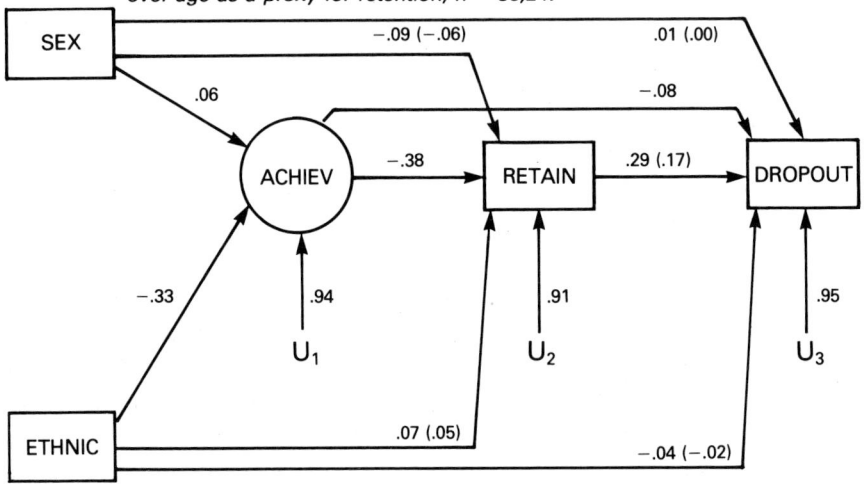

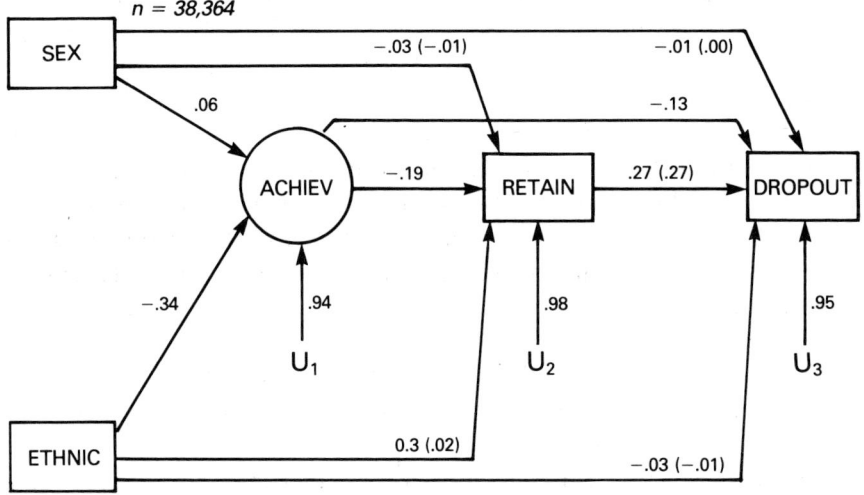

Figure 5: Causal Model of Dropping Out: Estimated from a High-Socialeconomic District
(a) Using known retentions in the past three years plus an exaggerated definition of overage as a proxy for retention, n = 35,247
(b) Using only known retentions in the past three years to indicate retention, n = 38,364

coefficients are quite different, however, suggesting that a student who is made to repeat during grades 7–12 has a greater increase in the probability of dropping out (27 percentage points) than the total mix of overage students, many of whom were retained in earlier grades. As would be expected when many students are misclassified on the retention variable, the retention-dropping out relation was much weaker when the exact definition of overage was used to infer retention, with standardized and unstandardized coefficients of only .21 and .10; all other paths in this analysis, however, remained very close to those in figure 5(a). The results in figure 5 are conservative because students from all grade levels were included. If only students in grades 10-12 were included, because only these students would have had a chance to graduate (or be still enrolled in their senior year), then the retention-dropout relation using the exaggerated definition of overage becomes .34(.22).

With student background factors and achievement accounted for, retention still had a direct effect on dropping out in District 3. The strength of the effect was surprising in several respects. First, a high socioeconomic district had been selected because it was thought that in a more advantaged setting family and community support to stay in school might counter the negative effects of retention. In addition, on purely statistical grounds we would expect it to be very difficult to observe a strong relationship between two variables that occur at such different rates. In District 3, only 4 per cent of the population had dropped out while 13 per cent had been retained, according to the definition used in figure 5(a). Furthermore, all of the definitional problems with overage and retention work to attenuate the relationships. For example, when verified retentions for just the last three years are used as the predictor, a great number of students retained in the previous ten years of their schooling are falsely classified as not retained. Similarly we know from other policy studies that teachers are most likely to retain poor-achieving children who are also youngest in their class. Therefore, the effort to create a more defensible measure of overage by removing the four months at the cutoff undoubtedly eliminates many genuine retentions.

Limitations of the Causal Analysis

We have discussed previously omissions from a more elegant causal model and the limitations of specific measures, especially using overage to represent retention. An additional caveat is needed about the time precedence of achievement. In the conceptual model, achievement occurs before grade retention. Except for the eighth grade retainees in Chicago and some unspecified number of later grade retentions in Austin, most subjects were actually retained before the achievement tests were administered. Thus we have used these measures as if they were indicators of relatively enduring levels of achievement. Advocates who believe that retention increases achievement would say that the scores of retained children were higher, then, by some amount than they would have been previously. Based on Holmes' meta-analysis (chapter 2), however, the reverse is more likely true, i.e., achievement could actually have been depressed by prior retention. In the latter event the lowering of achievement due to retention would falsely increase the apparent effect of achievement on dropping out at the expense of the retention-dropping out relation. Following this reasoning, the unavailability of achievement measures in the early grades should not seriously distort results. We have persisted in modeling the data with achievement predicting retention because achievement is logically prior. We also had more than one year's worth of achievement data for many students in Austin and District 3. Our achievement estimate was an average of these years making it a more stable indicator of achievement.

Interpreting the Retention-Dropping Out Relation

Analyses that adjust for achievement and various background variables suggest that there may indeed be a causal connection between retention and dropping out. Statistical controls help to assure us that the apparent relationship between retention and dropping out is not merely a correlational artifact. The causal model is not, however, truly explanatory. It does not tell *why* retained students are more likely to drop out. The causal model does not rest on an underlying theory, for example, that some students carry a grudge from the time they are made to repeat first grade and finally decide to leave school in the tenth grade as an act of defiance.

Repeating a grade undoubtedly contributes in subtle and interactive ways to an already complex constellation of causes for school leaving. Mann (1986) examined the reasons students give for dropping out and suggested that some students are 'pushed out' by the aversiveness of their experiences in school while others are 'pulled out' by circumstances outside of school. Different aspects of retention may be more or less salient when considering existing influences on dropping out.

From nationally representative data, Erkstrom, Goertz, Pollack and Rock (1986) found that dropouts said they left because they 'did not like school' (33 per cent) or had 'poor grades' (33 per cent). Rumberger (1983) had reported similar results from the National Longitudinal Survey; 44 per cent of dropouts gave school related reasons for leaving. They disliked school, had poor performance, or had been expelled or suspended. Looking at the same High School and Beyond data analyzed by Eksrom *et al.*, Wehlage and Rutter (1986) described a mutual process of rejection whereby students, who had originally said they intended to finish high school, eventually found it more comfortable to leave: 'It begins with negative messages from the school concerning academic and discipline problems. As these messages accumulate into concrete problems — failing courses and thereby lacking credits required for graduation — the choice is between continuing an extra year or more in a setting that offers increasingly negative experiences and dropping out' (p. 81). Given this picture, it is very plausible that flunking a grade, especially in high school or junior high, would add to the feeling of alienation and contribute to a student's sense that graduation was out of reach.

The next most frequent category of reasons for dropping out reflects the pull of out-of-school factors. For males, getting a job or helping to support their family are major reasons for dropping out. For females, getting married or having a baby are the most prevalent responses (Ekstrom *et al.*, 1986; Rumberger, 1983). Dropout interviews suggest that sometimes students feel trapped by necessity, 'mother got tired of taking care of my baby', but others are attracted to leave by what they see as more satisfying alternatives (Doss, 1983). If we speculate that both marriage and jobs represent the taking on of adult roles, then it is plausible to say that students who are a year too old for their grade may find it more and more difficult to postpone leaving school. One could argue that in the culture of public schools students are treated as children and assigned subordinant roles. The older the student, the more he or she perceives the disparity between adult demands thrown upon him or her outside of school and the necessity to be a powerless child within the confines of the school building. From this perspective, previous retention could work to make a student more likely to drop out even if the student had no memory of stigma or injured self-esteem from the original decision. To the extent that overage is a salient aspect of what it means to have been retained, the effect would be the same whether the child had repeated grade 1 or grade 10.

These explanations are not mutually exclusive. Regardless of what students are able to voice as the primary reason for quitting, multiple factors may all be operating, both pushing and pulling students away from school.

Conclusions

Whenever high school dropouts and graduates are compared, it is always the case that a substantially larger proportion of the dropouts have repeated a grade. This observation has had little influence on school promotion policies, however, because it has been logical to say that grade retention is just another symptom of poor achievement, which is the real cause of dropping out. The purpose of this chapter was to analyze whether the retention decision itself increases the risk of dropping out.

When student background, sex and achievement are controlled, there remains a significant effect for grade retention on dropping out. The magnitude of the effect varies from one school system to the next. For black males in Austin repeating a grade increases the risk of not finishing high school by 27 percentage points. For white females in a high socioeconomic district, retention increases the chances of not graduating by 21 percentage points. Although causal modeling techniques can never produce unequivocal conclusions from correlational data, the consistency of findings across many analyses supports the conclusion that retention adds to the risk of dropping out. Even the most advantaged groups, those who are least likely to leave school, experience a practically significant increase in dropout rate when they are a year too old.

For a school district contemplating tougher promotion policies it is possible to estimate what the effect might be on the district's dropout rate. If annual retention rates are increased, say, from 5 per cent to 7 per cent, the cumulative retention rate will go up on the order of 20 per cent (chapter 1). That is, an additional 20 per cent of students will experience retention sometime in their school career. Following from the extra retentions, the district's dropout rate will go up by 3 to 6 percentage points. A district that had had a 20 per cent dropout rate could anticipate a new rate of 25 per cent as groups of previously retained students reached high school age.

Students leave school for a variety of reasons, often because they are not good at school or because the attractions of job, marriage, or associations with out-of-school peers become harder to resist. In many cases dropouts may not be very articulate or perceptive in explaining their reasons for leaving to survey researchers. Grade retention is a discrete policy intervention that appears to contribute to the dropout problem. Whether it is a part of a negative set of experiences that convince the student he can't make it or merely a temporal dislocation that makes the student too old for his classmates and a year further from graduation, the negative consequences of the extra year are clear. As noted by Rice *et al.* (1987), the repeat year would have to produce achievement gains of thirty months to compensate for the negative effects of being made a year too old.

Notes

1 This research was supported in part by a grant to the Center for Research on Evaluation, Standards, and Student Testing from the Office of Educational Research and Improvement/Department of Education (OERI/ED). However, the opinions expressed herein do not necessarily reflect the policy of the OERI/ED, and no official endorsement by the OERI/ED should be inferred. We thank the researchers in the Austin Independent School District, Chicago Public Schools, and District 3 for their efforts in making comprehensive data sets available to us. We also thank Robert L. Linn and Charles S. Reichardt for their advice on methodological issues.
2 On several occasions throughout the chapter, we refer to the relative weight of predictors in a regression system. Although standardized coefficients make variables comparable in standard deviation units, it should be noted that the relative contribution of each will be constrained by the variability and intercorrelations among variables in a particular context.
3 Duplicate analyses were also conducted using LISREL VI (Joreskog and Sorbon, 1984) maximum likelihood estimation. Because the model is fully recursive, LISREL and multiple regression will produce very similar numerical results. Multiple regression estimates are reported because they do not rest on the questionable assumption of normality with these several dichotomous variables.
4 As explained in a previous note, comparisons regarding the relative size of effects on dropping out are dependent on the standard deviations of each variable in a particular context. The lay person has some common understanding of the effect of achievement on dropping out. Thus we wish to compare the magnitude of the retention effect, when retention has typical variance, to the achievement effect, under conditions of typical

variability, from which these common understandings derive. The Austin ITBS average within-grade standard deviation was 22 NCEs compared to the national norm standard deviation of 21.06 NCEs. The retention proportion in figure 3a was 36 per cent which is typical (or an underestimate) of cumulative retention rates inferred from data reported in chapter 1; (for dichotomous variables variance is a function of proportion). Therefore, these data provide a realistic contrast between achievement and retention effects on dropping out.

5   The relative size of effects between the two school systems holds true whether the comparison is made in standardized or unstandardized regression weights or percent of variance accounted for.

References

ASSOCIATION OF CALIFORNIA URBAN SCHOOL DISTRICTS (ACUSD) (1985) *Dropouts from California's Urban School Districts: Who Are They? How Do We Count Them? How Can We Hold Them (or at Least Educate Them)?*, Los Angeles, CA, ACUSD.

BACHMAN, J. G., GREEN, S. and WIRTANEN, I. D. (1971) *Youth in Transition, Volume III: Dropping Out — Problem or Symptom?*, Ann Arbor, MI, Institute for Social Research, University of Michigan.

CURTIS, J., DOSS, D., MACDONALD, J. and DAVIS, W. (1983) 'Dropout prediction', paper presented at the annual meeting of the American Educational Research Association, Montreal, April.

DOSS, D. A. (1983) *Mother Got Tired of Taking Care of My Baby. A Study of Dropouts from AISD*, Austin, TX, Austin Independent School District, Office of Research and Evaluation (Publication No. 82.44).

EKSTROM, R. B., GOERTZ, M. E., POLLACK, J. M. and ROCK, D. A. (1986) 'Who drops out of high school and why? Findings from a national study', *Teachers College Record*, 87, pp. 356–73.

GRISSOM, J. (1988) *Structural Equation Modeling of Retention and Overage Effects on Dropping Out of School*, unpublished doctoral dissertation, University of Colorado, Boulder, CO.

HESS, G. A. and LAUBER, D. (1985) *Dropouts from the Chicago Public Schools: An Analysis of the Classes of 1982, 1983, 1984*, Chicago, IL, Chicago Panel on Public School Finances (ERIC Document Reproduction Service No. ED 258 095).

JÖRESKOG, K. G. and SÖRBOM, D. (1984) *LISREL VI: Analysis of linear Structural Relationships by the Method of Maximum Likelihood, Instrumental Variables, and Least Squares Methods. User's Guide*, Mooresville, IN, Scientific Software.

LLOYD, D. N. (1978) 'Prediction of school failure from third-grade data', *Educational and Psychological Measurement*, 38, pp. 1193–200.

MANN, D. (1986) 'Can we help dropouts? Thinking about the undoable', *Teachers College Record*, 87, pp. 307–23.

NATRIELLO, G. (Ed.) (1987) *School Dropouts: Patterns and Policies*, New York, Teachers College Press.

NOTH, N. and O'NEILL, B. (1981) *Dropout Identification: A Preliminary Study of the Pasco School District*, Pullman, WA, Pasco School District 1; Washington State University (ERIC Document Reproduction Service No. ED 215 013).

RANDALL, C. V. (1966) *A Study of Early School Leavers and Significant Causes*, Bloomington, MN, Bloomington Public Schools.

RICE, W. K., TOLES, R. E., SCHULZ, E. M., HARVEY, J. T. and FOSTER, D. L. (1987) 'A longitudinal investigation of effectiveness of increased promotion standards at eighth grade on high school graduation', paper presented at the annual meeting of the American Educational Research Association, Washington, D.C., April.

RUMBERGER, R. W. (1983) 'Dropping out of high school: The influence of race, sex, and family background', *American Educational Research Journal*, 20, pp. 199–220.

RUMBERGER, R. W. (1987) 'High school dropouts: A review of issues and evidence', *Review of Educational Research*, 57, pp. 101–21.

SCHULZ, E. M., TOLES, R., RICE, W. K., BRAUER, I. and HARVEY, J. (1986) 'Association of dropout rates with student attributes', paper presented at the annual meeting of the American Educational Research Association, San Francisco, April.

SHEPARD, L. A. and SMITH, M. L. (1985) *Boulder Valley Kindergarten Study: Retention Practices and Retention Effects*, Boulder, CO, Boulder Valley Public Schools, March.

STEPHENSON, R. S. (1985) *A Study of the Longitudinal Dropout Rate: 1980 Eighth-grade Cohort Followed from June 1980 through February 1985*, Miami, Office of Educational Accountability, Dade County Public Schools, March.

STROUP, A. L. and ROBINS, L. N. (1972) 'Elementary school predictors of high school dropout among Black males', *Sociology of Education*, 45, pp. 212–22.

WEHLAGE, G. G. and RUTTER, R. A. (1986) 'Dropping out: How much do schools contribute to the problem?', *Teachers College Record*, 87, pp. 374–92.

Chapter 4:
A Review of Research on Kindergarten Retention

Lorrie A. Shepard

Editors' Introduction

Repeating kindergarten is intended to be different from non-promotion at other grade levels. Because it comes before academic failure it is meant to be a preventative treatment. The populations served and its social effects are thought to be different. Often children are selected for kindergarten retention because of immaturity rather than poor academic skills. And, many believe that being held back in kindergarten does not carry the stigma associated with retention later on.

Given these arguments, it is unwise to generalize the findings from research on later-grades retention to what might happen in kindergarten. Advocates for kindergarten retention deny that conclusions from Holmes' review (chapter 2) are pertinent. Separate studies aimed directly at the effect of repeating kindergarten are needed.

This chapter is a review of available research on kindergarten retention in its several forms: transition classrooms before first grade, developmental kindergarten before kindergarten; and straight repeating of kindergarten. Research findings are summarized for both academic and personal adjustment outcomes. Studies are categorized as to their degree of control in accounting for the initial readiness of retained and promoted children and studies with more adequate control are given greater weight in formulating conclusions. Methodological issues unique to this topic are discussed, especially the odd occurrence that retained children are often more advanced on readiness measures (before repeating) than at-risk controls who are promoted to first grade.

Holding children back in kindergarten in large numbers is a phenomenon of the 1980s. In the past, a relatively small number of school districts have followed the recommendation of the Gesell Institute (1982) to have immature children repeat kindergarten. But nationally the number of children affected by such policies has been quite small. Recently, however, state level retention rates show that the most consistent and dramatic increases are in kindergarten (chapter 1). In California local district practices vary such that 0 to 50 per cent of kindergartners are made to repeat (School Readiness Task Force, 1988). One school district in New York state required two-thirds of its children to spend two years in kindergarten (Liebfred, 1987).

Retention in kindergarten is sometimes considered to be an extra year of preparation before first grade. According to this theory, retaining a child for a second year in kindergarten is only one of three alternative tactics aimed at early prevention of school failure. Perhaps the most popular extra-year program is the transition room, sometimes called the readiness room, junior first grade, or pre-first. The advantage of transition classes, as seen by their advocates, is that they do not simply repeat the kindergarten program but provide an intermediate step between kindergarten and first grade. In many cases transition rooms have the status of special programs and have a reduced class size, fifteen or sixteen children (Dolan, 1982; Jones, 1985; Kilby, 1982); in other school systems, transition classes are equal in size to other first grades. A third form of retention is a developmental kindergarten, or pre-kindergarten, followed by regular kindergarten. Children who are the normal age for kindergarten are usually placed in developmental kindergarten on the basis of readiness tests or developmental tests given before the start of school. All of these two-year kindergarten placements have a common purpose, to provide a more appropriate curriculum for children judged to be unready for the learning demands of first grade.

Are extra-year programs effective? Do they prevent subsequent failure? Do they improve achievement over what it would have been had the child been promoted to first grade? And, since academic progress is not the only issue, is similar achievement obtained with less emotional distress? Is there evidence that retention in kindergarten is a fundamentally different intervention from retention in later grades?

In this chapter, extant studies of the effects of extra-year programs are reviewed and methodological issues are raised. This review is different from that of Holmes (chapter 2) because it focuses on retentions and transition placements prior to first grade. In 1984,

Gredler provided the only review of research on transition rooms. Here, Gredler's major findings are recapitulated. Then the results of more recent studies are summarized.

Gredler's Review

Unlike the 800 references on grade retention and sixty empirical studies found by Holmes (chapter 2), relatively few controlled studies exist on the effects of kindergarten retention or transition room placement. Gredler (1984) located several dissertations (Bell, 1972; Matthews, 1977; Raygor, 1972; Talmadge, 1981) and published studies which compared transition room children with 'at-risk' children who had been socially promoted to first grade. He concluded that 'transition room children either do not perform as well or at most are equal in achievement levels to transition room-eligible children placed in regular classrooms' (p. 469). Gredler also noted that educators express a great deal of faith in their transition room program, although 'few, if any, schools have gathered any data to indicate the educational status of children so placed' (p. 469).

Bell's (1972) investigation is worth special attention, because it was the only study to examine the effect of program placement on self-concept as well as achievement. At-risk, control children were identified by teachers' opinions and two tests but attended a school that did not have a readiness room. At the end of one year and again after two years, the control children significantly outperformed the retained children on achievement test measures. During the same period, self-concept scores for the control children had increased slightly while those for the readiness room children dropped significantly. Raygor's (1972) study likewise deserves special comment because it provided a more long-term comparison of transition room children and the 'potential first-grade failure' group. Although the retained children scored higher on a standardized measure of achievement at the end of first grade, their advantage had washed out by the end of third grade; furthermore, the achievement of the 'potential first grade failure' group had become indistinguishable from that of their fourth-grade classmates.

Finally, Gredler (1984) gave special status to a study published by Leinhardt (1980). Leinhardt's investigation was exemplary because she examined the effect of an individualized reading program as well as the effect of transition room. Transition room children who also received individualized instruction were no better off at the end of first grade than at-risk children who had been promoted with no special instruction. The group that did best of all, however, was the transition-room-eligible children who had been promoted but received individualized instruction in the regular classroom.

Additional Studies

In order to expand Gredler's review, especially to include more recent studies, computer-assisted searches were conducted of education and psychology data bases using the following descriptors: transition room, kindergarten retention, pre-first, and developmental kindergarten. Reference lists were also cross-checked to identify additional studies. School districts identified by the Gesell Institute (1988) as having successful developmental programs were contacted for copies of their evaluation or research reports. The resulting fifteen new empirical studies, primarily dissertations, were read and categorized along two dimensions. First, studies were typed by their degree of control. 'No control' meant that only data for the retained group were reported or that the retained group was inappropriately compared to normal grade peers. Studies with 'minimal control' were those with comparison groups who had been recommended for retention, sometimes called the 'refusal' group; but there was no measure of the initial equivalence of the two groups. Studies with 'adequate control' compared retained children to promoted, at-risk children only after matching on initial readiness or using some form of statistical adjustment. Then, the outcomes of controlled studies were classified as positive, negative, or no difference.

Rather than recount the design and findings of each study (as was done exhaustively in every one of the dissertations referenced), a brief summary is provided from the controlled studies for each outcome category. Within each category, greater attention is given to research with more adequate controls. The results of studies without control groups are mentioned briefly to make the references accessible to the reader but were not given weight in forming conclusions. Are there general conclusions that can be drawn from this expanded set of studies?

Among the newly-identified studies, the predominant finding was one of no difference. After having been retained in kindergarten, children were no better off in first grade (or later) than similarly at-risk children who went directly to first grade. For example, Kilby (1982) compared graduates of a Junior First Grade program with program-eligible students across three separate years. Initial readiness scores were used to make covariance adjustments. There were no significant differences between the groups on achievement measures at the end of first grade, second grade, or fourth grade; (tests were not available in third grade). Kilby also examined several years of test scores for a small group of junior first graders (n = 12) who were then completing eighth grade. They were consistently behind in achievement compared to a representative sample of classmates in grades 4 through 8. When covariance adjustments were applied to these same data, the children who had been junior first graders were above their own expected scores in reading for three years. Then in seventh and eighth grade, their reading scores fell below expectation. Through their entire school career they were below their own expectation scores in math. Junior first graders and program-eligible students did not differ in subsequent special education placements nor in measured attitude toward school. Junior first grade children had significantly fewer grade retentions, but in arriving at that conclusion the extra year of kindergarten was not counted. If junior first grade had been counted as retention, the junior first graders would have had by far the greater number of retentions. Questions surrounding the use of subsequent retentions as an outcome measure in retention research are discussed in the section on methodological issues.

Jones (1985) studied groups of transition children in first through third grades and in each case compared them to at-risk children whose parents had refused transition placement. Jones' data are particularly noteworthy because of the large pretest advantage for the transition children; in some cases they started transition with as much as a 1.9 standard deviation advantage over their at-risk counterparts. Gain scores from the beginning to end of first grade showed no differences between the two groups. By the end of second grade the advantage of the transition group had substantially diminished; and by third grade there were no significant differences on four tests. In fact, in one third grade group, a non-significant difference favored the at-risk, non-transition group.

Four other studies showing no differences were also identified. In May and Welch's (1984) study, the Gesell Developmental Test was used to identify children who were developmentally immature and in need of an extra year. Children whose parents refused the extra-year placement comprised the control group. There were no significant differences between these groups on achievement tests given at the end of their second, third, fourth, and sixth grade years, respectively. Similarly, Caggiano (1984) found no difference on standardized achievement measures at the end of second, fourth, and sixth grades between Gesell identified children who spent an extra year in transition room and those whose parents refused the extra year. Caggiano did, however, find statistically significant differences favoring the transition group on two of four behavioral rating scales. In contrast, the transition group had significantly more referrals to special education in subsequent years and significantly more special education placements. (The study was classified as 'no difference' because most of the outcomes showed no difference and significant findings did not consistently favor one group.)

An evaluation of transition rooms in the Kirkwood School District (1984) found that children who had 'barely passed' into first grade outperformed transition children. However, because the negative findings were no greater than might have been expected from the initial differences between the groups, this minimally controlled study was classified as a no difference result. Conversely, generally positive effects for transition reported by Stapleford (1982) were also treated as no difference findings because the comparison group began far behind the group that agreed to retention; no adjustments had been made in the study to control for initial differences.

One well-controlled, negative study was located, that by Mossburg (1987). Relatively large samples, 149 in each group, were matched on sex, socioeconomic level, age when first entering kindergarten (within four months) and kindergarten readiness. The negative study results were especially compelling because the readiness room children were ahead at the end of first grade (though not significantly so). By the end of the second, third and fourth grades, however, the control children had surpassed the extra-year children and were significantly higher on reading, math and composite standardized achievement test scores. The developmentally immature children who had refused the extra year were also significantly higher on social, emotional, and academic readiness for middle school as judged by fifth grade teachers.

At the opposite extreme, Turley (1979) found a strong positive effect for kindergarten retention. Measured at the end of first grade, the retained children were approximately eight months ahead in reading and math compared to those who had been recommended to repeat. Because the district was in a very high socioeconomic community, the unready, non-retained children were themselves eight or more months above national norms. Although covariance adjustments were used to permit some degree of control, comparative data were not provided beyond first grade. The only other positive study was reported by Dolan (1982). Dolan's study had only five or six children in the 'parent refusal' group in follow-up grades and most of the specific contrasts between transition children and the refusal group were not statistically significant. However, when significant results did obtain, they favored the transition group. For example, children who spent a year in transition subsequently had better second grade math scores and less need for special services. The groups were not significantly different in second grade reading or fifth grade math and reading. Dolan's analysis did not adjust for initial differences between the groups.

Three studies by Hunter (1975), Sheets (1977) and Wilson and Hewett (1978) were classified as uncontrolled because transition children were compared to a sample of normal grade peers rather than with children who had been judged similarly unready at the end of the first year of kindergarten. In each case, the results were negative, transition room children were behind their younger classmates on achievement measures.

Three other uncontrolled studies claimed to show the benefit of extra-year placements. A study in the Brevard County public schools (c. 1987) compared transition children, developmental kindergartners and those retained in kindergarten, to each other on subsequent achievement measures. Transitional students were the best group achieving at the district average and 30 percentile points above the national norms at the end of third grade. Despite the fact that the district as a whole was very high achieving and that no data were available on initial characteristics of the groups the above evidence was used to conclude that 'the effect on achievement appears to be of long-term benefit' (Highlights, p. 2). This conclusion is obviously unsupportable given the serious invalidity of the study design. Comparing transition children to other retained samples is not the same as comparing them to unready but promoted children. Before attributing high third grade scores (consistent with the district average) to the transition room placement, the evaluators would have to know whether these children were below the district average going into the transition year.

Duhe', Green, Taylor, Frank and Dunlap (1984) did not isolate the scores for students participating in developmental programs. Instead they noted that school and district averages on standardized achievement tests at the end of regular kindergarten had climbed dramatically, for example, a 28 percentile point gain in reading, from 1980 to 1985 during the period when development kindergartens had been implemented. The authors noted that 'the gift of time provided by developmental placement *appears* to be the only altered variable that may account for this significant growth in kindergarten achievement test scores during the five-year span' (p. 3). A careful reading of their data, however, reveals that schools without developmental programs gained an average of 7.3 percentile points per year compared to average gains of 7.7 points per year in schools where the program had been in place for two or three years, suggesting that scores were going up regardless of the special program. Furthermore, the average reading scores then dropped by 25 percentile points from 1985 to 1987. A study reported by Ford (1985) had no control group but compared readiness scores for transition participants at the end of their transition year to their own readiness scores at the end of the first year of kindergarten. Gains in readiness scores were striking, an average of 55 percentile points in one year. Transition children were not followed up in first grade. It was presumed that they would fare as well as more ready children who had achieved similarly high readiness scores their first year in kindergarten. Such a presumption cannot be supported by existing predictive validity data on the Metropolitan Readiness Tests and could only be confirmed by following these children into first grade and making the appropriate controlled comparisons. In the measurement literature there are many instances where a test is correlated with a subsequent criterion but artificial increases in the predictive measure are not followed by gains on the criterion.

Methodological Issues

In the course of reading and categorizing kindergarten retention studies, important methodological issues arose pertaining to populations studied. First, with respect to external validity, there were differences between studies in the types of children served that could make a difference in conclusions about program effectiveness. For example, transition rooms might work for immature children with average ability but appear to be ineffective when tried with slow learners. Secondly, within studies, systematic differences between retained and control children could influence the direction of findings. If transition children are selected to be more able than other at-risk children who are passed on, then initial ability differences would create spurious results in favor of the transition program. Each of these population issues will be considered in turn.

Although all two-year kindergarten programs have the intention of protecting at-risk children from first-grade failure, there are sometimes sharp philosophical differences about the definition of readiness and the selection of children who might benefit from an extra year. At one extreme, transition rooms are seen as a pre-special education intervention and are intended for children with poor academic prognosis. At the other extreme, children who have normal intelligence but immature development are judged to be the best candidates for extra-year placements. Programs of this type, advocated by proponents of the Gesell philosophy, specifically exclude potential special education children (see Jones, 1985). For example, Scott and Ames (1969) argued that, 'Repeating should be the solution for children who are too immature for the work of a grade in question and thus need to be older to succeed...' (p. 434). They dismissed negative findings from previous research saying that, 'There is no reason to assume that repeating can correct low intelligence, emotional disturbance, brain damage or many of the other difficulties that produce poor school work.' In their study, Scott and Ames (*ibid.*) eliminated subjects who had been retained for reasons others than immaturity; no control data were provided.

Because children selected for immaturity are academically more able than children identified because of pre-academic deficiencies, the effects of retention could be quite different for the two populations. Thus, a review of literature that fails to acknowledge the distinction in types of kindergarten retentions could mask an effective treatment for one or the other group. In fact, however, the predominant finding of no difference between extra-year and control children holds true whether children were placed for academic unreadiness or developmental immaturity. Both the most positive and the most negative studies (by Turley, 1979, and Mossburg, 1987) were examples in which children were retained on the basis of the Gesell tests. Three other controlled studies, by Jones (1985), May and Welch (1984) and Caggiano (1984) found essentially no benefit for *immature* children assigned to extra-year placements.

The practice of identifying either slow learners or immature children for kindergarten retention also has implications for the internal validity of comparative studies. In Jackson's (1975) often-cited review of retention research, the case is made that non-random controlled studies will tend to have hidden biases favoring the control group. Even when the controls were themselves candidates for retention, the final decision to promote these children implies that their characteristics were not as severe as those for the retained group. From what we can see, however, on the basis of studies with pre-measures, this portrayal is not necessarily an accurate depiction in the case of kindergarten retention. The reverse is more likely true; i.e., transition children might be systematically more able than promoted at-risk children. As noted previously, transition children in Jones's (1985) study began with an initial advantage over control children of 1.9 and 1.5 standard deviations in reading and math, respectively. Similarly, in Stapleford (1982) and Turley (1979) the retained groups began ahead of their respective controls. We know of school districts in California, Connecticut, Florida and New Jersey where the explicit policy is to follow the advice of Scott and Ames (1969), passing slow learners on to first grade but holding 'bright immature' children in transition classes. In chapter 5, we present data from a specific school where there were systematic differences between the children whose parents agreed to an extra-year placement and those who refused; the children whose parents agreed had had significantly higher readiness scores at the start of school. Although there were also examples in studies cited earlier that had the more traditional bias favoring controls, such a pattern should not be presumed. Researchers seeking validly controlled comparisons should be equally cautious that the promoted, refusal group might be the more seriously deficient group.

The occasional placement of academically able groups into transition rooms also alters the perspective for interpreting uncontrolled studies. For example, Sandoval and Fitzgerald (1985) conducted a retrospective study of high school students who had either attended a junior first grade or had repeated a later grade in school. In high school, the junior first grade participants were achieving on a par with their grade peers while repeaters had significantly poorer academic performance. Advocates for pre-first grade retentions might take these results as proof that early retention works, in contrast to later-grades retention. These findings are exactly what would be expected, however, if there had been no benefit to the extra-year placement but the junior first graders had been selected for immaturity (with average academic ability) and the subsequent grade repeaters had been selected for academic failure. As the authors pointed out, the study could not determine if the junior first graders were doing better than they would have done without the extra year, because they did not have a comparison group of equivalent children who did not spend the year in junior first.

A final methodological issue concerns the use of subsequent grade retention as an outcome measure to judge the benefit of extra-year placements. Because kindergarten retention is intended to prevent failure later on, researchers are led naturally to count subsequent retentions (the fewer the better) as a quantification of program benefits. Such data are spurious, however, for two reasons. First, in studies where comparisons are made between later retentions for control and kindergarten retainees, kindergarten retentions are not counted, thus the control group invariably has more retentions. Second, a reduction in future retentions is an artifact of implicit policies against 'double retentions'.

Consider, for example, the findings reported by Kilby (1982). When two sets of junior first grade participants and non-attending controls were followed up through second and fourth grades, respectively, only two of eighty-two program participants had been retained subsequently and none had been retained twice. On the other hand, eight of thirty non-attending candidates (27 per cent) were later retained and four (13 per cent) were retained twice. If kindergarten retentions had been counted, however, the rates of single retentions would have been 98 per cent for junior first graders versus 27 per cent for non-attending candidates: and rates of double retentions would have been 2 per cent and 13 per cent, respectively. If it is argued that early retention is better than later retention, then 40 per cent of the junior first graders benefited by being 'saved from' later retentions, as judged by the control group rates. By the same reasoning, however, 60 per cent of the junior first graders were harmed by the early retention because they were retained in kindergarten to forestall a subsequent retention that never would have occurred, again judged by the control group rates.

The inference that kindergarten retainees are recommended to repeat later grades less frequently because they are more successful in school is invalid. Teachers' recommendations to hold children back are governed by explicit and implicit policies to avoid double retentions within the primary grades. For example, Ellwein and Glass (chapter 8) describe in one school district both formal and informal policies against retaining children twice within the 1–3, 4–6, and 7–8 grade spans. In addition, teachers use age as a significant factor in deciding whether to retain a child. Consideration of a child's age when recommending retention was documented in both a judgment-capturing experiment and a simple rating task (Shepard and Smith, 1985). For example, if two boys had equally poor academic skills, but one was the youngest and the other the oldest in his class, teachers are likely to retain the youngest boy but promote the oldest.

Achievement data obtained in conjunction with the study reported in chapter 5 further corroborate the disassociation between actual achievement and retention decisions for previously retained children. In the study reported by Shepard and Smith (1987) kindergarten retainees were compared at the end of first grade to an equally unready control group that went directly to first grade. Teachers rated the children on five sets of scales reflecting both academic success and adjustment. On these scales from 1 to 7 of the control children and none of the previously retained children were suggested for possible first grade retention. However, on these same scales essentially the same numbers of retained and control children were judged to be below grade level in reading and roughly equal numbers were judged to be in the 'bottom five' in their respective classes (e.g., 10 vs. 12). Therefore, it cannot be said that the difference in retention recommendations represented performance differences.

Based on these observations, the literature review in this chapter was rewritten giving much less credence to retention as an outcome measure. For example, Caggiano (1984), Stapleford (1982), and Turley (1979) also reported that controls suffered significantly more retentions, ranging from 8 per cent to 54 per cent of controls subsequently retained. At a minimum, the meaning of this program benefit should be kept in perspective by acknowledging extra-year programs as retentions; couched in these terms, results *always* favor controls. Further, it would seem that subsequent retention should not be interpreted as an indicator of poor achievement to the extent that older and previously retained children are excused from repeating.

Summary of Research Findings

In summary, the expanded purview of available research studies corroborates the conclusions of Gredler's (1984) review. Kindergarten retention and transition rooms are ineffective. Although a year older than their new grade peers, transition children perform no better academically than transition-eligible children who went directly on to first grade. The finding of no difference or no benefit is true whether children were placed on the basis of pre-academic problems or developmental immaturity. Children who spend an extra year before first grade are just as likely to end up at the bottom of their first or third grade class as unready children who refused the special placement. Academically able but immature children who repeat kindergarten may well be at the top of their first grade class but are not ahead of where they would have been without the added year, as shown by equivalent controls. Only one adequately-controlled positive study was found among twenty-one; it did not follow the comparison groups beyond first grade. Several other controlled studies found an advantage for transition children in first grade that disappeared when groups were followed up in third and fourth grades. Self-concept or attitude measures, only rarely included in research studies, showed no difference or negative effects from the extra-year placements. In this respect retention, whether it is called by a special name (transition), occurs for special reason (immaturity), or takes place in kindergarten rather than later, is still retention — and still ineffective.

References

BELL, M. (1972) 'A study of the readiness room program in a small school district in suburban Detroit, Michigan', unpublished doctoral dissertation, Wayne State University.

BREVARD COUNTY PUBLIC SCHOOLS (c. 1987) *Developmental Placement Program Evaluation: 1986-87*, Rockledge, FL, Brevard County Public Schools.

CAGGIANO, J. A. (1984) 'A study of the effectiveness of transitional first grade in a suburban school district', unpublished doctoral dissertation, Temple University.

DOLAN, L. (1982) 'A follow-up evaluation of a transition class program for children with school and learning readiness problems', *The Exceptional Child*, 29, pp. 101–10.

DUHE', G., GREEN, V., TAYLOR, J., FRANK, M. and DUNLAP, C. (1984) *Report on Developmental Placement*, Luling, LA, St. Charles Parish Public Schools.

FORD, J. (1985) *The Transitional Classes: A Report to the Elementary Principals*, Norman, OK, Norman Public Schools, (mimeo), 22 October.

GESELL INSTITUTE OF HUMAN DEVELOPMENT (1982) *A Gift of Time... A Developmental Point of View*, New Haven, CT, Gesell Institute of Human Development.

GESELL INSTITUTE OF HUMAN DEVELOPMENT (1988) 'Extending appropriate practices in the elementary school', *Education Week*, 7, 13 April.

GREDLER, G. R. (1984) 'Transition classes: A viable alternative for the at-risk child?', *Psychology in the Schools*, 21, pp. 463–70.

HUNTER, B. B. (1975) 'An evaluation of the effectiveness of a transition grade between kindergarten and first grade upon later academic achievement', unpublished doctoral dissertation, Ball State University.

JACKSON, G. B. (1975) 'The research evidence on the effects of grade retention', *Review of Educational Research*, 45, pp. 613–35.

JONES, R. R. (1985) 'The effect of a transition program on low achieving kindergarten students when entering first grade', unpublished doctoral dissertation, Northern Arizona University.

KILBY, G. A. (1982) 'An ex post facto evaluation of the junior first grade program in Sioux Falls, South Dakota', unpublished doctoral dissertation, University of South Dakota.

KIRKWOOD SCHOOL DISTRICT (1984) *Evaluation of Transition Room*, Kirkwood School District, January.

LEINHARDT, G. (1980) 'Transition rooms: Promoting maturation or reducing education?', *Journal of Educational Psychology*, 72, pp. 55–61.

In the matter of Liebfred (1987) Petition, State of New York Department of Education, 30 November.

MATTHEWS, H. W. (1977) 'The effect of transition education, a year of readiness, and beginning reading instruction between kindergarten and first grade', unpublished doctoral dissertation, St. Louis University.

MAY, D. C. and WELCH, E. L. (1984) 'The effects of developmental placement and early retention on children's later scores on standardized tests', *Psychology in the Schools*, 21, pp. 381–5.

MOSSBURG, J. W. (1987) 'The effects of transition room placement on selected achievement variables and readiness for middle school', unpublished doctoral dissertation, Ball State University.

RAYGOR, B. (1972) 'A five-year followup study comparing the school achievement and school adjustment of children retained in kindergarten and children placed in transition class', unpublished doctoral dissertation, University of Minnesota.

SANDOVAL, J. and FITZGERALD, P. (1985) 'A high school follow-up of children who were nonpromoted or attended a junior first grade', *Psychology in the Schools*, 22, pp. 164–70.

SCHOOL READINESS TASK FORCE (1988) *Here They Come: Ready or Not*, Sacramento, CA, California State Department of Education.

SCOTT, B. A. and AMES, L. B. (1969) 'Improved academic, personal, and social adjustment in selected primary school repeaters', *The Elementary School Journal*, 69, pp. 431–9.

SHEETS, C. (1977) unpublished research paper, University of Northern Iowa, cited in WILSON, B. J., HEWETT, G., SHEETS, C. and THOMAS, J. (1978) 'Early recognition: Proceed with caution and evaluate', paper presented at the annual meeting of the Iowa Association for Children with Learning Disabilities.

SHEPARD, L. A. and SMITH, M. L. (1985) *Boulder Valley Kindergarten Study: Retention Practices and Retention Effects*, Boulder, CO, Boulder Valley Public Schools.

SHEPARD, L. A. and SMITH, M. L. (1987) 'Effects of kindergarten retention at the end of first grade', *Psychology in the Schools*, 24, pp. 346–57.

STAPLEFORD, D. C. (1982) 'The effects of a second year in kindergarten on later school achievement and self-concept', unpublished doctoral dissertation, Michigan State University.

TALMADGE, S. J. (1981) 'Descriptive and predictive relationships among family environments, cognitive characteristics, behavioral ratings, transi-

tion room placement, and early reading achievement', unpublished doctoral dissertation, University of Oregon.
TURLEY, C. C. (1979) 'A study of elementary school children for whom a second year of kindergarten was recommended', unpublished doctoral dissertation, University of San Francisco.
WILSON, B. and HEWETT, G. (1978) 'Long-term effects of a transition room program on student achievement', paper presented at the annual meeting of the American Educational Research Association, Toronto.

Chapter 5:
Academic and Emotional Effects of Kindergarten Retention in One School District[1]

Lorrie A. Shepard and Mary Lee Smith

Editors' Introduction

In a climate of extreme opinions, for and against repeating kindergarten, it is unlikely that dry, summarized research findings will be persuasive to those who hold contrary opinions. There is always the thought that somehow the groups were inappropriately selected or the outcome measures too narrowly focused to grant credence to the findings. Chapter 5 presents an in-depth study of kindergarten retention in one school district, intended to give flesh to the research reviewed in chapter 4. In a single study it is possible to describe methods in greater detail thus enabling the reader to examine critically the integrity of study conclusions.

The research reported here also had the benefit of issues raised by previous studies. The question as to whether children were placed in extra-year programs because of immaturity, learning difficulties, or both, was addressed directly by studying the characteristics of retained children when they first entered school. More rigorously equivalent comparisons could be established by selecting control children from similar schools where retention was not practiced rather than relying on the comparability of children whose parents refused retention. Outcomes were measured in a way that respected the claimed benefits of those who advocate an extra year of kindergarten. For example, retained children were always measured in relation to their new, younger peer group where the advantage of being older would most likely be seen, and important affective outcomes were assessed such as learner self-concept, social maturity in relation to classmates, and appropriate attention span.

Perhaps the most important contribution of the chapter is the extended analysis of parent interview data on the effects of kindergarten retention for their children. Verbatim quotations reveal, in a way not captured by survey rating scales, how parents can hold simultaneously both positive and negative feelings about program effects.

Is an extra year of kindergarten safe haven for immature children whose 'time clocks tick slower?' Will they have a happier and more successful first-grade experience for having waited? Or, as some parents fear, is staying back in kindergarten simply a case of 'flunking', just like repeating any other grade? This chapter presents detailed results of a comparative study undertaken as part of a policy analysis for a Colorado school district (Shepard and Smith, 1985). The purpose of the study was to evaluate the effects of kindergarten retention. Were the retained children more successful academically than they would have been without the extra year of school? Did they feel better about themselves because they were not pushed ahead before they were ready?

The literature review pertinent to this research is presented in chapter 4. When the study was begun in 1984, Gredler's (1984) review had already concluded that transition or readiness rooms are ineffective means to prevent school failure. There was and continues to be, however, sharp disagreement between research findings and the beliefs of local educators about the benefits of such programs. In a context of controversy, methodological issues that might bias results become especially salient. Our research was undertaken to replicate controlled studies of the effects of kindergarten retention but with an eye to correcting the methodological limitations of previous investigations.

The naturally occurring variation in retention rates among schools within the district allowed us to institute more rigorous controls than had previous researchers over the initial comparability of retained and non-retained groups. Alerted to the issues of population differences in candidates for retention (see chapter 4), it was possible to examine the characteristics of children selected for retention and to ensure that controls were matched on relevant dimensions. Because the research was intended to inform policy decisions in the district, both program advocates and detractors influenced the design of the study. Social-emotional outcomes were deemed as important as measures of achievement in judging program success. Therefore, the study methods were intended to improve on previous research by including multiple outcome measures and more adequate controls.

Sample Characteristics

Elementary schools within the district differed markedly in the percentage of children spending two years before first grade, from 0 to 25 per cent. In some schools as many as 38 per cent of kindergartners were recommended to repeat. The 'high-retaining schools' were not of one particular type or location, i.e., they were spread throughout the district and served both higher and lower socioeconomic neighborhoods. Because the schools were so different in retention rates, the present study did not have to rely on the questionable practice of selecting control (promoted) subjects from the same school as the retained children. Thus we could avoid the threat that control children were systematically more or less able. Instead, more comparable subjects from matched schools could be selected who were equally young or unready and who would clearly have been candidates for retention had they attended a high-retaining school.

A two-stage sampling procedure was used to identify comparable schools and matched pairs of subjects within the schools. Data on kindergarten retention rates by school were collected at the end of the 1982/83 school year. Four schools with the highest retention rates were identified for study as the high-retaining schools. These schools, labeled A through D, in table 1 retained from 16 to 20 per cent of their kindergartners. Then, control schools were selected so as to be matched as closely as possible on percent receiving reduced or free lunch and mean scores on the Comprehensive Test of Basic Skills (CTBS) but with retention rates of 4 per cent or less.

The characteristics of the high-retaining and low-retaining schools are summarized in table 1. The percent of children receiving free and reduced-priced lunches (FRL) was used as a crude index of the school's socioeconomic status (SES). However, other knowledge of SES factors was also considered. For example, schools D and (d) both have significant English as Second Language (ESL) populations. Schools B and (b) serve adjacent attendance areas and are believed to be more similar in SES than the FRL measure would suggest. Finally, third grade mean CTBS scores were used to identify schools whose populations have similar achievement-ability levels. Schools (e1) and (e2) served as additional control schools. For example, at the pupil level, if an accurate match could not be found from control school (a) for a retained child at school A, the control child might be selected from school (e1). Especially, because of missing entry-level data at school (c), school (e2)

L. A. Shepard and M. L. Smith

Table 1: *Characteristics of High-Retaining and Matched Control, Low-Retaining Schools (in Matched Pairs)*

	High-retaining schools	Low-retaining schools	
	School A	*School (a)*	*School (e1)*
n*	559	225	477
FRL**	13%	14%	3%
CTBS***	5.0/4.9	5.1/5.0	5.0/4.8
% R in K****	16%	0%	2%
	School B	*School (b)*	
n	590	607	
FRL	7%	24%	
CTBS	5.0/4.7	4.2/4.2	
% R in K	20%	4%	
	School C	*School (c)*	*School (e2)*
n	593	483	302
FRL	3%	16%	8%
CTBS	4.4/4.4	4.5/4.5	4.9/4.9
% R in K	19%	4%	1%
	School D	*School (d)*	
n	520	415	
FRL	37%	38%	
CTBS	4.2/4.1	4.0/3.6	
	high ESL pop.	high ESL pop.	
% R in K	18%	3%	

    * K-6 enrollment
    ** % of school population receiving free or reduced lunch (FRL)
    *** Third grade CTBS school means in grade equivalent units for total battery and/or 'expected' grade equivalent based on short form aptitude tests
    **** % retained in kindergarten, based on 1982/83 data in all schools except school (e2) where the rate reported is for 1981/82

served as an alternate control for school C to which it is a close neighbor.

At the second stage of sampling, entry-level data and school histories were coded for all first graders at both the high-retaining and low-retaining schools. Data included sex, birthdate, retention in first grade or in kindergarten, participation in the reduced-price lunch program, first language other than English, and scores on a kindergarten readiness measure. The Santa Clara Inventory is an individually administered measure of developmental tasks. It is administered to kindergartners district-wide in September. The Santa Clara has eight sub-tests like those typically found on school readiness measures: conceptual development, language development, auditory memory, auditory perception, visual memory, visual perception, visual motor performance and motor coordination.

At the high-retaining schools all first graders who spent two years prior to first grade were identified. Included in this category were

Academic and Emotional Effects of Kindergarten Retention

children who had attended pre-first grade or developmental kindergarten as well as those who had repeated regular kindergarten. These children, called the retained group, were automatically in the study if they had been given the Santa Clara at the beginning of their first year of kindergarten. The lack of entering Santa Clara scores resulted in some attrition from the sample. The final sample of forty retainees was comprised as follows: twelve of seventeen children retained at school A, sixteen of seventeen children retained at school B, nine of nine children retained at school C, and three of four children retained at school D. Follow-up analyses are provided later to determine if the children with missing data had been systematically more or less able (on outcome measures) than the children studied. It should also be noted that the only children eligible for inclusion in the retained sample were those who had not only repeated kindergarten in 1982/83 at schools A through D, but who also were still attending the same school at the end of first grade. Some children were lost to the study either because of normal migration out of district and between schools or because parents specifically changed schools as a result of the retention decision or to avoid retention. For example, we found several children in the control schools who had been recommended for retention at school A or C but whose parents wanted them to repeat with different classmates.

The characteristics of children retained in kindergarten are depicted in figures 1 and 2 for the three schools with the largest retained samples. These distributions were constructed to facilitate matching with control children as described below. However, these graphs also convey important information about implicit differences in school policies as to who should be retained. Teachers in school A tended to recommend children to repeat kindergarten who had been low on the readiness measure (figure 1). As shown in figure 2, these extra-year placements bore almost no relation to children's sex or age in months. School B appeared to apply more joint criteria. That is, children recommended to repeat were low on the readiness measure but also tended to be either male or in the younger half of their class. When the readiness distribution was constructed for school C the results were surprising and inexplicable; this anomaly was the reason, in fact, for adding figure 2. Readiness performance was uncorrelated with retention recommendations at school C; instead, children had been asked to repeat most often if they were boys or in the younger half of their class.

In addition, an important policy implication was noted for school C. Because the parents of the more ready kindergarten children had acceded to the recommendation for an extra year, and generally the

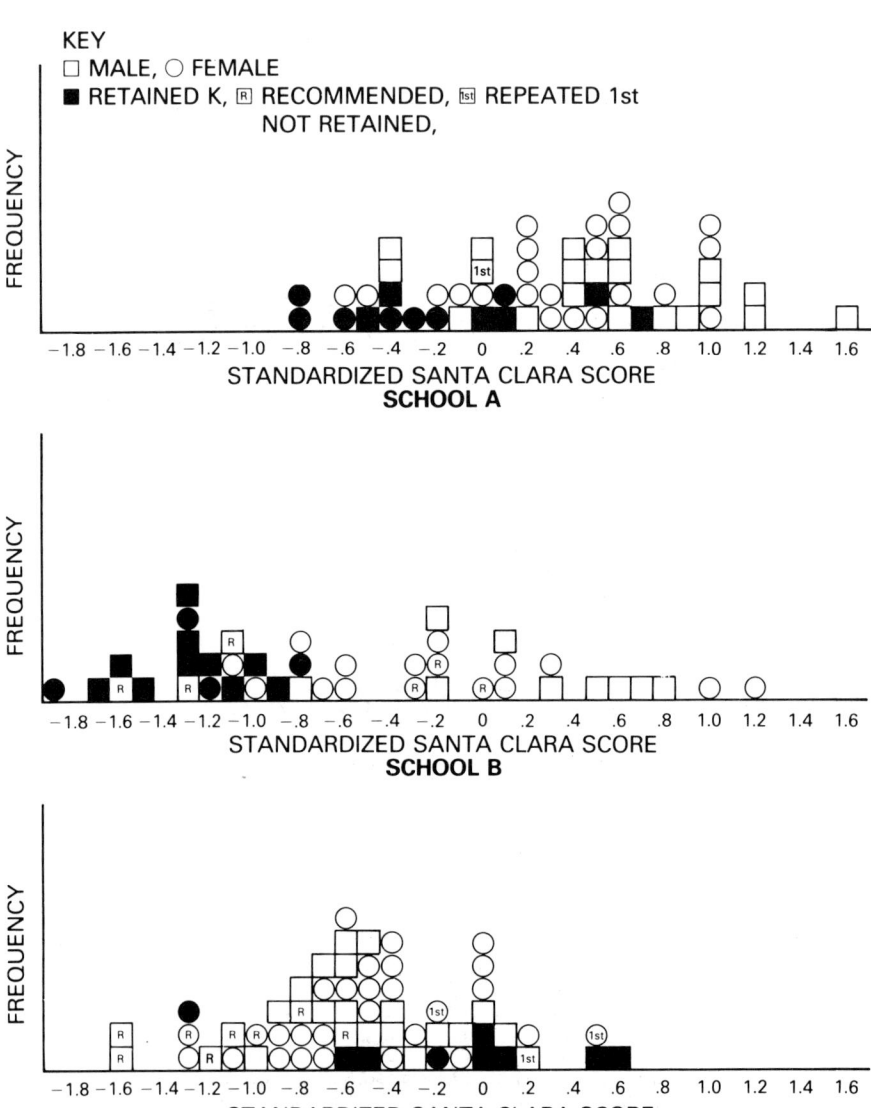

Figure 1: Distribution of Entering Kindergarten Santa Clara Scores for Retained and Non-retaining First Graders in Three High-retaining Schools

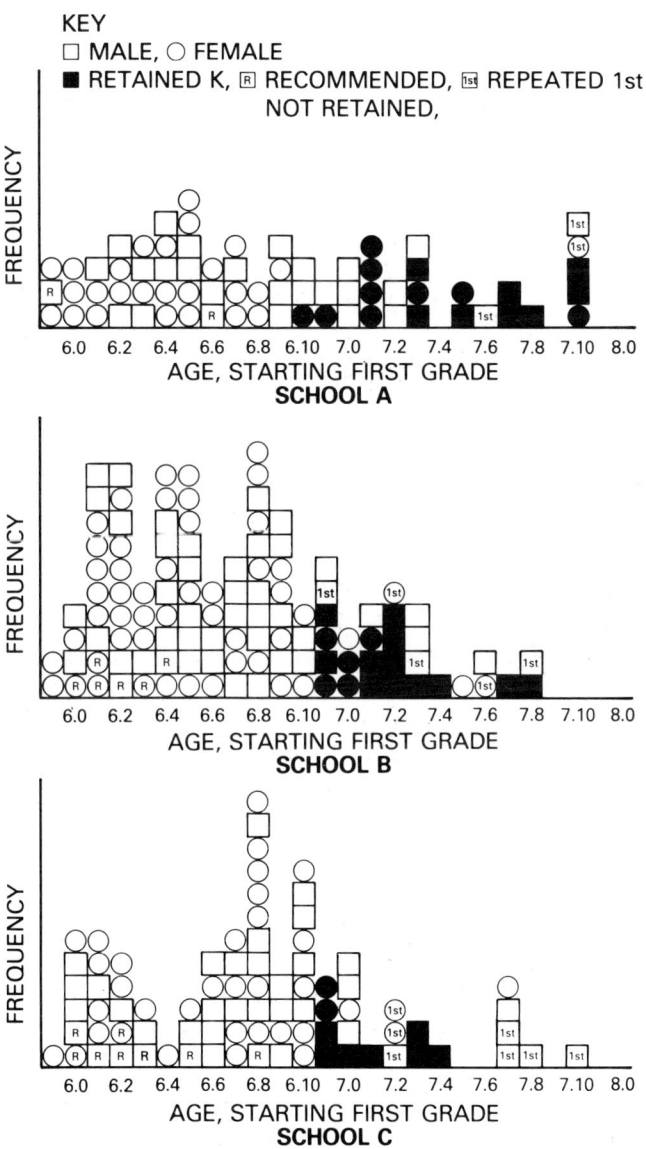

Figure 2: Distribution of Ages When Entering First Grade for Retained and Non-retained Pupils in Three High-retaining Schools

parents of the least ready children had not, the practice of kindergarten retention in this school had greatly increased the heterogeneity of the first-grade class. Children who were average or above on readiness measures when they came to school then spent an extra year in kindergarten and were 7 years old when they entered first grade. These already advantaged children were then in the same class with just barely 6-year-olds who had been the lowest scorers on readiness measures. If what occurred in school C were to generalize to other school districts, then parent choice as well as teacher selection criteria might explain the occasions where transition children are more able than the parent-refusal control group (chapter 4 in this volume).

In the second stage of sampling, a matched-control child was selected for each retained child from the corresponding low-retaining school or schools. Retained and control children were matched on sex, birthday, SES factors, and entry Santa Clara scores. In creating the matched pairs, there was never any deviation from the requirement that the children be the same sex. We judged it better, for example, sometimes to have birthdates or scores deviate by two or three months than to pair a boy with a girl. Birthdays were used, lagged by a year, so that the retained and control children were the same age when they entered kindergarten *for the first time*. Thus, retained children were a year older at the time of the first-grade outcome measures, but at the time they first presented for kindergarten, they were the same age within one or two months. Of the forty matched cases, thirty-two had what we considered to be good matches for age at entrance, i.e., birthdays were within two months of each other (in fact, twenty-three were within one month). Four matched pairs differed by three or four months in entrance age; these and the remaining four cases were flagged as either 'favoring controls' or 'favoring the retained' group; i.e., if the retained child was three months older than his counterpart, this was considered a selection bias 'in favor of' the retained group. Later, when we did separate analyses for only identical matches or those favoring one group or the other, we were able to examine the effect of any inaccuracies in the match of initial characteristics on the final results. Two retained children for whom English is a second language were matched with comparable low SES (reduced-price lunch), second language control children.

Retained and control children were also matched on Santa Clara scores obtained at the start of their first year in kindergarten. Thus, these two groups of children were comparable when they first entered school. Because the Santa Clara does not have adequate normative data for combining separate item responses, a scoring procedure had to be devised for the purposes of this study. Separate sub-test scores were computed for each child as the sum of the item scores. Then, based on the September kindergarten data for all 700 first graders in the ten sampled schools, means and standard deviations were calculated for each sub-test. These statistics could then be used to determine each child's standard score on each sub-test. Finally, each child received a total Santa Clara score that was the average of his or her separate z scores. These total or composite scores were used to match children who started school with the same level of academic readiness. Of the forty matched cases, twenty-three were matched on initial Santa Clara scores with z-score differences of less than .2; an additional six pairs had z differences between .2 and .3. The remaining eleven matched pairs were noted to favor one group or the other on z scores and were excluded from later analyses designed to test the effect of initial matching on outcomes.

To summarize, the two-stage sampling procedure produced forty matched pairs. First graders from high-retaining schools who had repeated kindergarten (and hence were completing three years of school) were matched on sex, birthday, initial readiness, and dominant language with first graders from low-retaining schools who had not been retained. Whenever the initial data were suspect or the data were certain but the match was imperfect, the pairs were flagged so that the effect of these biases could be checked in subsequent analyses.

Outcome Measures

Retained and non-retained children were compared on seven outcome measures, including five teacher ratings and two standardized test scores as described below. Each first grade teacher in the ten participating schools rated all of the children in his or her class during the last two weeks of school in spring 1984. The teachers rated each child in the following areas: reading achievement, math achievement, social maturity, learning self-concept and appropriateness of attention to school work. For each of these five areas, teachers made a normative judgment about each child *in relation to other children* in their first grade class. These normative comparisons were on a five-point scale: 1 = bottom group (the child is one of the lowest five children in this class), 2 = next-to-bottom group (next-to-lowest five children), 3 = average children in this class, 4 = next-to-top group (next-to-top five children), and

5 = top group (the five top children in this class). The purpose of having teachers rate all these first graders and not merely those involved in the study was not only to ensure true relative comparisons but to control for reactivity and the instrumentation threat to internal validity. The teachers in the low-retaining schools could not have been aware of which children had been selected as control cases. To the extent that the first-grade teachers in the high-retaining schools were aware that the ratings were part of the 'kindergarten study', they might have surmised that the ratings of children who had been repeaters would be of special interest. Teachers were also asked to report how much time was spent in completing the rating forms, which ranged from thirty minutes to five hours. All of the teachers appeared to take the rating task seriously, many reported that they got out their grade books or looked at their reading groups to assign children to categories.

The two standardized test scores were the reading and math total scores from the Comprehensive Tests of Basic Skills (CTBS) (Level B, Form S). The CTBS is routinely administered district-wide to all first grade children in April each year.

To supplement test scores and teacher ratings, we collected information from the parents of the children. Parents of the retained and non-retained samples of first grade children were surveyed by the first author and a trained graduate assistant by means of a structured telephone interview. Two additional samples of parents were also interviewed: those who had refused to have their children repeat kindergarten and a group whose children had repeated first grade. The interviews were intended to answer several questions regarding parents' perceptions of their child's readiness when first entering kindergarten, the nature of screening and orientation to school, and perceptions of progress in kindergarten and first grade. (These narrative data were analyzed in Shepard and Smith, 1985.) Parents were also asked to rate their children on four dimensions reflecting their progress and adjustment at the end of first grade.

Teacher Ratings and Test Score Results

The overall results based on teacher ratings and test scores for forty retained children and forty matched controls are reported in table 2. In this study, significance tests to check for random sampling error are inappropriate because subjects were not randomly assigned to groups. We instead addressed the related question regrading the effects of initial

Table 2: First Grade Outrcome Measures for Previously Retained Children and Matched Controls

	Retained (in kindergarten)			Matched controls		
	$\bar{X}$	s	n	$\bar{X}$	s	n
Teacher Ratings (Compared to classmates, 1 = lowest group, 5 = highest group)						
Reading	2.65	1.31	40	2.50	1.32	40
Math	2.80	1.29	40	2.68	1.33	40
Social Maturity	2.83	1.15	40	2.65	1.29	40
Learner Self-Concept	2.90	1.30	40	2.55	1.20	40
Attention	2.73	1.20	40	2.63	1.35	40
Standardized Tests						
CTBS Reading						
Raw Score	69.85	9.78	40	64.55	12.96	40
National percentile	63rd			56th		
Grade eqivalent	1.9			1.8		
CTBS Math						
Raw Score	44.65	8.94	40	45.93	7.50	40
National percentile	78th			81st		
Grade equivalent	2.2			2.3		

matching on the stability and magnitude of effects. The concern about the size of the differences is addressed using the more appropriate metric of effect sizes. Effect sizes are defined as the difference between the experimental and control (retained minus control) in standard deviation units, i.e., divided by the pooled standard deviation (Glass, McGaw, and Smith, 1981). For the CTBS scores we had the benefit of national percentiles and grade equivalent scores for interpreting the magnitude of effects. We also obtained overall distributions for both teacher ratings and CTBS scores in the ten schools as another way of interpreting the distribution of outcome measures for retained and control groups.

Overall, the picture in table 2 is one of very small or no differences. The only real difference (measured in effect size or by statistical significance) occurred on the CTBS reading sub-test where the retained children were five raw-score points higher than the control group. This difference translates into seven percentile points on the national normative scale. In grade equivalent units this difference amounted to a one month gain. That is, children who repeated kindergarten were one month ahead of where they would have been if they had been promoted to first grade instead of spending two years in kindergarten. The benefit of retained over control children on CTBS reading is highlighted by the frequency distribution in figure 3. The five-point gain at the mean

L. A. Shepard and M. L. Smith

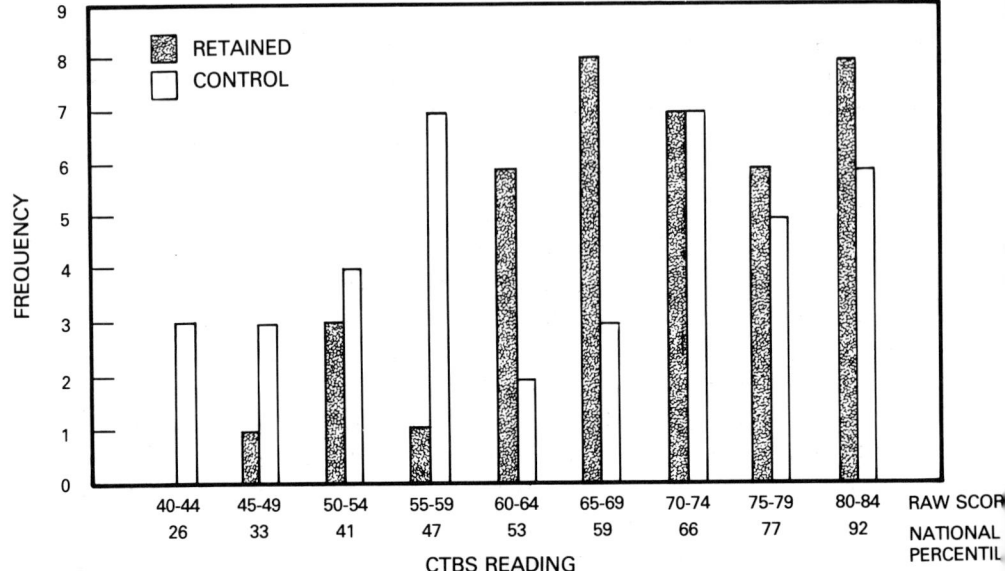

Figure 3: *Distribution of Retained vs Control Scores on CTBS Reading*

appears to be fairly stable across the distribution (i.e., the retained distribution is shifted one score interval to the right). For example, children who would have been at the twenty-fifth percentile nationally are improved to the thirty-third percentile as a result of the extra year. An average improvement of one month may seem trivial to some, important to others. In any case, it is correct to say that the effect is real but that these children spent a year to gain one month in reading achievement. Other effect sizes were either zero, or were considered to be zero if removal of one or two extreme cases would eliminate the effect.

On the CTBS math test the effect was reversed. The control group was ahead of the retained group by three percentile points, or by one month in grade equivalent units (however, the effect size was quite small). It is worth noting that in an absolute sense both the retained children and their matched controls performed well in comparison to national norms. In reading the retained group was at the sixty-third percentile; the control group, who were younger and low in academic readiness compared to other children in the district, was at the fifty-sixth percentile nationally. In math the retained and control children were at the seventy-eighth and eighty-first percentiles, respectively. The very lowest child in either group on either test was at the twenty-second percentile nationally in reading.

With the exception of CTBS reading, the other variables in table 2 show essentially no difference between groups. Thus, the extra year before first grade did not raise academic performance in comparison to classmates. As rated by first grade teachers, there was no harm to self-concept for the retained group in comparison to the control group. Interestingly, the retained group was not better off after an additional year in terms of social maturity or attention to school work. The claims that an extra year will move immature children to the head of the class or make them leaders are not borne out. Extra-year children were no different in comparison to their respective classmates than a group of very young and unready children who were sent directly on to first grade. More than 40 per cent of the retained children were rated as below average in social maturity by their first grade teachers despite the fact that they were now a year older than normal first graders. This last finding caused us to speculate that perhaps when teachers or Gesell examiners identify kindergarten children as immature they are responding to relatively enduring personality traits (such as shyness or hyperactivity) that are not altered by the passing of time. Or viewed another way, Gesell examiners might be responding to a child's context-bound response to the testing situation with an unfamiliar adult.

How can these results be explained? If it can be shown that 'ready' children do better than 'unready' children in first grade, why don't unready children gain substantially when they are given time to become ready? It may surprise many to realize that the small gain in reading (7 percentile points) is precisely what would be predicted by a sizable portion of the research used to justify kindergarten retention. Many advocates for extra-year programs do not cite evidence from controlled studies. Instead, they point to the research literature on the 'youngness' effect, whereby children in first and second grade are at a disadvantage on achievement measures if they are youngest in their grade. It is presumed that by holding children for an extra year in kindergarten they will perform in first grade like the oldest children. And indeed, such a result sometimes occurs in controlled comparisons (but the effect is small or non-significant). A computational review of the youngness literature reveals that the advantage of the oldest group was never very large, on average across studies only about 7 or 8 percentile points (Shepard and Smith, 1986). Thus, the result in this study of 7 percentile points gain in one subject area is consistent with the predicted effect of making the children a year older before receiving first-grade instruction. This interpretation is also consistent with findings from a few controlled studies (chapter 4) showing an initial benefit for kindergarten retention at the end of first grade but no benefit when retainees are followed to third grade. The youngness effect also disappears by about third grade (*ibid.*). Thus, the lack of benefit from waiting a year is not surprising, if one has a realistic rather than an exaggerated conception about the average difference between the oldest and youngest first graders.

Controls over Internal and External Validity

In any quasi-experiment, researchers should consider whether limitations in design threaten its conclusions. Since random assignment is impossible and unethical in studies such as the one reported here, the initial comparability of groups is open to question. In this case, however, the groups were well matched on those variables thought to be most related to development and early school achievement; that is, chronological age, sex, measured readiness, and dominant language. In addition, the schools were comparable in socioeconomic status and typical achievement levels. The stability of the foregoing effects was tested across pairs of schools and across comparison groups that differed in the exactness of the original matching data. The most reliable effects were for the CTBS data; i.e., the small negative effect (favoring controls) in math and the slightly larger positive effect (favoring retained children) in reading held up over all the crossbreaks of the data. By selecting the most favorable school comparison the benefit on CTBS reading for retention could be boosted to two months (based on nine cases), whereas in the worst case the effect was reduced to zero (based on twelve cases). Nevertheless, the total data give a good picture of the pattern of effects across schools and types of two-year programs.

As one might expect when the average is roughly zero, the effects for the teaching rating variables tended to be sometimes positive and sometimes negative. One school had all negative effects (i.e., the control children were higher on all five dimensions), another school had all positive effects, and a third school had zero effects except for the retained children being seriously behind on social maturity and attention even after an extra year. These positive and negative effects averaged out to the near zero effects reported in table 2. When only the exact matches (n = 14 pairs) were used, virtually identical effect sizes were obtained as those found for the total sample (n = 40 pairs). Thus, the no difference result on the teacher ratings fluctuates a little, but is corroborated when the quality of the original matching is taken into account.

Even careful matching does not preclude regression artifacts when the treated and control groups are chosen from different populations or different regions of a distribution. In traditional grade retention research, control groups are likely to be systematically more able, thus potentially masking outcomes favorable to retention (Jackson, 1975). Conversely, several studies of kindergarten retention reviewed in chapter 4 placed more able groups in extra-year programs than the at-risk group who were promoted to first grade and served as controls. The present study is less susceptible to regression or selection threats than studies in which the control group consists of children in the same school as the retained group, who were recommended for retention but not retained. The type of bias identified in chapter 4 would have occurred here, for example, if the low-readiness children in school C whose parents refused retention had been compared to the high-readiness children whose parents agreed to retention (see figure 1). In our study non-retained children in low-retaining schools had the same readiness abilities as retained children in high-retaining schools; furthermore to achieve the matches, cases were selected from the same regions of the respective distributions. In the few cases where retained children were more extremely low on entry scores than were their matched controls, we actually treated the difference as a selection bias favoring the controls. Regression artifacts like this, which occurred in only one school, would in fact mitigate against the selection effect.

However, selecting groups from different schools confounds treatment (retention or non-retention) with school culture. It is conceivable, for example, that less ready children do equally well without retention because the instruction in their schools is geared to their level of development. It might not follow then that the retained children would have done equally well in their schools if they had gone on to a more aversive curriculum. We addressed this question by analyzing data from one group of parents interviewed, those who had refused the extra-year placement for their children. These children were part of the same culture of the high-retaining schools as their retained counterparts. Furthermore, those who were retained actually were slightly more able, initially, than those who were recommended but not retained. By the end of the first grade, the ratings given by the parents of the two groups did not differ (see table 3 in the next section). These findings of no difference between retained and non-retained children in the same schools are consistent with the controlled comparisons between schools.

A check was made on the possible bias created by the omission of six cases (four from school A) prior to matching because of missing entry level data; a seventh case was left out of the study because no extremely low counterpart could be found. The six retained children with missing entry data had mean first grade CTBS scores of 72.5 and 45.7 in reading and math, respectively. These values are slightly above the total retained group means (see table 2) but are the same as school A means (71.83 and 45.33) where most of the missing data occurred. Because these children would have been matched with correspondingly more able children as was done for school A, there is no reason to believe that the six missing cases created any systematic bias in the results. In general, then, we believe that the findings are robust with respect to the initial comparability of the groups and generalize to the complete population of retained kindergartners in this district.

Parent Ratings and Descriptions of Retention

Parent interviews for four samples of first graders were conducted following a chronological protocol. Parents were asked to think back to their feelings about their child's readiness before starting school, to describe their perceptions of progress in kindergarten, to recall the discussion of the extra-year decision (where relevant), and to report on several aspects of their child's progress in first grade. These interviews were recorded with the permission of the parents and transcribed. More complete analyses of the narrative responses are provided in Shepard and Smith (1985). For the purposes of this chapter, results are presented for the quantitative rating scales. In addition, qualitative results are reported from the sample of parents (n = 30) whose children were retained in kindergarten.

Parent ratings at the end of first grade are summarized in table 3. These data show that the two key comparison groups, those retained or not retained in kindergarten, differ only slightly from each other according to parents' perceptions. The differences that do exist favor the non-retained matched-control group. Both the non-retained children, who had been selected from low-retaining schools, and the recommended-but-not-retained children, who attended the high-retaining schools, appear to have better attitudes toward school than the retained children as judged by their parents.

Parents are also an appropriate source for information about the effects of kindergarten retention. In the interviews, parents often told about what retention had meant to their child or family in response to

Table 3: Quantitative Ratings from Parent Interviews

'Now at the end of first grade, how would you describe your child's progress in school subjects?' (Doing extremely well = 5; Having serious difficulty = 1)

	Retained	At Risk Not Retained	Recommended Not Retained	First Grade Retained
$\bar{X}$	3.38	3.43	3.46	3.14
s	.82	.42	.52	1.07
$s_{\bar{x}}$	.15	.08	.16	.40
n	29	28	10	7

'How would you describe his attitude toward school?' (Very positive, loves school = 5; Has a very negative attitude toward school = 1)

	Retained	At Risk Not Retained	Recommended Not Retained	First Grade Retained
$\bar{X}$	3.93	4.50	4.36	4.14
s	1.14	.75	.81	.90
$s_{\bar{x}}$	.21	.14	.26	.34
n	30	28	10	7

'How would you describe his(her) relationship with his(her) peers?' (Is very popular, gets along very well with peers = 5; Has a great deal of difficulty getting along with others = 1)

	Retained	At Risk Not Retained	Recommended Not Retained	First Grade Retained
$\bar{X}$	3.43	3.89	3.36	3.43
s	1.01	.83	.51	.79
$s_{\bar{x}}$	.18	.16	.16	.30
n	30	28	10	7

'How ready would you say your child is now for second grade?' (Very ready, I expect him to be very successful in second grade = 5; Definitely not ready, we expect difficulties = 1)

	Retained	At Risk Not Retained	Recommended Not Retained	First Grade Retained
$\bar{X}$	3.00	3.38	3.30	3.43
s	.98	.81	.68	1.41
$s_{\bar{x}}$	.18	.15	.22	.53
n	30	28	10	7

the following standard questions:

> What were the reasons for repeating kindergarten?
>
> What were your feelings about the decision at the time?

At the end of the interview, parents of retained children were also asked this question:

> Now looking back, what would you say are some of the benefits or drawbacks to having your child spend two years in kindergarten?

Full-length transcripts from parent interviews were read and coded. Responses describing the effects of retention were coded whether they occurred in response to standard questions or incidentally in answer to other questions.

Narrative data were analyzed using qualitative methods as suggested by Miles and Huberman (1984). Verbatim quotations were excerpted summarizing each parent's descriptions of the effects of retention. A continuum of positive to negative effects was identified. Excerpts that were similar in attitude or valence were grouped together and located on the continuum. The analysis proceeded iteratively until all cases had been assigned to relatively homogeneous categories, and the distinctions between the categories could be typified. The results of the analysis are presented in table 4. Six categories or degrees of positive versus negative effects are presented followed by quotations from parents that gave rise to the category. Excerpts have been altered slightly to correct for errors in grammar; names and class references have been changed to disguise the identity of individuals and schools.

The frequencies of responses from parents of retained children were distributed from the most positive to the most negative category as follows, indicating a greater preponderance of positive conclusions about retention:

Category	**Category Label**	**N**
Category 1	Unambiguously positive	7
Category 2	Very positive; misgivings are expressed but are only in the background	5
Category 3	Benefits outweigh the drawbacks; but negative effects had to be overcome	7
Category 4	It was the right decision but negative impact was keenly felt	5
Category 5	It wasn't necessary and we worry about negative effects	4
Category 6	Very negative	2

Responses in the first two categories, representing 40 per cent of the cases, reflected fairly enthusiastic endorsements of the extra year for their child. In fact, if parent comments were to be reduced to a single vote, 'Yes or no, did the retention help more than it hurt?', responses in the first *four* categories would be considered 'yes' votes, representing 80 per cent of the cases. Positive effects of retention as seen by the parents were an extra year to mature, an academic advantage or 'boost', and more self-confidence.

At the same time that a very large majority of parents expressed an overall positive effect of retention, an equally large proportion reported on negative experiences that had been a part of retention for their child. The continuum which was constructed reflected the relative salience or weight these negative occurrences seemed to have for the parents (rather than the presence or absence of negative events). For example, parents in all of the categories mentioned hurtful comments from other children or adults: but the overall tone of the responses placed in category 1 were so positive that these negative side effects seemed to have very little import. In contrast, category 4 was created expressly to represent the parents who wanted to give a positive overall vote for the program but whose extended comments reflected largely negative emotional effects that had to be overcome. Although only 20 per cent of parents gave pervasively negative answers, an additional 40 per cent gave accounts of unhappy or distressing problems that weighed against benefits to some significant degree. The most seriously negative effects reported by the parents were teasing by other children for being kept back and the child's own sense of failure. Other negative effects were being too big for one's grade, careless work habits (from work being too easy and repetitive), and the persistence after an extra year of behaviors that the extra year had been intended to correct. Some behaviors, originally attributed to immaturity, such as 'antsiness' and lack of social skills had not been corrected either by the program or by time alone.

Issues of non-response bias were treated more fully in our complete report (Shepard and Smith, 1985). For example, two non-English speaking families had been eliminated from both the retained and non-retained samples; half of the remaining non-respondents in both samples were accounted for by disconnected telephones; obviously, more mobile families were underrepresented in the interview portion of the study. Further, the positive to negative continuum represented in table 4 is naturally, systematically biased (by some unknown amount) toward the positive end of the scale because, by definition, all of the parents in this group agreed to the retention decision. Although in some cases parents were under considerable pressure to agree, being told that the school would not accept responsibility if the child was pushed ahead before he was ready, the district policy gave parents the final authority for retention decisions. As was mentioned previously, some number of parents had moved their children to have them repeat with other

Table 4: Parent Reports of the Effects of Kindergarten Retention: A Continuum of Excerpts from Positive to Negative

CATEGORY 1: UNAMBIGUOUSLY POSITIVE

She got that extra year in, which I believe will help her throughout, until she graduates from high school. Just that added boost that she needed was to me the most beneficial part. She didn't attend pre-school, and I don't know whether that might have had anything to do with the decision, but I think that's the biggest thing right there. ... The only (drawback) would be other people who would say, 'Why isn't Abby in first grade? She should be, you know'. But it didn't bother me. It seemed to bother some people, but for me and my husband, it didn't bother us at all.

Overall it was a good decision and I support the program and I think it was very good for her. They were very helpful and she had a real good experience in special ed.

The extra year gave him a chance to strive ahead instead of always catching up. It has already proven itself. We felt he was exactly where he belongs. He wouldn't have made it in a straight academic kindergarten. He was not ready to sit and learn to do the things that his sister had done in one year of kindergarten.

We felt that he was not really developed and mature enough to do the concentration. He could have (gone) on but it would have put him at a disadvantage in that he would have struggled from there on through school, for the rest of his life, rather than really letting him be on top from the beginning. He has shown that (theory) has proven to be successful all the way through first grade also. ... He has no problems socially at all. He relates well and tends to be maybe a little timid at times. He's probably more of a follower than a leader in some respects, but yet there doesn't seem to be any problem for him.

It gave her that extra year to develop. Without that she would have been withdrawn or a clown.

He didn't have the patience. He was a fidgety type person, was not good at concentrating at all ... (The extra year) helps the child adjust more to the classroom setting and the speed. Brian's trouble area used to be the reading. He caught up a lot in the areas where he had been having trouble. It helped him in getting along with the other kids. It was slower paced — he's on a slower speed scale — he's very meticulous. That helped him because he would get very frustrated.

I would say the benefits far outweigh the disadvantages, especially in her situation. (Also repeating first) I would say the maturity level is a real big thing, just giving them a chance socially to adjust to the school, and keeping it less academic. It gives you the freedom as a parent to say, 'It's O.K. if you don't catch it this year, don't worry about it, you'll get it next.'

CATEGORY 2: VERY POSITIVE: MISGIVINGS ARE EXPRESSED BUT ARE ONLY IN THE BACKGROUND

During the second year, I asked how those students that went on to first grade (despite the teacher's recommendation) were doing — if they were keeping track of them. She said, 'Yes, that they weren't doing as well in first grade, that they still weren't emotionally ready to be there.' So I felt a lot better about Collin's staying back a year. Well not staying back, but being in that particular program. ... I think that if he had just jumped into kindergarten and then gone on to first grade, I don't think he'd be doing well at all. It's hard to know, because I look around at some of these other kids on our block who have moved from other states, and they're the same age as my son and they're a year ahead, because they didn't go through the two year program ... But, it really doesn't make that much difference, just as long as he enjoys what he's doing

Table 4   (Continued)

and he learns. That's the important thing, and I think that's what going to two years of kindergarten did.

Well, the benefits were that if she would have pushed on she wouldn't have made it anyway. She would have failed. It was beneficial to hold her back. What would be the point of pushing her ahead and being totally frustrated not being able to do the work and keep up?

He has done very well. He still has a few problems of antsiness but he's doing a lot better ... The only drawback is he's extremely tall. So he overtowers most of the kids in first grade. I think that might bother him, maybe not. I feel that it's the best thing I could have done for him and I feel he's done very well. If I had not kept him back it would have been harder for him to stay back in first grade than it would be in kindergarten ... I wish David had gone to a pre-school before I put him in kindergarten. I think he would have learned to adapt to strangers and would have been more drilled in the fact that he has to sit still.

They call it a 'gift of time' and I think that is probably the best way to describe it. Going over the same stuff again gives him an advantage over some of the other kids ... It was a different program (from kindergarten) but it didn't seem that it was very challenging. It wasn't very hard for him to do. It was mostly busywork compared to this year (first grade).

He was one of the lowest in reading and they thought that as the years go on he was going to have more difficulty. They thought they could hold him back and catch up in reading; and it would make it a lot easier for his school work in later years because reading is one of the big essentials ... When Elliot was taken out of first grade and put into pre-first, it made him more prepared for the first grade level. So when he did enter that first grade, I think that they may have given him too much confidence. They may have prepared him too much because he was finishing his work a lot sooner than most of the students.

CATEGORY 3: BENEFITS OUTWEIGH THE DRAWBACKS: BUT NEGATIVE EFFECTS HAD TO BE OVERCOME

I think the benefit is that he has more confidence. He's older and I think boys should be older. He's kind of small physically, so this puts him with kids his own size. It has its drawbacks in that he's older. This year he'll be 9 and going into the second grade. On our block he's playing with 9-year-olds who are in fourth grade or going into third. I only regretted it one time when a woman at the shopping center asked me about his grade and I told her I had retained him, and her kids were standing there. At that point I regretted it only for his ego, not for his mind.

He was doing real well in reading and math. I attribute that to the two years he had in kindergarten because he was able to sit still and listen better and know what school's all about. But (I worry about) the fact that they placed him with the first grade teacher that is considered to have a little more patience and (they said) she takes things at a slower pace. I thought, 'Is he going to be behind throughout?' But, he's got friends who have other first grade teachers and they seemed to have all learned the same things, but maybe at a slower pace.

To him it made all the difference in the world. He's blossomed. He participated; he wasn't withdrawn. (But we still cannot talk about it at home.)

I'd say its going to help her in the long run. She got the basics and the readiness; she got socially more mature and the motor development. A disadvantage I would say is

Continued

Table 4 (Continued)

that she's a real tall girl. She probably was one of the biggest in the first kindergarten class so she's really big in all of these classes. I think she probably feels older and stuff than the other kids.

I knew he was struggling and he knew that he wasn't doing what the other kids were doing so I thought this was right. He seemed to be pleased about it. He's OK now. He does refer back once in a while. He says, 'If I would have made it through kindergarten, I would be in second grade instead of first.' But he doesn't harp on it ... He wasn't ready to do it. But I think going through a second time he was able to retain what he learned. So, I felt it was the right thing to do, to go through the second time. If they are to be held back at any grade, I think kindergarten is it.

Well, the only drawback was that he wasn't going to be going with the rest of his class into the next grade. But it was only because I told him that he was so special that his teacher wanted to keep him. But anyway, the positive thing about it, the advantage, was that he just did so much better and it just made him feel good about himself — because he was right up there with the rest of them then ... If I had to do it all over again, I think I probably would have had him tested (earlier) or put him in preschool or something.

I think the biggest drawback is the attitude of other children and adults. Not so much from the teachers, but parents of other children remarking on how he looks so much older, 'he should be here', 'he should be there', and other children picking up on the fact that he was going to remain in kindergarten, giving him a hard time about that. It was difficult for him to handle it until the teacher was real supportive and explained what was happening and that there were other children that were going to an advanced kindergarten because they weren't quite ready for first grade yet ... I think the positive aspects are just him feeling better about himself, and having more confidence, and the fact that we did it early enough in his education that it's not going to damage him socially and emotionally farther down the road.

CATEGORY 4: IT WAS THE RIGHT DECISION BUT NEGATIVE IMPACT WAS KEENLY FELT

I think it was more of a social thing. It was really hard to explain to her that her friends would be going on and she wouldn't be. That was a real hard part of it. I think it helped her more than it hindered her. I just wished it had been done in a different way. There's got to be some kind of program that they can have so they don't have to do that. A lot of kids would react negatively, like, 'there go my friends into first grade and I have to go back there'. I wouldn't want to go through it again. I never want to go through it again.

The benefits are that she has —, again it almost sounds negative, but the fact that she wouldn't be so terribly behind her peer group. I personally think it's better that we've held her back and she has the possibility of being a little closer to the top than being a grade ahead and being at the very bottom. Some of the negative aspects of it are her own problems dealing with it and saying that she's been held back. It's very strange because we had attempted to deal with this in a very positive manner, never really saying that she's been held back. We pretty much said it was my decision, a conscious decision on my part that she take kindergarten over again, so she'd have some more chances. But, she's still picked up on the fact that she's been held back.

I think putting Frankie in pre-first grade was one of the best things that ever happened to him, but I don't feel he would have had to, I think he would have been ready for first grade had he had a more qualified teacher in kindergarten. He had a lousy year. After having a lousy year, there was no way he could be ready for first grade.

The benefits far outweigh the drawbacks. The only drawback we had was in the first

Table 4 (Continued)

month or two of the second year. The kids he went to kindergarten with who went on to first grade made life miserable. Unfortunately, there are about five of them in the neighborhood. We tried to help him cope with it and by about December, it was just assumed in the neighborhood that he was a kindergartener and they were first grade. We haven't had any trouble since then.

I'll tell you the drawbacks first. I think it decreased her attention and I was upset at the kindergarten teachers. They said to hold her back and she knew everything so she went to kindergarten the second time and she got everything checked the first quarter and the child learned zero for three quarters. She didn't learn anything and she figured she didn't have to pay attention. I think that carried into first grade because that was one of the bad things on her report card ... But, she caught up. I could see a difference in her the second time. (It helped) that she was allowed to mature another year. But maybe I was a little upset because they didn't teach her anything (the second year) ... Another drawback was what the other kids would say to her, especially a couple of the older ones who knew that she had been retained. But I don't think it fazed her. I don't think she considered it a failure. If she was older it may have been a blow.

CATEGORY 5: IT WASN'T NECESSARY AND WE WORRY ABOUT NEGATIVE EFFECTS

He's doing OK academically but behaviorally and socially we still have some concerns ... The benefits are that he's one of the older ones in his class instead of one of the younger ones. He likes to feel that he's a leader and have people follow what he tells them; so if that comes with age, then he feels better about that now. One of the drawbacks was having him repeat the same program even with another teacher. Throughout the year, he'd come home with the same thing or he'd say, 'Well, we did this again.' That was not a major problem, but it was a minor problem. Another drawback is that he doesn't, I've tried to explain (sigh), he doesn't understand why he went to kindergarten twice, and he wondered if he wouldn't go to first grade twice. He looks on himself as having failed that first time even though he didn't fail, and it was us that held him back. Then another drawback is, if this is indeed just behaviorally and socially a part of him, you know, that he has trouble dealing with other children, then I don't think he gained anything by holding him back.

I don't think two years does them good or harm really. I really don't know what two years of kindergarten is going to accomplish for any of them. There hasn't really been a benefit because he didn't feel top of the class at all; and the drawback is, of course, my children are all bigger than life. They're tall. Every once in a while he'll come to me, 'I'm the biggest kid in my class.' On the other hand, he'll say, 'I'm the toughest too, so it's O.K.' It hasn't been a real detriment, but I think it could be.

The teachers told us (that first year), 'well, we're not trained in working with younger kids. What they were doing, I guess when Greg was going to kindergarten, was weeding out the younger 5-year-olds and just taking the older ones that, you know, would sit down and listen to instruction and be able to do what they instructed them to do ... I think that if the teacher had spent more time with him, he would have done really well in kindergarten. I don't think being out of his seat was a valid enough reason to hold him back. But, I think he more or less accepts it, and keeps on going. As far as advantages go, he's older and probably will pick up a lot from the teacher a lot easier than some of the other children in his class.

They said he wasn't prepared. I was very shocked because he did enter kindergarten at the age of 6. My husband was against it because he was already a year older. We're afraid that we may not be able to keep him in school when he's older, which is

Table 4 (Continued)

Table 4 (Continued)

important also. The way they explained it to me, I could understand their point, and I just thought maybe it would be best for him ... I don't think that it has hurt him in any way. I think that sometime maybe later that someone will say, 'Oh, you're such and such an age and you're supposed to be in this grade.' If he has brought it up to me, oh maybe one time, we've sat and talked about it and I've explained it to him. Several of his friends have had to repeat and go to pre-first. I think he's accepted it at that level. He seems fairly well adjusted. I just hope that in years to come that everything will work out. It's a very, very important thing. I guess, I hope everything will be ok.

CATEGORY 6: VERY NEGATIVE

To me, his kindergarten teacher ruined him for a whole year and then the (second year) teacher helped him (recover). Henry lost all his self-esteem, his self confidence. He would come home saying, 'I'm stupid.' 'I don't know anything, I can't learn anything.' And before that time he was a very confident, happy little boy. He knew he was smart, he knew he was someone special. And then when he had this kindergarten teacher, that was just blown away. In fact, his teacher bent over and put her face in his face and said you are definitely going to be in ____(class) next year. I am not letting you go on to first grade. His second year teacher gave his confidence back to him; but he wouldn't have had to be there if he'd had the proper kindergarten teacher.

My only regret is that I didn't take him to another school when I put him back in, because of the teachers ... If you have a child who does not fit exactly within the mold of the setup that they've got going, they have no time for him. They don't want to take time for him. Now with Issac I don't know that he will ever like school. He is a typical little boy that would rather play than do anything else. His first grade teacher has given him motivation to do something and to like school. Even with all the trouble we had in kindergarten he never hated it. He has the type of personality that he just kind of developed the attitude, 'I'm damned if I do and I'm damned if I don't', and he went from there.

---

schoolmates. Obviously, this group of parents had a greater foreboding initially about the negative stigma of repeating and took action to protect their children from it. Other parents had removed their children from the high-retaining schools to avoid retention. This phenomenon was detected when files for children recommended for retention turned up in the low-retaining schools and is consistent with Turley's (1979) finding that many parents withdrew their children to private schools rather than have them repeat kindergarten. A final group of parents whose children were not in the retained group were those who had refused the extra-year placement but remained in the same school.

Based on the above omissions from the population of children recommended for retention, the parent sample was clearly a select group who tended to favor retention from the outset. To convey how much more negative the results might have been if parents opposed to retention had had their children retained, consider the following interview example typical of parents who refused kindergarten retention.

We were somewhat disappointed with (his progress in kindergarten). The teachers had segregated him pretty much from the rest of the kids in the class because of his age (entry age 5.3). They put him in this category that he was underdeveloped and that no matter what they would do he would continue that way. They structured his class around that fact. This was due to a prejudice in my opinion.

Results in table 4 should be interpreted with the understanding that the respondent group were on average somewhat favorably disposed toward the potential benefits of retention.

Concerning parents' views two years later, the interview data suggest that the majority of parents who had agreed to retention still believed in positive gains from retention. Most of the parent conclusions in table 4 appear to rest on the assumption that the extra year moved their child ahead of where they would have been otherwise. 'If she had pushed on, she wouldn't have made it.' 'Without the extra year, she would have been withdrawn or a clown.' 'It gave him a chance to strive ahead.' 'I attribute his success in reading and math to the two years in kindergarten.' Even if their child was still struggling, they believed the situation would have been even worse if they had pushed on. When the idea of retaining their child had first been discussed, parents were told that the extra year would give their child greater confidence and better preparation for first grade. And, they had been warned that immature children 'never catch up', if they are pushed on too soon.

The results of the controlled comparison presented earlier indicate that these retained children were not any further ahead. Some were at the top of their class and some were at the bottom, in equal numbers with the at-risk control children. We believe it would have been unethical to present these data to parents of retained children and then ask them how it affected their feelings about the benefits of retention. Lacking the insights provided by a control group, however, parents are likely to believe what the school said would occur, or what they themselves expected would be the benefits of retention. For example, if their son is in the top reading group in first grade, they are likely to believe this happened *because* he repeated kindergarten. According to cognitive dissonance theory (Festinger, 1957), it would be very difficult for parents to maintain a negative conclusion about retention even if they had been skeptical initially. Once having acted on the belief that retention is beneficial, by agreeing to the decision, they are under pressure psychologically to reduce dissonance by bringing their beliefs in line with their action.

Had it been ethical to inform parents about the lack of program benefits, it is reasonable to suppose that information of this kind might shift the balance of positive over negative effects in the minds of some parents. Consider especially parents in the middle of the distribution (categories 3 and 4) who expressed ambivalence. They reported mild to serious negative side-effects for their child but cast a positive vote for retention. Theirs are the opinions most likely to be changed by access to knowledge about program effects.

The largely positive program endorsement by parents of retained children is consistent with the results of other parent surveys on grade retention (Ames, 1980; Chase, 1968). In her survey of parents whose children had participated in junior first grade, Kilby (1982) obtained the very highest agreements for general program items; 90 per cent agreed, 'I'm glad my child was in junior first grade'. Greater dissonance occurred on specific items such as 'unkind remarks from others' (24 per cent) and 'Being in junior first grade made my child feel "different" from other children in school' (14 per cent). Even so, the majority of parents gave positive ratings to the extra year. In Kilby's study as well, parents were probably not aware of the lack of significant achievement gains found by the author.

Summary and Conclusions

This study was designed to assess the efficacy of kindergarten retention. It was intended to add to the existing body of research studies by instituting more rigorous controls, by testing the generality of findings for both immature and slow learner retainees, and by measuring affective as well as academic outcomes. Results are summarized as follows:

1 Kindergarten Retention Does Not Improve Achievement

Gredler's (1984) review concluded that at-risk children, promoted to first grade, achieved as well or better than children who spent an extra year in transition rooms. In chapter 4, fifteen additional studies were located and analyzed as to degree of control; they confirmed Gredler's conclusion of no benefit. Long-term follow-up studies, especially, found no difference in achievement between transition-eligible and transition participants even though transition children had sometimes shown an initial advantage.

In our study, children who had repeated kindergarten were compared at the end of first grade to matched control children who had been equally young and unready when they first began school. The retained children were, of course, one year older when measured at the end of first grade. On teacher ratings of reading and math achievement there were no differences between the groups. On CTBS math the groups were the same; on CTBS reading, the retained group was one month ahead. The one month advantage in reading is equivalent to a 7 percentile point difference, which is the same as the average difference between the youngest and oldest first graders in research on the within-grade age effect. When parents were asked to rate the relative academic standing of retained and non-retained children in their respective schools, there were no differences. Thus, the findings from this study are consistent with previous research showing no boost or academic advantage from the extra year to mature.

2 *Extra-year Kindergarten Programs Are Intended to Serve Different Populations but the Finding of No Benefit Is True for Both Immature and Slow Learner Populations*

Extra-year programs differ sharply from one locale to the next in the type of child expected to benefit. Some programs are intended for slow learners and others for academically able but immature children. Those studies, where extra-year placements had been made on the basis of developmental immaturity, also showed no differences in comparison to controls. In this study, it was possible to analyze the characteristics of children selected by teachers for a second year of kindergarten. At one extreme children tended to be recommended for retention if they were young and male, regardless of readiness scores; at another school, academic readiness appeared to be the basis of extra-year decisions. The study findings of essentially no differences between retained children and their comparable controls were consistent across schools, regardless of the type of child selected for retention. The research review in chapter 4 prompted the same conclusion. Kindergarten retention was ineffective regardless of whether children had been placed for developmental immaturity or deficient academic skills.

3 Retention in Kindergarten Produces either No Difference or Harm on Social-emotional Outcomes. Parents Rate Extra-year Programs Positively but Describe Negative Side Effects from Retention

Most controlled studies have not included affective outcomes. Bell (1972) reported a negative effect on the self-concept of readiness room children but Kilby (1982) showed no difference in attitude toward school between junior first graders and controls. Mossburg (1987) found that extra-year children were significantly behind 'non-readiness' children on ratings of social and emotional behaviors at the end of elementary school.

In the comparative study reported here, the extra year had produced no benefit for retained children over controls on teacher ratings of social maturity, learner self-concept, or attention at the end of first grade. Thus there was no evidence to substantiate the claim that retained children will become leaders, have greater self-confidence, and longer attention spans than if they went unready to first grade. In the interview data, several parents of retained children had noted that characteristics such as lack of attention and poor social skills had not been corrected by the extra year to grow, causing us to speculate that when teachers identify children as immature they may be attending to relatively enduring personality characteristics rather than developmental readiness.

Parents of children who repeated kindergarten reported that their children had slightly poorer attitudes toward school then either matched controls or the group of at-risk children whose parents had refused to have them repeat. Interview data from parents of retained children reflected both positive ratings of the program and negative side-effects which had to be overcome. The majority of parents believed that their children were ahead of where they would have been without the extra year (a belief contradicted by the results of the controlled experiment); the most serious negative effects were teasing by other children and the child's own sense of failure. Although only 20 per cent of parents described pervasively negative effects, the large majority told of emotional disruption for their child associated with not making normal progress.

The intention that extra-year programs will give at-risk children a boost, in academic achievement or in self-concept, has not been borne out by research. Kindergarten retention is not fundamentally different in its effects from retention in later grades. Negative associations with 'staying back', communicated by other children and adults, are the same as in higher grades.

Note

1 Substantial portions of this chapter are reproduced with permission from Shepard, L.A. and Smith, M.L. (1987) 'Effects of kindergarten retention at the end of first grade', *Psychology in the Schools*, 24, pp. 346–57. Readers familiar with previous work are referred to new data and analysis based on parent interviews, pp. 94–104.

References

AMES, L.B. (1980) 'Retention: A step forward', *Early Years*, 11, pp. 10–11.
BELL, M. (1972) '*A study of the readiness room program in a small school district in suburban Detroit, Michigan*', unpublished doctoral dissertation, Wayne State University.
CHASE, J.A. (1968) 'A study of the impact of grade retention on primary school children', *Journal of Psychology*, 70, pp. 169–77.
FESTINGER, L. (1957) *A Theory of Cognitive Dissonance*, Stanford, CA, Stanford University Press.
GLASS, G., MCGAW, B. and SMITH, M.L. (1981) *Meta-analysis in Social Research*, Beverly Hills, CA, Sage.
GREDLER, G.R. (1984) 'Transition classes: A viable alternative for the at-risk child?', *Psychology in the Schools*, 21, pp. 463–70.
JACKSON, G.B. (1975) 'The research evidence on the effects of grade retention', *Review of Educational Research*, 45, pp. 613–35.
KILBY, G.A. (1982) '*An ex post facto evaluation of the junior first grade program in Sioux Falls, South Dakota*', unpublished doctoral dissertation, University of South Dakota.
MILES, M.B. and HUBERMAN, A.M. (1984) *Qualitative Data Analysis*, Beverly Hills, CA, Sage.
MOSSBURG, J.W. (1987) '*The effects of transition room placement on selected achievement variables and readiness for middle school*', unpublished doctoral dissertation, Ball State University.
SHEPARD, L.A. and SMITH, M.L. (1985) *Boulder Valley Kindergarten Study: Retention Practices and Retention Effects*, Boulder, CO, Boulder Valley Public Schools.
SHEPARD, L.A. and SMITH, M.L. (1986) 'Synthesis of research on school readiness and kindergarten retention', *Educational Leadership*, 44, pp. 78–86.
SHEPARD, L.A. and SMITH, M.L. (1987) 'Effects of kindergarten retention at the end of first grade', *Psychology in the Schools*, 24, pp. 346–57.
TURLEY, C.C. (1979) '*A study of elementary school children for whom a second year of kindergarten was recommended*', unpublished doctoral dissertation, University of San Francisco.

Chapter 6:
Attitudes of Students, Parents, and Educators toward Repeating a Grade[1]

Deborah A. Byrnes

Editors' Introduction

This chapter marks the divide in the book between research on the consequences of retention and research about practice. Byrnes provides both types of data and draws the contrast between beliefs about retention and its verified effects.

Parent, teacher and principal opinions about the advisability of retention were gathered using large-scale survey techniques. The large majority of each group, even parents of retained children, applaud retention to correct deficient academic skills. Making students repeat is an accepted and expected school practice. Parents and educators have slightly different opinions about using criteria such as immaturity for retention and about who should have the final say.

Byrnes also contributes the only study we know of in the literature where retained children are interviewed. The accounts of these children, about what it meant to be held back, are not just opinion data. They are measures of the effects of retention in a metric other than standardized test scores or self-concept ratings.

Finally, responses from able students as well as those who were held back give a consistent picture of what retention means in the school culture. All of the children were well on their way to seeing retention as a deserved punishment for poor work, in much the way that parents and teachers saw it as a necessary corrective.

To be held back or retained, to repeat a grade, or as one first grader clarified for me, 'Oh, you mean, flunking', is a phenomenon increasingly prevalent in American schools. Because this procedure has shown a resurgence in many school districts as an ostensible answer to low pupil achievement, it is important to understand the meaning of this experience for children and to look more closely at how parents, teachers and principals view the use of retention.

General policies on school retention tend to be mandated by school boards and are often established after the local community expresses dissatisfaction with the academic gains of its children (Thompson, 1979). The choice of many school districts to improve public school credibility by developing strong retention policies appears to be due to traditional beliefs in the value of retention, the ease of implementation, and the need to satisfy the public outcry for quick, noticeable action. Academic retention appears to be popular, at least in part, because it does not disrupt the organization of the district, local school, and classroom (Labaree, 1984).

Unfortunately, there is little in the research literature to support retention as a pedagogically sound strategy. The majority of past research strongly indicates broad retention policies accomplish little of what they are intended to achieve (Bossing and Brien, 1979; Holmes and Matthews, 1984; Jackson, 1975; Shepard and Smith, 1985). Specifically the research indicates that:

(i) Grade retention does not ensure significant gains in achievement for children who are academically below grade level (Holmes and Matthews, 1984; Jackson, 1975).
(ii) The threat of non-promotion is not a motivating force for students (Bossing and Brien, 1979).
(iii) Grade retention does not generally improve achievement or adjustment for developmentally immature students (May and Welch, 1985; Shepard and Smith, 1985).
(iv) Economically, grade retention is a poor use of the education dollar, because it increases the cost of education (the retained child spends an additional year in the public school system) without any benefits for the vast majority of retained children (Haddad, 1979).
(v) Characteristics such as low socioeconomic status (SES) and poor classroom conduct affect the likelihood that a child will be retained (Bossing and Brien, 1979).

The Study

The study consisted of two parts, a questionnaire on the views of grade repetition given to parents, teachers and principals; and personal interviews with non-promoted children and their teachers. Both parts of the study were conducted in a school district of 26,000 elementary students in a large southwestern US border city. This district is composed of two quite diverse communities separated for the most part by a freeway. On one side of the freeway the community is middle to low SES with the majority of families speaking both Spanish and English, while on the other side the families are middle to upper SES with fewer bilingual families. The school district in which the study took place had recently implemented a strict non-promotion policy based on mastery of grade level objectives that resulted in an overall (K-12) annual retention rate of 9.5 per cent.[2] The highest rate at the elementary school level was in grade one (11.5 per cent), followed by grades two (6.6 per cent), three (4.6 per cent), four (4.4 per cent), five (2.8 per cent), and six (1.6 per cent). (Kindergartners were not retained in this district.) The rates at the junior high level zoomed to 19, 20, and 21 per cent respectively, creating the overall average.

Survey on Views of Grade Retention

The opinions of parents, teachers and principals toward retention were surveyed better to understand their viewpoints and to provide a backdrop and contrast for the children's views of the experience. In addition, the questionnaire made it possible to identify differences or similarities in the viewpoints of parents, teachers and principals toward grade retention. An overview of the survey findings will be presented here. For a more detailed report see Byrnes and Yamamoto (1986).

The questionnaire was sent to 2000 parents of students in grades 1–6, 200 teachers in seven elementary schools and forty-five principals and assistant principals in thirty elementary schools. Approximately half of the survey sample was drawn from each of the income areas. The numbers of usable returns were: parents — 1063; teachers — 145; and principals — thirty-five. There was a parent, teacher and administrator version of the questionnaire. The parent version was written in Spanish and English.

Response rates were reasonably good for educators, 72 per cent and 78 per cent respectively. Parent response rate was only 53 per cent; however, demographic characteristics of parents were known thus permitting analysis by sub-group. Answers from parents of retained children were analyzed both separately and as part of the total group;

the 27 per cent of parents in this category is roughly proportional to their share in the population (see note 2). Lower and middle class parents tended to respond at equal rates. However, there may have been other untested biases in who responded related to opinions about retention; thus, analyses should be taken to represent views from the population of respondents.

Survey Findings

The majority of responding parents, teachers and principals in this district supported grade retention for children who did not meet requirements of the grade. Seventy-four per cent of the principals, 65 per cent of the teachers, and 59 per cent of the parents in this study felt children should 'usually' or 'always' be retained if they did not meet grade level requirements. 'Occasionally' was selected by 17 per cent of the principals, 25 per cent of the teachers and 24 per cent of the parents. 'Rarely' or 'never' were marked by 9 per cent of the principals, 11 per cent of the teachers, and 17 per cent of the parents. Differences in the views of parents, teachers and principals were significant.

Parents, teachers and principals varied greatly on what should be considered an appropriate reason for academic retention. Not surprisingly, 'lack of basic skills' was the most widely supported response in all groups (principals — 94 per cent; teachers — 85 per cent; and parents — 63 per cent). A fairly large percentage of teachers and principals, significantly more than parents, supported 'emotional immaturity' (principals — 54 per cent; teachers — 53 per cent; parents — 19 per cent), 'academic failure for reasons other than lack of basic skills' (principals — 57 per cent; teachers — 37 per cent; parents — 30 per cent), and 'excessive absences' (principals — 69 per cent; teachers — 39 per cent; parents — 14 per cent) as reasons for grade retention. 'Parental request' for retention was the least supported reason in all of the groups (principals — 20 per cent; teachers — 16 per cent; and parents — 15 per cent).

There were significant differences found in parents', teachers' and principals' responses to the question about who should have the final say on whether a child is retained. The majority of principals (54 per cent) felt it should be left to them. In contrast, the majority of the teachers (66 per cent) felt the final decision should be made by teachers. Parents (48 per cent), especially those from lower income communities, were also most likely to feel that teachers should make the final decision to retain. A fairly large percentage of parents (20 per cent), in contrast to principals (3 per cent) and teachers (3 per cent), felt the parent should have the final say. Parents who felt they should have the final say tended to be from higher income communities.

Of the 1063 parents who completed the survey, 285 (27 per cent) had a child of theirs retained at some time. When responses of parents with and without a retained child were compared, several interesting differences were evident. Parents with a retained child were more likely to be from lower income neighborhoods, to speak Spanish, have more school-aged children, report less school involvement, and mark the school's performance lower than those without a retained child. However, there were no significant differences in their support for the use of grade retention, what constitutes appropriate reasons for retention or who should have the final say in the retention decision.

Teachers and principals were asked to check three characteristics from the following list that they observed most often in children who have been selected for retention: (a) low self-esteem; (b) learning disabled; (c) low motivation; (d) low intelligence; (e) developmentally immature; (f) emotionally unstable; (g) disciplinary problem; (h) shy and non-assertive; or (i) lack of English proficiency. The three most frequently marked characteristics (in order) were developmentally immature, low self-esteem and low motivation. These were followed by lack of English proficiency, low intelligence, discipline problem, learning disabled, shy and non-assertive, and emotionally unstable. Only one characteristic, low self-esteem, showed a significant rank difference between rating groups. Sixty per cent of the principals vs. 34 per cent of the teachers marked this response.

Teachers and principals were asked to check any of the following they saw as preferable to retention as a way of handling inadequate academic progress: (a) development of transitional maturity classes; (b) remedial instruction opportunities increased; (c) smaller classes with more individual instruction; (d) establishment of school readiness of a child prior to entrance to kindergarten versus entrance by age alone; and (e) use of multi-grade grouping or a non-graded school structure. The two most frequently checked responses were smaller classes with more individual instruction (teachers – 70 per cent; principals — 77 per cent) and increased remedial instruction opportunities (teachers — 50 per cent, principals — 80 per cent). The remaining three alternatives were selected as positive strategies by less than 35 per cent of the teachers and principals.

Attitudes of Students, Parents and Educators toward Repeating a Grade

Discussion of Survey Findings

Research findings indicate that repeating a grade does not improve a student's subsequent performance. Yet the majority of parents, teachers and principals in this school district felt that students should be retained if they do not meet grade level expectations. It is apparent that the retention of children in grade is not a school district policy being put into effect by school administrators and board members against the wishes of educators and parents in the community. Interestingly, parents who have had children retained are no different in their views toward retention than parents who have not.

The responses of parents, teachers and principals to what are appropriate reasons for retention indicate that children are not being retained only because they need to gain skills in reading, writing and arithmetic. Academic ability is only part of school failure. Many children, as indicated in Humphrey's review (1965), are retained on the basis of attitude, work habits, attendance, conduct and maturity. Interestingly, parents in this survey were less supportive of reasons that were not directly related to academic skills. For example, the vast majority of parents believed that reasons such as excessive absences and emotional immaturity should not, in and of themselves, be used as a basis for a child's promotion or non-promotion.

Each group of educators thinks it knows best what is in the best interest of the retained child. That the majority of principals responded that they should have the final say on whether a child is retained probably reflects the fact that principals are inevitably responsible for what goes on within their schools. Teachers, no doubt, feel they should make the final decision because they know best the child's academic strengths and weaknesses. Because many parents also felt that teachers should make the final decision, it appears that parents accede to the professional judgments of their children's teachers. This pattern varies somewhat with the socioeconomic status of the community. Higher income parents tend to want more power in decisions regarding whether their children repeat a grade.

There was surprising consistency in the way teachers and principals characterized retained students. The picture of the typical retained child emerges as an immature child, who is not motivated to work and has fairly low self-esteem. There is a good chance that in this district the child will also lack English proficiency.

Principals and teachers supported several alternatives to retention.

However, those options chosen most frequently, smaller classes with more individualized instruction, and increased remedial instruction opportunities, are also alternatives which are the least threatening to the current structure of the school. Ideas such as flexible entry age, transitional maturity classes, and multi- or non-graded school structure, which involve a greater change in the structure of the school, were not supported by the majority of the teachers and principals.

Interviews with Non-promoted Students and Their Teachers

For the second part of the study, the views of seventy-one retained children in grades 1, 3 and 6 were gained through structured personal interviews by the author or, in the seven cases where Spanish was the dominant language, by her bilingual assistant. The study looked particularly at the students in the first grade (fifty-two retained children: thirteen girls, thirty-nine boys) because younger children are most likely to be retained and particularly because parents and teachers often think retention is less socially stigmatizing for younger children. A small group of third (nine retained children: six girls, three boys) and sixth (ten retained children: four girls, six boys) graders were also interviewed to examine the varied impressions among non-promoted middle and upper elementary students. Approximately half of the children were from upper-middle income schools and half from the lower-middle income schools.

These children were all currently repeating a grade in one of twenty-five classrooms within four schools. The interviewer was introduced to all the students in these classes as a person interested in finding out what children think about school. The retained children, an equal number of 'good' students, as well as some students slated for possible retention the following year, were individually called out of the room to talk in private. It was hoped that by talking with these other children, as well as the non-promoted ones, the students would not infer the intention of the study. Also, it was hoped that the procedure would in no way call specific attention to the target children. For the same purpose, all the questions asked of the children pertaining to retention were nested within a longer discussion of school in general. Retention information from school records was also collected and brief personal interviews were held with the twenty-five teachers of the seventy-one non-promoted children.

Attitudes of Students, Parents and Educators toward Repeating a Grade

Views of Children

All students were introduced to the topic of retention in the following way: 'Some students who need more time to learn spend another year in the same grade. Have you or any of the students in your class ever had that happen?' (Interestingly, despite the efforts of the researcher and her assistant to stay away from any negative labeling of the retention experience, it was at this point that many of the children automatically referred to the experience as 'flunking'.) Of the seventy-one children who were repeating a grade, 73 per cent named themselves. Interestingly, only 57 per cent of the retained girls included themselves, whereas 81 per cent of the boys named themselves. First grade girls in particular were the most likely children not to admit they had been retained, even after the question was clarified or repeated.

Most of the children who did not name themselves did, however, accurately name other children in their classrooms who had been retained. It became obvious that their denial of being retained was not because they did not understand the concept of retention. For example, Nancy[3] (first grade) told the interviewer that she had never spent two years in the same grade; she then proceeded to name accurately two children who had. She also stated that 'nobody' in her family had been retained. In actuality, according to school records, all four of her siblings had been retained. Denise (third grade) accurately named the other child who had been retained in her room but throughout the interview never admitted that she had experienced retention. She went so far as to say that, 'Last year I thought I was going to flunk' in response to the question 'Do you ever worry about being retained?' But she never admitted to the interviewer that it had actually happened. Debra (first grade) did not name herself as a child who had been retained but did, with great pride, name herself as a child who 'did really good work in school'. Her current teacher ranked Debra academically in the top 25 per cent of the class. It was obvious that Debra took pride in her high academic standing and was not willing to admit that she had ever performed otherwise.

One of the most interesting cases was a first grade girl, Renae, who correctly named several other individuals but not herself when asked about retention. She then asked that I interview her best friend next. I obliged. When her friend was asked the same question, she named several students and added, 'But not Renae'. I wrote down 'not Renae' next to the other names in my notes. Seeing me writing something down, she said sternly, 'I said not Renae'. I assured her that was what I had written. It became evident from responses such as the above that many of these children did not feel comfortable admitting that they had been retained. At least one child called on a friend to help her keep the secret. The fact that fewer girls than boys were willing to name themselves may indicate that girls' identities are more tied up with school success or that girls are more aware of the social stigma of grade retention.

Students, depending on their earlier responses to the question of whether they had been retained or not, were asked how they 'felt' or 'would feel' about being retained. Of the sixty-four responses, the vast majority (84 per cent) centered on 'sad', 'bad', and 'upset'. This feeling was expressed in many different ways. Eduardo (first grade), who did not name himself as retained, replied that if he was retained, he would feel 'sad, because you did wrong things. They [children who are retained] are dumb and get in trouble.' Anna (first grade) confided that she felt 'sad, it's not fun not to pass'. Jorge (first grade) responded that he felt 'sad, I wanted to pass. Kids sing and tease if you don't pass.' Diego (first grade) responded, 'bad! I don't like being in first'. Janis (third grade) replied, 'real sad. Kids start calling me names', and Connie, another third grader, responded, similarly, 'sad. People laugh at me'. Ellen (sixth grade) responded, 'sad. Friends were going on and I was staying' and Herberto, a sixth grader who did not admit to being retained replied, succinctly, 'terribly bad'.

Closely related to the predominant responses of 'bad', or 'sad', were the few children (3 per cent) who used the word 'embarrassed' to describe how they felt about being retained. Victor (first grade) whose response was more elaborate than most of the other first grade children said, 'I'm afraid to tell someone I flunked. On my birthday I'll be embarrassed. I don't want it to come because then the teacher will ask how old I am'. Jennifer (first grade) replied that 'My mother told me it's okay that you stay [in the same grade] but I feel embarrassed'.

Six per cent of the students reported positive feelings such as 'happy' when asked about retention. Juan (first grade) said, 'Kinda happy, because the teacher would always get all mad [last year]. Now I do better work.' However, later in the interview, when Juan was asked if he thought it was a good idea for him to stay in the same grade, he replied, 'No, I should have gone to second. Kids tease and say I flunked'. Similarly, Frankie (first grade) responded that he was 'happy, cause I didn't want to go to second'. In response to whether he should have been retained he said, 'No! We be good. I should gone on to second so I learn more'. In contrast, Sarah (first grade) said she was 'happy' to stay in first because 'I can learn more'. In response to whether she should have been retained she replied, 'yes'. It is evident that several of the children who responded positively had mixed feelings about the experience. Notably, none of the nineteen (27 per cent) children who denied being retained responded positively about how it would feel. This finding lends weight to the interpretation that a child's declining to say that he or she was retained reflects some shame or negative association with that fact.

The responses of the remaining 7 per cent of the students were idiosyncratic and did not fit into any of the above categories. When Steven (sixth grade) was asked how he felt about being retained he replied that he felt 'shy and nervous — out of place' but also agreed that he should have been retained because he 'didn't know a lot'. Vince (first grade) said he felt 'mad at myself. I think I stayed back because I hurried and got bad grades.' He also felt he shouldn't have been held back because when you 'grow older you'll be dumb'. Jorge (third grade) felt it was 'good' he was retained because 'otherwise I'd just flunk fourth grade instead'.

When the non-promoted students were asked how their parents 'felt' or 'would feel' about them repeating a grade, 46 per cent of the seventy-one respondents replied 'mad', 28 per cent 'sad', while 8 per cent seemed to feel their parents 'didn't care or had or would not react at all'. The other 18 per cent of the responses could not be categorized. A follow up question, 'Were you punished at all?' was asked of those children who admitted to being retained. Forty-seven percent of them replied 'yes'. Examples of responses to these questions follow:

Angela (first grade): They were mad and real sad. They spanked me and [I got] grounded. I didn't get to go to Disneyland.

Tommy [first grade]: 'Mad'! Dad paddled me and kicked me out of the house.

Miguel (first grade): They were sad. They said, 'Be good at school'.

Will [first grade]: They didn't care. They were mad at school because my teacher didn't teach me barely anything.

Veronica [third grade]: 'Mad! They said I didn't try hard. No TV for a month. I couldn't go anywhere. I got grounded.

Carol [third grade]: They were okay. They hope I pass this year.

Robert [sixth grade]: They were mad. They said that I better pass cause I need a good education.

These comments may not accurately reflect what their parents' actual responses were but they do reflect how children interpreted and remembered their parents' feelings about their retention. Interestingly, children who were good students (in the top 25 per cent of their class) and children who were slated for possible retention the following year responded similarly when the hypothetical question, 'How would your parents feel?' was presented to them. One high achieving first grade girl replied, 'Whew! They'd be mad'. A first grade child who was being considered for retention responded, 'I'd get a whippin'.

In order to understand better children's perceptions of the retention experience, children who admitted to being retained (fifty-two of the respondents) were asked how they had found out they were going to be retained. This question was difficult for some of the first graders to understand. In those cases, children were asked if they found out from their parents, teacher, their report card, or some other way. Forty-two per cent of the children answered 'by their report cards'. The next most common response was 'parents' (31 per cent), followed by 'my teacher' (20 per cent). The remaining 7 per cent made comments such as 'my sister', 'the principal', and most distressingly, 'the list of names on the door at the beginning of this school year'. It was so surprising that teachers were not mentioned in the vast majority of cases that we often asked children outright, 'Did the teacher talk to you about it?' Their yes-no responses to this form of question merely confirmed the original assertions.

The fact that so many children replied that they found out they were going to be retained from their report cards is surprising. However, several of the high achieving children who were interviewed mentioned they were always a little scared to look at the promotion box on their final report card just in case they didn't pass. Regardless of how well or poorly one might be doing in school, it appears that promotion or non-promotion may only be realized for sure when one gets his or her final report card. Decisions such as promotion or non-promotion appear to be quite arbitrary to many children.

When the children who acknowledged repeating were asked why they thought they had been retained, their responses were diverse. Responses related to 'not getting good grades' were the most common (25 per cent). Children made such comments as 'I got a lot of U's'; 'I got bad grades in reading and math. I couldn't do them'; and 'Because of my report card'. Statements regarding behavior problems (14 per cent) were the next most frequently given responses. Diego, Joshua, Victor and Johnny (all first grade boys) answered, respectively, 'I don't know. I flunked. I kept playing'. 'I always played and talked to my friend.' 'I didn't act good.' 'Because a kid always talked to me and he didn't get in trouble and I did.' Work habits followed (13 per cent), usually being mentioned by the older children in terms of lack of studying or listening. Eleven per cent of the remarks focused on missing school. Robert (sixth grade) said, 'I was absent too much. I was sick with colds and ear aches'. Juan and Jennifer (first graders) both reported that they were retained because they had 'chicken pox', and missed too much school. A few children responded with 'not knowing English' (9 per cent), and 'I don't know why' (9 per cent). The remaining responses (19 per cent), which could not be typified, included such statements as:

Frankie (first grade): I ran out of medicine [Ritalin] for the last two weeks and didn't do any work. I think that's why.'

Richard (sixth grade): 'The teacher didn't like me. I was in fights. She always said I didn't hand in work but I did.

David [third grade]: The first time I came to school I couldn't see real well. I have glasses now.

When the children's perceptions of why they were retained were compared with school records of why they were retained, the first grade children were accurate or partially accurate 50 per cent of the time. The third and sixth graders were accurate or partially accurate 66 per cent of the time. (Children who responded 'I don't know' were not included in this analysis of accuracy.) A partially accurate response from a child would be one such as 'I played around and got in trouble'. In actuality, the child was retained because he did poorly in reading which was attributed to immaturity (he played around, wouldn't attend to his work). 'Immaturity' was frequently used in the formal school reports as an euphemism for 'misbehavior', and 'not following directions or getting one's work done'. The fact that 50 per cent of the first grade children and 34 per cent of the third and sixth graders totally misidentified why they were retained may be partially due to the fact that teachers and parents actually gave them false information or did not give them information at all. This point will be discussed further in the teacher interview section of this chapter.

Curious as to whether teachers talk about non-promotion to their classes, we asked all the retained respondents if they had ever heard their teachers talk about keeping children in the same grade. Seventy per cent of the students reported 'yes'. When asked what kinds of things teachers say, children mentioned such statements as: 'If you don't want to do it, we won't force you. You will be here next year, too'; 'If you don't follow directions, you are going to flunk'; 'All of you kids who didn't hand in your papers, stand up. These will be the ones that are here next year'; 'Start working or ...'; 'Get busy or ...'; and, 'If you don't shape up ...'. The 'good' students who were interviewed responded similarly to this question giving credence to the picture understood by retained children.

When the retained students were asked if they felt keeping children in the same grade was a good idea, 42 per cent said 'yes'. However, when these same children were asked if they felt it was a good idea for them personally, many of them said 'no'. The most frequent reason given for a 'yes' response was something like 'they can learn more'. Some of the reasons given tended to take on moralistic qualities. For example, 'It will teach them a good lesson'; 'If they don't act right and talk too much they should flunk'; and 'They should flunk because they didn't try'. Such responses, with one exception, came from third or sixth graders. Representative comments of first grade children who said 'no' are: 'It ain't no fun. Kids want to be in second'; 'It makes you sad'; 'You get in trouble'; 'No, cause if I don't go on to the next grade, I will never learn'; 'You get the same stuff'; and 'They'll tell us and kids will laugh, boo and those things'. Interestingly, when the high academic children were asked this same question, 60 per cent of them responded 'yes'. Generally, they were more likely than retained students to feel children who didn't behave, work or learn should not be promoted.

The non-promoted children were all asked what they felt was (or would be) the worst thing about not passing, as well as what they thought had been (or would be) good about it. The most common negative response was 'being laughed at and teased' (22 per cent). 'Not being with friends' (16 per cent), 'being punished' (14 per cent), 'being sad' (10 per cent), 'getting bad grades' (8 per cent), 'being embarrassed' (4 per cent) and 'doing the same work' (4 per cent) were also mentioned. Twenty-two per cent of the responses were unique to the individual child. Comments included 'the teacher yelling at me', 'not knowing how to do the work', 'like to feel bigger', 'not catching up with my cousin', 'thinking you do good and then flunking', and 'my sister talking about it' were also mentioned.

Most of the retained children found it difficult to think of something good about not being promoted, and a few seemed incredulous that they were even being asked. Twenty-one per cent said there was 'nothing good about it'. Fifteen per cent of the children responded with 'I don't know'. Several children felt their new friends they had made were the best part (15 per cent), while others mentioned their teachers were nice (5 per cent) or they like doing their work better this year (5 per cent). Others, representing a total of 39 per cent, said: 'I learned a lot'; 'I'm doing better'; 'Different things to do this year'; 'It taught me a lesson'; 'The work is easy'; and 'I don't get in as much trouble'.

When the non-promoted children with older or younger school-age siblings were asked if they had any brothers or sisters who had repeated grades, 76 per cent replied 'yes'. Two of these children, one with five and the other with six siblings, said everyone in their family had failed at least one grade. One of these children added spontaneously 'my parents are used to us not doing good in school'. The attitudes of parents toward education and the home environment in general certainly cannot be ignored as factors related to non-promotion.

Character Sketches of Retained Children

The following brief sketches, all of first graders, have been prepared to illustrate more clearly the variety of experiences and perceptions that characterize these retained children. Data for these character sketches were integrated from several sources: child interviews, teacher interviews, school files, sociometric questionnaires and classroom observations. Through these short vignettes it is hoped that a view of young non-promoted children may be gained that goes beyond percentages and numbers.

Happy to be retained

Without hesitation, Stacey admitted to the interviewer that she had been retained. She commented that she was happy she had been retained in first grade because she 'needed to learn more math'. She felt that she had been retained because she 'did not do good math' and also because she was a 'ding dong'. She added that her mother agreed that she should

be retained and had talked to her about it long before Stacey saw it on her report card. Stacey asserted that children should be retained 'if they didn't do good on stuff'.

According to Stacey's current teacher, Stacey's mother, a teacher at a private school in the area, had requested that Stacey be retained. Despite Stacey's comments that she did not do well in math, her school records indicate she has always made satisfactory progress in math. In fact, the only area in which Stacey received an unsatisfactory grade was handwriting. From information in her school file, it was apparent that her mother and school officials actually retained Stacey because she acted immaturely and had poor work skills. Stacey's mother was reported to have said that if there was any question about Stacey's ability to do well in second grade, Stacey should be retained. Apparently, this is partly in reaction to the fact that Stacey's older sister was not retained and is now doing poorly in the sixth grade. Not surprisingly, Stacey is now one of the top students in her first grade class. (However, she still has poor handwriting skills.) Stacey was not seen as being immature or having behavior problems during her second year in first grade. On a class sociogram she appeared neither as an isolate nor a star.

It would be difficult to say that Stacey benefitted academically from the experience of retention. She was not particularly low academically to begin with. Her positive acceptance of the retention experience leads the author to believe that although Stacey may have advanced further academically had she been promoted, she did not appear to be experiencing any negative social or emotional effects from the retention. For Stacey, the experience of retention, although not challenging, at least did not appear to be stigmatizing.

A problem of language

Ivette hesitated to include herself among those children in her class who had been retained. It was only after she was specifically asked if it had ever happened to her that she included herself. Ivette reported that she felt 'very sad' that she had been retained. She stated that she did not know she was going to be retained until she received her report card. Ivette commented that her parents were 'mad and real sad when they found out'. She remembers being 'spanked and grounded' at the time. With head down and in a barely audible whisper, she told the interviewer that she did not know why she had been retained. Ivette felt

that keeping children in the same grade was not a good idea because it made them sad.

School records indicate that Ivette was retained because she did not know English. Her original first grade teacher described her as well behaved, a hard worker and a good student, one who did not do well in school only because she predominantly spoke Spanish. Records indicate that her parents (who speak only Spanish) agreed to the retention. Her current first grade teacher indicated that Ivette is now in the top 25 per cent of the class and is well adjusted socially and emotionally. When Ivette's current first grade teacher was asked if Ivette received any individual instruction in her classroom, the teacher replied 'no'. However, she did inform the interviewer that Ivette had been receiving ESL (English as a Second Language) instruction for two years. On a class sociogram Ivette was chosen two times as a friend. Only one of these choices was mutual.

Classroom observations indicated that in her second year of first grade, Ivette spent very little time actually intent on work in her classroom. Yet, she was ranked by her classroom teacher as one of the five best students in the class. Ivette appeared to have no understanding of why she was retained and the experience was reported to be a sad one for her.

Social concerns

George named himself right off when he was asked if he knew anyone who had been retained. He said he felt 'sad' about the retention 'because everybody laughs at you'. George told the interviewer that he first found out about being retained from his report card. He added that his sister and friend also told him he had 'flunked' when they checked the signs that tell students in what room they will be at the beginning of the school year.

George reported that his parents didn't say anything about his repeating a grade; they were just a little sad. He believed that he was retained because he missed a lot of school and didn't get his homework done. He felt the worst thing about being retained was 'kids say "flunker"'. When asked what had been good about it, he replied incredulously, 'If it happened to you, do you think there would be anything good?' When asked if children should ever be kept in the same grade, George said, 'I don't know', and then added, 'they've got to if they have real bad grades'. Despite the fact that George generally saw retention as a negative experience, he believed that it was justifiable for academic reasons that he was retained.

School records indicate that George was retained because he just wouldn't work. His initial first grade teacher commented that 'George got along well with other children but was very immature. He is just not interested in school'. This teacher also mentioned that George often complained of illness. He missed sixteen days of school his first year in first grade. However, no mention was made in the school records that these absences were even partially the cause of his retention. George's mother approved of his retention, but George's father was vehemently against it.

His current teacher sees him as being slightly above average in his school work but believes he knows a lot more than he lets on. When asked, his teacher admitted that she had done nothing to individualize George's academic program. She also described George as 'very quiet and frightened; he shies away from risks'. On a class sociogram he was selected two times as a friend. The children who selected George and the three children George selected had also been retained in first grade. There was one mutual choice.

George seemed to feel quite concerned about being retained in first grade. His comments about children laughing at him, being called 'flunker' and his friendship circle being made up entirely of other retained children, indicate that he felt socially stigmatized by the experience. His father's non-acceptance of George's retention may also have contributed to his negative feelings about this experience. It is unfortunate that there were no efforts made to help George cope with the social and emotional impact of retention or to individualize his academic program.

An angry child

Johnny openly admitted that he had been retained. He said the experience made him 'very sad', especially because 'Daddy said I was going to get a new bike but I didn't cause I didn't pass'. Johnny felt his parents were 'very mad' at him because he failed first grade. He believed he had been retained because he 'was talking a lot and standing up'. Also, he 'didn't color great'. Johnny was one of the few children who said that his teacher told him he would be retained. He felt that children shouldn't be retained because 'they get the same stuff and it makes you sad. You don't learn'. He adamantly stated that he shouldn't have been retained.

School records indicate that Johnny was retained because he was immature (i.e., had major behavior problems) and was academically very low. He began going to the resource room and speech therapy in his initial first grade experience. His parents, who speak very little English, accepted the school's plan to retain Johnny. According to his teacher, at the time the decision was being made to retain Johnny, his parents, who had been separated for several months, were going through a rather difficult divorce.

In his second year of first grade, Johnny's teacher commented that he was still in the resource room and that he was one of the lowest children in her class academically. She commented that she relied on the resource teacher to provide Johnny with the individualized help he needed. The classroom teacher believed that Johnny was better, socially and emotionally, than the year before but added that he would still have angry emotional outbursts that were difficult to handle. On the classroom sociogram, Johnny was chosen only once and this was by a child who received no friendship choices and was himself slated for retention.

Johnny's retention was one more stressful experience in an already unstable life. In three years he had moved three times, attended three different schools and his parents had divorced. Added to that, Johnny appeared to have no friends in his class. It was obvious that Johnny was going to need a great deal of help if he was to succeed in school. Repeating first grade appeared to be more like putting Johnny in a 'holding tank' than a specific effort to assist this child.

The Teachers' Perspective

The teachers of these retained children (fifteen first, six third and four sixth grade teachers) were all concerned educators who volunteered to participate in this study. The vast majority of them worried about the decisions they made to retain children or promote them. They were open and eager to gain new information on the topic. All of them agreed to meet with the author to discuss the non-promoted children in their classes. While many of the questions were only relevant to individual cases, a few questions shed additional light on children's experience of school retention.

Making sure parents were aware of their child's poor progress early in the year was considered essential by teachers so as to prevent the familiar lament, 'Why didn't you tell me that he (or she) was having problems?' The perceived need for warning parents well in advance often led to teachers labeling children as future retainees as early in the academic year as January. Discussing the matter with the children was another story. The question 'How do you let the children know they will be repeating a grade?' elicited varied and interesting responses. Sixty per cent of the teachers left it up to the parents, either directly or indirectly. Some specifically discussed how the parents should handle it, while others assumed the parent would naturally discuss it with the child in a constructive way. With the sixth grade children it was often assumed, due to a frequently verbalized policy concerning grades for promotion to junior high, that they were well aware of their status. At one school, however, the principal tried to meet personally with all sixth grade students to be retained.

First grade teachers seemed to have a particularly difficult time discussing non-promotion with their students. Even those who did talk directly to the children gave euphemistic or even untrue explanations at times out of concern for the child's feelings. Children were told, 'You'll be the best in the class next year'; 'It's only because you missed a lot of school'; or, 'You're just a lot younger than the other children'. Explanations such as these appeared to be used most frequently in cases where the child was considered a 'good student' (i.e., did not misbehave and tried hard) but was a slow learner. Other teachers tried to help children come to the conclusion themselves. 'I tell them how hard second grade work is and ask them how they think they would do'. 'I ask the child if they would like to read real well'. 'I tell them to look around at the other kids so they'll understand why they need to stay in first'. Generally, teachers appeared uncomfortable informing the child of their retention. Some waited until the last week of school so as not to discourage the children from working and to keep from upsetting them in school. Only two of the twenty-five teachers interviewed mentioned discussing the non-promotion with both parents and child together.

According to the teachers, the children whom they did tell almost always accepted the news without comment. Only one teacher reported a child who cried and begged not to be retained. This child, according to the teacher, seemingly adjusted to the idea over the summer. In fact, in the interview with the researcher three months into the repeat year, the child stated that retention made him feel 'sad not to be good' and that children shouldn't be retained because 'it makes you feel bad'.

In contrast to the complacency with which most children accepted the decision, parents' reactions were quite often emotional, and teachers were sometimes openly blamed and criticized. Of the sixty children on whom information regarding parents' attitudes toward retention could be gained, 33 per cent of the children had at least one parent who originally objected to their child's non-promotion. As reported by teachers, those parents expressed such feelings as: retention was not a good solution to their child's problem, if teachers were better at their jobs their child wouldn't have a problem, and their child did not have a problem. It is important to note that the comments of teachers as well as school records regarding individual retention cases indicate that parents were not always in agreement with each other regarding their child's retention. Additionally, teachers frequently noted that most of the objecting parents eventually came to accept and cooperate with the school's decision. The majority of parents (66 per cent) were reported as agreeable, supportive and accepting regarding their child's retention. These percentages, although indicating a somewhat greater dissatisfaction with retention on the part of these parents, are generally supportive of the results of the parent survey reported earlier in this chapter.

The majority of teachers (60 per cent) felt they treated repeating children the same as any other students, both academically and socially. They made no mention of their non-promotion to the children or the class, and they were treated just like any other children starting first, third or sixth grade. Academically, their programs and lessons were the same as their classmates', which varied according to each teacher's style. Many teachers felt strongly that by concealing the child's retention, they were helping the child to escape the stigma of non-promotion. One teacher even had her returning third graders print so as not to stand out by their cursive.

Those teachers who reported special interaction of some sort (40 per cent) varied immensely in their approach. Some, especially first grade teachers, gave the children extra responsibilities, such as delivering messages or setting out supplies. Others made special efforts to encourage these children with praise and attention. Two teachers reported giving the children harder work, while two others automatically started these children in middle or top groups. One teacher automatically began the fairly involved process of having a full assessment done on each retained child so as to be assured the child was not in need of special services. Several of the retained children in this class, as well as in other classes, were identified during their repeating year as having visual, auditory or learning disabilities. By implication it appears that children had typically been retained without any special intervention, either adaptation of instruction or indepth assessment.

Throughout personal interviews with these twenty-five teachers their concern for each of the children they retained was evident. Many spontaneously expressed the difficulty they experienced in making the decision to retain. For example, one teacher stated that she often lost sleep over such decisions. However, all the teachers felt that although retention could be stressful for the child, it would be worse for the child if he or she was promoted. They felt that the next grade teacher would not be able to accommodate the child's level of skills or emotional development and the child would experience even more failure. Several teachers also mentioned their fear of being ridiculed by the colleagues of the following grade for creating more work for them by sending such ill-prepared students.

In two cases first grade teachers did mention that if specific children could have received remedial assistance outside of the classroom, they might not have retained these students. However, as one teacher explained, 'When there are open slots in the resource room they go to the older children who are experiencing problems. I feel I have no alternative but to retain the young ones. It takes so long for them to get additional help. They will be lost if they go on to second'.

Only two of the teachers mentioned in their spontaneous comments that retention was not helpful to some children. Both felt that some children, particularly the ones who were slow to learn, may begin to feel they are failures as a result of being retained. Additional insight into teachers' beliefs about the helpfulness of retention may be gleaned from their comments regarding the success of individual students' retention experiences. Of the sixty-two recorded responses to the question, 'How effective do you believe retaining (*child's name*) has been?' teachers believed that retention was effective or very effective in helping the child in 89 per cent of the cases. Comments made included: 'He has really turned around.' 'She never would have succeeded in second grade.' 'He's not doing well but imagine how poorly he'd be doing in second grade.' 'Karen has really matured this year. She has more self-confidence now.' In 8 per cent of the cases the teacher commented that the retention experience had been of questionable assistance. Examples of the teachers' comments are: 'In some ways Joe is more mature but his work hasn't improved much.' 'Tony is still doing very poorly in his work. He should be in special education.' 'Sue does better in her work but she has become a behavior problem.' The remaining 3 per cent of the retentions were considered to be unnecessary by the reporting teachers. In these cases the teachers commented that they did not believe they would have retained these particular students because they believed the students were already capable of succeeding in the next higher grade. Consistent with survey data reported earlier in this chapter, it appears that teachers, for the most part, believe grade retention is effective in assisting unsuccessful elementary school students.

Discussion of Interviews with Retained Children and Teachers

The interviews with these retained children and their teachers indicate that many of our concerns about school retention are well justified. Children do feel anxious about the reactions of their peers and others to their status as 'school failures'. Non-promotion is generally looked on as a punishment, a testimony to one's inability to succeed in school.

In a culture that places so much emphasis on what one (allegedly) has in, and does with, her or his brains, retention is indeed a particularly devastating indictment of a person's whole being (Edgerton, 1967). It should be remembered that children are, in fact, quite sensitive to teacher evaluation, conveyed through school marks, even as they remain uncertain of the exact basis for the appraisal (Boehm and White, 1967).

Teachers, although sensitive to the feelings of individual children repeating a grade within their class, often provide little more than a repeat of the previous year's curriculum. The vast majority of these teachers see the retention experience as effective in helping low achieving students. Unfortunately, when speaking about repeating to students, they tend to create a view of retention as punishment by frequently using it as a threat to those students they see as lacking in motivation to achieve.

To add to the stress of those who repeat grades, there are few, if any, attempts to help children deal with their fears and reservations about the experience. The responsibility of this task is frequently left to chance, with teachers often allocating the responsibility to parents who may be unprepared to help the child feel more comfortable with and understand his or her retention. 'A reservoir without water cannot take water to those who are thirsty. Neither can a starved person feed another out of full bounty' (Baruch, 1964, p. 24). To many parents, the world of schools is unfamiliar and intimidating and, even with the best of intentions, they are in a poor position to guide their children along. Parents who are poorly educated and who themselves had difficulty in school are over represented among the parents of non-promoted children. Indeed, the parents frequently add to the seriousness of the situation by punishing the child for her or his failure to be promoted.

Conclusion

A survey of principals', teachers' and parents' views of retention in grade revealed that non-promotion is a popular means of improving poor school achievement. Grade repetition is intuitively thought to help children who are considered unable to deal responsibly with tasks typically assigned to students in the next grade. Children who lack basic skills, have poor work habits or are immature are all likely candidates for retention in grade. These children, who are characterized as not being motivated to work, having poor self-esteem, and being immature, are given another year in the same grade in the hope that time and a repeat of the same curriculum will make them more capable students in the future. Unfortunately, children who are retained generally do no better than their matched counterparts who have been promoted (see chapter 2 in this volume). Retention is generally not an effective remedial strategy. Retained children perceive retention as a punishment and a stigma, not as a positive event designed to help them.

Notes

1 Portions of this chapter are based on previously published articles: Byrnes and Yamamoto (1985, 1986).
2 Annual retention rates should not be confused with cumulative retention rates (which are rarely computed by school districts). If these data were stable from year to year and discounting double retentions, then by sixth grade the cumulative rate in this district would be 31.5 per cent; i.e., nearly one third of all pupils would have been retained at some time before sixth grade.
3 All names used in this analysis are fictitious but were chosen to preserve the sex and ethnic group identity of the subjects.

References

BARUCH, D. W. (1964) *One Little Boy*, New York, Dell.
BOEHM, A. E. and WHITE, A. W. (1967) 'Pupils' perceptions of school marks', *Elementary School Journal*, 67, pp. 237–40.

BOSSING, L. and BRIEN, P. (1979) *A Review of the Elementary School Promotion Retention Dilemma*, Murray, Kentucky, Murray State University (ERIC Document Reproduction Service No. ED 212-362).

BYRNES, D. and YAMAMOTO, K. (1985) 'Academic retention: An inside look', *Education*, 106, pp. 208–14.

BYRNES, D. and YAMAMOTO, K. (1986) 'Views on grade repetition', *Journal of Research and Development in Education*, 20, pp. 14–20.

EDGERTON, R. B. (1967) *The Cloak of Competence*, Berkeley, CA, University of California Press.

HADDAD, W. D. (1979) *Educational and Economic Effects of Promotion and Repetition Practices*, Washington, DC, The World Bank (ERIC Document Reproduction Service, No. ED 195 003).

HOLMES, C. T. and MATTHEWS, K. M. (1984) 'The effects of nonpromotion on elementary and junior high school pupils: A meta-analysis', *Review of Educational Research*, 54, pp. 225–36.

HUMPHREYS, P. (1965) 'The school's concern in non-promotion', *Theory into Practice*, 4, pp. 88–92.

JACKSON, G. B. (1975) 'The research evidence on the effects of grade retention', *Review of Educational Research*, 45, pp. 613–35.

LABAREE, D. F. (1984) 'Setting the standard: Alternative policies for student promotion', *Harvard Education Review*, 54, pp. 67–87.

MAY, D. C. and WELCH, G. L. (1985) 'The effects of developmental placement and early retention on children's later scores on standardized tests', *Psychology in the Schools*, 21, pp. 381–5.

NATIONAL ASSOCIATION FOR THE EDUCATION OF YOUNG CHILDREN (1986) 'Position statement on developmentally appropriate practice in early childhood programs serving children from birth through age 8', *Young Children*, 41, 6, pp. 4–19.

SHEPARD, L. A. and SMITH, M. L. (1985) *Boulder Valley Kindergarten Study: Retention Practices and Retention Effects*, Boulder, CO, Boulder Valley Public Schools.

THOMPSON, M. (1979) 'Because schools are burying social promotion, kids must perform to pass', *American School Board Journal*, 166, pp. 30–2.

Chapter 7:
Teachers' Beliefs about Retention

Mary Lee Smith

Editors' Introduction

In recent years, educational researchers have begun to study teacher thinking as a powerful determinant of classroom practices and student learning. If we can understand teachers' beliefs or mental constructs about how children learn, then we will have an insight into the myriad of day-to-day instructional decisions that teachers make about what to teach when, how to organize lessons, and even whom to teach.

In this chapter Mary Lee Smith uses clinical interviews and observational data to examine teacher beliefs about retention. In the minds of teachers, what kind of child is eligible for retention? What are its perceived effects on students? How is the use of grade retention related to views about child development and learning?

At the most superficial level, Smith's findings are congruent with surveys of educators' opinions. Grade retention is seen as a benevolent intervention that will help the students who need it. Retention is seen as efficacious, with virtually no ill effects, even by teachers who have a history of retaining very few children.

Extensive narrative data permitted analyses beyond a simple tally of teacher votes for or against retention. Given that nearly all teachers think that retention is good, teacher decisions to hold children back were better explained by their beliefs about which children could learn in which learning contexts than by an endorsement of retention per se. Unknown to teachers in individual school environments, the need to retain many or few children might be explained by artifacts of school structure and not by incompetencies in the children retained.

In earlier chapters of this book, the results of research on the effects of retention have been made explicit. That is, controlled studies show with very few exceptions, that children who have been retained for a second year in a grade are not better off than initially equivalent children who have been promoted. This is true whether the outcome is achievement or adjustment and whether the reason for the retention was low academic performance or immaturity.

Teachers conduct their daily activities — decide what to teach and how to teach it, when to intervene and correct improper pupil behavior, and whether to alter the pupil's progress through the grades — based on sets of beliefs about the nature of learning and development and images of what school should be. Research evidence is either not accessible to them or seems not to apply in their particular circumstances. Instead, teachers rely on practical knowledge.

Studying practical knowledge and beliefs of teachers is a recent phenomenon. Its methods are controversial. Some people cannot articulate what they know; therefore asking directly for them to state their theories is unenlightening. As Feiman-Nemser and Floden (1986) noted, 'Practical knowledge is difficult to describe. People often know how to do things without being able to state what they know. Furthermore, neither teachers nor researchers have an adequate vocabulary for describing practical knowledge, much of which is tacit ... If teachers are pressed to give general descriptions of themselves and their work, they often use the same language that social and behavioral scientists do' (p. 506).

One solution to this problem has been the use of the clinical interview with teachers. In the study reported here, the purpose of the interview was to be able to infer the teacher's beliefs about retention by reference to that teacher's practical knowledge. Practical knowledge is based on the first-hand experience of a teacher with specific children and concrete circumstances. Unlike formal knowledge, practical knowledge cannot be stated in the form of generalized propositions of this type: 'On the average, children who have been retained have better self-concepts than comparable children who have been promoted'. Instead, practical knowledge is often in the form of stories of particular events and particular children in specific circumstances: 'When my own son was retained, it was because he was too young for his age, and the next year he was a real leader in his class, and we never have regretted that decision; and ever since then I have recommended that parents of young children in my class take the same step'.

According to Feiman-Nemser and Floden (1986), practical knowledge is 'Personally compelling' and 'oriented to action (p. 512)'. In other words, it helps the teacher decide what to do in a given circumstance. For example, a kindergarten teacher is confronted with the following situation. Every child except one in her class is proceeding through the curriculum. Invariably, one boy leaves his seatwork to crawl to the kitchen center; moreover, he does not seem to remember letter-sound associations. The teacher forms a judgment that this boy is falling behind his classmates in the kindergarten sequence and may not be ready to progress to first grade. She decides that he must have more consistent individual attention to enable him to concentrate and catch up with his pre-reading skills. She bases her decision on previous encounters with similar children in her kindergarten or those of her mentors, as well as the feedback she has received from parents, teachers and administrators about the results of these earlier interventions. Thus, she knows *what* to do without necessarily being able to state directly her underlying belief that 'children who are ill-prepared for first grade may make up for their lack of preparation if given intensive, individual academic assistance'. This latter kind of general proposition can be inferred by the researcher from the teacher's narrated practical knowledge or from observations of her actions in similar circumstances.

The study reported here is based on clinical interviews with kindergarten teachers in the multi-method policy study (Shepard and Smith, 1985) described in chapter 5. The interview agenda was designed on the principle that beliefs can be inferred from recountings of practical knowledge. Rather than asking directly for each teacher to state her philosophy, we framed a series of indirect questions that would elicit narrated stories. For example, we asked teachers to recall specific children in their own classes who had manifested characteristics that might cause them to be considered for retention, to describe these children in detail, including the curricular, instructional and organizational choices that had been made for those children, the consequences of these decisions and any lessons they learned from the case. From the reported practical knowledge we would then be able to make an inference about the teacher's beliefs.

The interviews averaged one hour in length. The teachers were promised anonymity and a report of the results. From previous statements from the project director as well as district administrators, they understood the nature of the policy study. The purpose of the interviews was explained in the orienting statement, as follows:

> The study is about practices in the school district relating to providing an extra year prior to first grade for children who need it. As you know, the extra year is provided either by

retaining a child for an extra year in kindergarten or by screening children into a prekindergarten or transition kindergarten. I know that such practices differ from school to school and that responsible professionals differ in their opinion about this issue. I would like to know your thoughts about this issue, in your own words.

All interviews were conducted by the author. An effort was made to keep the teacher focused on concrete episodes and specific children in the teacher's personal experience. The interview agenda progressed from indirect to direct questions, under the assumption that the most valid and least reactive data are expressed in the teacher's own words, prompted by neutral, fact-oriented questions and minimal leads and non-directive probes by the interviewer. Toward the end of the interview, if sufficient practical knowledge had not disclosed the teacher's implicit theories, more direct questions were posed. For example, if at the end of the interview we could not readily infer the teacher's beliefs about retention, a more direct question was posed such as the following. 'Which do you think poses the greatest risk, retaining a child who needs it or promoting a child who needs to be retained?'

This part of the study can best be understood as a semi-structured interview. Its advantage is its unlikely reactivity with the purpose of the study because of a reliance on teachers' narrations rather than direct questions. Its disadvantage is an absence of standardization of question and response categories.

The interviews were tape recorded and the tapes transcribed. For the analysis of the transcripts, we followed some procedures suggested by Miles and Huberman (1984). We developed a list of categories from the goals of the study and from initial reading of a sample of transcripts. We then coded the transcripts. This chapter emphasizes the data from categories related to teachers' implicit theories about retention and its effects. Other categories have received more attention elsewhere (Smith and Shepard, in press).

As a control against invalid inferences that might have been made from self-report data, we triangulated interview data with data from classroom observations and district documents on retention rates and the like. We judged the interview data provided a fair representation of the day-to-day workings of the teachers and the knowledge upon which they draw. In addition, the teacher interview data were cross-referenced with data obtained in interviews with parents of retained and promoted children. The topics of the interviews (in addition to perceptions about the outcome of retention reported in chapter 5) included the parents' recollection of their interactions with teachers over the decision to retain as well as the parents' report of their children's reaction.

Findings

Teachers' Beliefs about Development

Teachers' beliefs about the mechanisms by which young children develop readiness for school and the role played by teachers in this development are the background for understanding their beliefs about retention. Responses to the questions in the interviews about children who appear to be ready for school, the characteristics of these children, evidence for readiness or lack of it, and causes of different degrees of readiness for school were extracted from the transcripts. A typology of beliefs was obvious. Teachers differed among themselves in the extent to which they construed the development of school readiness as an internal, organismic process unrelated to environmental intervention, or, in contrast, as a process amenable to influence by parents, teachers, and other forces in the child's environment. We used various methods, reported elsewhere, to confirm this typology, the components of which are described below.

Nativists

Nineteen of the forty teachers were classified as 'nativists'. They believe that, within some normal range of environments, children become prepared for school according to an evolutionary, physiological unfolding of abilities. This process, which unfolds in stages, is largely outside the influence of parents and teachers. The only thing teachers can do to help a child who is currently in a developmental stage that is not appropriate for kindergarten is to allow more time for the child to develop, and if possible to remove the child from the stresses of a developmentally inappropriate environment.

> Some children when they come to school are ready for the school situation so that they can be able to meet the school and with not a lot of stress. Other children are just not ready developmentally. And by that I mean they are not ready to let

go of mom, they're not ready to take directions from another person, and I just feel like this is a developmental stage. And that every child will eventually go through the stages. But right now in kindergarten the first part of school is just really hard on a lot of little children...All children develop at their own rate of speed, and we cannot push that development.

The remainder of the teachers were labeled 'non-nativists' and fell into three sub-groups.

Remediationists

These teachers believe that children of legal age for kindergarten are ready for school and can be taught. What the teacher does can influence the pupil's readiness and ability to learn. These teachers are active instructional and resource managers. They break the curriculum into segments and provide pupils with repeated opportunities to learn. Children who learn the material more slowly than their peers are given remediation with the help of volunteers, older tutors, academic assistance pull-out programs, and the like. Teachers in this group provide additional instruction to make up for deficits they perceive.

> If you take an average group of 6-year-olds and an average group of 5-year-olds, the 6-year-olds will be able to sit and do one thing longer. There is that. It is something that is a time kind of factor. But the timeline differs so much from child to child. I'm sure a lot of it has to do with the experiences that children have had, and whether they're familiar with the kind of thing you're doing ... I think we as educators have to give them the benefit of the doubt or do something different and help that child. And maybe the way we taught it is not correct toward their learning pattern. Maybe we ought to change our style or do something different and help that child.

Diagnostic-prescriptive teachers

Any inadequacies in school readiness in children of legal school age occur because one or more of several distinct traits necessary for learning and attention (for example, auditory memory, visual-motor integration) is not intact. A defect in any of these traits can be diagnosed and corrected by concentrated training tailored to the defect. If a diagnostician identifies a deficit in visual memory, she can prescribe a specific training program to correct it. After treatment, the child will be able to function more or less normally like his peers in kindergarten. The beliefs of diagnostic-prescriptive teachers differ from those of Remediationists in that the latter intensify general instruction and the former target therapies to diagnosed disorders.

> You always have children who can handle everything else but have problems with visual motor coordination, and those children probably are going to have those problems so that wouldn't be any reason for retention. We have our learning lab, and children that are showing these problems work there ... If a child absolutely couldn't listen, I'll certainly try very hard to find out what the problem is before wanting to keep him in kindergarten another year. The reasons he can't attend may be because he has an auditory problem...If he has this block or a problem, then he's got to learn to work around that to compensate for it, and that's what we'll try to give him, are ways to compensate.

Interactionists

This group believes in a complex pattern of interactions between the psychological nature of the child and the environments provided by teachers. They believe that the environment and materials should be arranged by the teacher based on an ongoing study of each child and what interest of his might awaken the learning process. Levels of developmental readiness can be influenced in this way.

> Maturity is the ability to focus and whether you can do it or not ... and to have their bodies working effectively for them or not. When these things are not in place, you have an immature child. The teacher can really help, even an immature child. They need more in terms of your time and effort and they need the environment to be set up in such a way that it's not confusing for them. And they need proper choices, not too many choices, but I think the teacher really can affect that and work with the child during the year so that those kinds of things are helped along. We can't get inside of the child and rearrange things, but I think there are some things we can do in the child's environment.

Retention Practices and Beliefs about Development

The next step in the analysis was to determine whether the retention practices of the teachers could be accounted for by their beliefs about the development of readiness for school. Table 1 shows the cross-tabulation of teachers by belief-system (nativist vs. non-nativists) and retention practices. Those who retained 10 per cent or more of kindergartners were classified as high retention and those who retained fewer than 10 per cent were classified as low retention teachers. The table makes it clear that those who believe that children develop readiness for school only as a physiological process, with little opportunity for correction by adults, are also likely to be those who practice retention at high rates. Nativists were also more likely than other teachers to rely heavily on such characteristics as measured level of developmental readiness, chronological age, physical size and gender (as opposed to academic skills) to decide whom to retain. Further analysis revealed that teachers were likely to share beliefs and retention practices with other teachers in their own school. Schools differed from one another in striking ways, some retaining as many as a third of their kindergartners for a second year, and others retaining only 1 or 2 per cent. Beliefs about developing readiness may have conditioned or been conditioned by this pattern of practice, for none of the obvious ways that schools differ from each other (for example, social class, economic opportunity, typical cognitive ability, minority composition, teacher background or ability) could be found to account for the difference in rates of retention.

Table 1: Relationship of Retention Practices and Teachers' Beliefs about Development

Belief system	Retention practices	
	High retaining	Low retaining
Nativist	16	3
Non-nativist	3	18

Beliefs about the Merits of Retention

Beliefs about the merits of retention were analyzed. We expected that teachers who retain few children would also entertain reservations about its use and endorse it less often than teachers, particularly nativists, who use it frequently. This expectation was not fulfilled. teachers of all belief types and those who retain relatively few pupils all endorsed retention as an effective solution to a perceived problem. They may have defined the problem differently, but what they said about the solution was the same. Presumably, low-retaining teachers would have judged retention to be less beneficial if applied to larger proportions of children.

Beliefs about retention and its consequences are detailed in this section along with representative excerpts from the data.

Retention is beneficial

The predominant view expressed by the teachers is that retention benefits the pupil. Specifically, because the pupil is older and more experienced the second time through kindergarten, he or she 'blooms', assumes 'leadership' in the class, is 'comfortable' with the environment and routine, becomes more 'a part of the social group', 'cooperates', has greater 'self-confidence', 'helps' the teacher, 'and achieves more academic success':

> I tend to get the children who are repeating, and it's just like night and day for most of them. The first year they just don't cooperate, have no idea what's going on, and the second year is just like a new child just walked in.

Not only short-term benefits but long-term ones were named:

> I think we owe it to him to tell his parents that, you know, he has another twelve years in school and if he's not functioning at a good level now, that we feel like another year, he would benefit from another year. To make his years happy in school.

> In my opinion, all I can say is, 'That lucky child!' Because they will be able to be a well-rounded child and can handle the peers in junior high and high school.

Several teachers specifically said that the retained child would move from the 'bottom' of his original class to the top of the class into which he has been retained. Those who claimed that retention moved a child from the bottom to the top tacitly assumed two things: that there is a single continuum (probably academic achievement) along which all students may be arranged; and that being on the bottom is undesirable. They failed to grasp, however, that if one child is removed from the bottom of this presumed distribution, another person must take his place.

> Retaining is really beneficial for some of those that just have to struggle and struggle because the next year they might be at the top of their class. And rather than push and put them ahead one year and let them struggle, it would be much more beneficial to the child to just wait, so they can be superstars at the head of the class.

Retention was believed to prevent a variety of ill effects, for example, 'struggle', 'frustration', 'stress', general difficulty in school, retention in a subsequent grade, and peer pressure and drug use later on. Those who mentioned struggle and stress always attached negative value to them.

> If he doesn't [get retained], school's going to be a struggle for him. You think about on down the road what is school going to be like for this child. If he is struggling right now in kindergarten what will it ever be like in first or second grade?

> We held our son back, number one because he was a boy and because we felt from observing him that he didn't have the maturity. We didn't want him to meet with failure, we wanted him to be a year older to cope. And of course then in junior high and high school ages we were delighted because he's had the maturity that so many of the kids haven't had to say no and to be his own man. And I am just a great one for letting children have the benefit of the doubt and not have to be followers all the time.

The quotation above also illustrates a common attribute of the interviews — the use of personal anecdotes from the teachers' own lives to recount or explain beliefs or sometimes to convince parents of the wisdom of retention for their child.

Teachers also claimed that they cannot recall a single instance when retaining a child had bad repercussions, and that there is no stigma attached to a retention in kindergarten (as opposed to subsequent grades).

> I think another year in kindergarten wouldn't hurt them, and it certainly would help them [developmentally young children].

> When they get older, it's harder for them to be kept back.

> There's not the stigma of failure in kindergarten, so that is the time to do it.

For nativist teachers particularly, the benefits of retention are simply the result of having more time to mature.

> Sometimes you just have to wait for Mother Nature to help the child.

A separate category of responses was generated from excerpts concerning the harmful effects of promoting a kindergartner who should have been retained. Children such as these were judged to be destined for failure, subsequent retention, or referral for special education. Several responses we labeled 'promotion disaster stories'. In addition, we noted several responses that referred to the mismatch between a developmentally unready child and the high degree of structure and high expectations for performance in the first grades.

> When I think about them going into first grade, it would have been failure, failure, failure.

> A child who when they come into kindergarten and they have a hard time with the structure here, and if I find by the end of the year that they're just now able to cope with the structure here and yet if I added any more structure to their day or to my expectations that they would have a hard time following it. Then I figure when they go to first grade they would be devastated by the structure, by sitting at a desk or by doing tasks for an hour at a time, by being given a packet of work and being responsible for going from page to page. That child is going to be devastated when he gets into first grade and is handed something and said, 'Do it'. They'll be in every recess getting their work done. They will have a horrible self-concept if they go through that trauma.

> If a child gets into first grade here, they are referred to special education very fast if they are unable to cope and go along with what is expected.

Benefits are conditional

Several teachers acknowledged that, although retention in its ideal form is beneficial, in reality several conditions may undo its effectiveness. The first has to do with how the decision is accepted by the parent and consequently how the parents present it to the child.

> If the parents let the child know they are happy with the decision ... if they're not happy and there's a lot of wavering on it, then I think it's almost — then I think it is probably harmful to the child. Because they are going to read that from the parent. And the kids really will read what you're feeling. And if you accept it, they accept it. So it depends on how the parent approaches the child.

How the teacher 'handles' the retention decision is also viewed as influencing whether retention will help or hurt the child:

> If it's handled correctly, there shouldn't be [any risks to retention]. I think if it's approached in a positive way, 'this is going to be terrific, it's going to be fun, you're going to have a new teacher and learn new things, and you're still going to be in kindergarten', make it a positive thing. I think that that has a great deal to do with what kids think.

Benefits of retention also can depend on the characteristics of the child involved, according to some teachers. For example, retention was seen as an effective device for solving the problems of general immaturity: wait a year for the child to grow into the kindergarten program that exists. For other kinds of children, however, those with low intellectual ability, low motivation, or educational handicaps, retention was not considered efficacious. Special education was deemed the more appropriate solution for children with learning disabilities or retardation. If teachers suspect that handicaps exist, some will promote the child so that he or she will be 'staffed' and placed as soon as possible, not delaying services over the course of the second year in kindergarten.

> I think over a period of twenty years, I can remember one child who I don't think it made any difference retaining that child. That child did not have the ability to be a good student.

> If I find that I'm repeating a child because I think that he's slow intellectually, then I'm not being of any benefit to that child. Yes, they're going to grow and they're going to get a little bit better, but in terms of what they need, they need to get into a special program.

Interactions with parents

Making the decision to retain a child places teachers in complex relationships with the child's parents. Few retentions are initiated by parents. Because some principals insist that parents make the final decision, teachers who have made the recommendation to retain must persuade the parents. Teachers talked about marshaling evidence from the child's performance throughout the year, passing out pamphlets like 'A Gift of Time', bringing in 'experts' to test the children and bolster the case, having the parents visit the classroom to see for themselves the putative difference between their child and his or her peers. Some schools where nativism was dominant conducted educational campaigns with people in their neighborhood, building up a base of support for delayed entry to school, kindergarten retentions, or placement in developmental kindergartens or transition classes.

> You see some parents just think retaining a child is a terrible stigma, you've labeled them for life. And you have to correct a lot of these attitudes. And there are some neighborhoods and some areas where the parents have been educated as to why this retention and everything has been going on, and the schools have worked very closely with the parents over a long period of years, and the whole thing is just a very easy thing. The parents have to know what's going on and why and you're just not picking on them or they're not going to be labeled for life.

Elsewhere, parents have not been so amenable to 'being educated'. In low income areas, particularly, parents need the full-time placement of first grade to fulfill the function of day care; they consider a second year for kindergarten to be frivolous. In the interviews, teachers directed a great deal of blame at parents for denying their recommendation for retention. Parents were seen as adversaries, not acting in their children's best interests.

> At the end of the year the parents said no, he will go to first grade. And we have a policy, when it comes down to that we will actually write a letter and have the parents return a letter stating that they want them to go to first grade even though it [retention] had been highly recommended. That's kind of to save our necks. It is almost always the men who will not go along with it. We think it's an ego thing.

> The thing that is hard on parents is that, 'Oh me. We bought all

Teachers' Beliefs about Retention

these kindergarten clothes and we want that child to go. All his friends are going to first grade. Oh, I can't stand for him to stay back.' But that's so minor in kindergarten.

They were willing to risk her whole future!

In some schools, the parents' point of view was genuinely respected, and the first grade teachers into whose classes the children were promoted made sincere efforts to individualize instruction and otherwise worked to ensure the children's success.

The teachers' interviews were cross-referenced with data from interviews with parents. Teachers consistently underplayed the extent of conflict with parents over the decision to retain and underestimated the degree of parents' active resistance or passive but unhappy compliance.

Negative effects of retention

Given opportunities and prompts for any negative effects that retention might produce, few teachers could name even one. Almost all stated clearly that they would rather err on the side of retaining a child who possibly might not need it than to promote one who might have needed to be retained. Some harm was mentioned, but it was either temporary harm, harm in other schools than the respondent's own, or reluctantly acknowledged, any harm being minor in relation to the positive effects.

> I always tell the parents the first month is hard for the kids that are repeating because they go out for recess and they see the first graders and stuff like that, but after that even I tend to forget which ones are repeating. They are just there.

> I sometimes wish there was another program for that child where then he wouldn't feel like maybe he was not doing as well as the other children.

> And about the first week I think bothers them. Then after that they pretty well fit in. But I guess you always have that stigma of having to be held back.

> I imagine there are risks. The risk would mainly be whether or not the next year you could provide the child with his needs, still let him go at his own speed and if he's a little bit ahead of some of the other children, to provide for him.

The sentiments above are in the minority. In most cases teachers discounted the possibility that children might be bored or frustrated by repeating work done before (either adequately or not), or that they might experience any more than the most minor and ephemeral emotions. The value of social promotion, that is, keeping a child with his age-mates for reasons of social and emotional cohesiveness, was absent from the responses. Nor was there doubt that children's achievement and adjustment would be enhanced by a second year before first grade. They had seen the evidence with their own eyes and took it as sufficient proof. Compared to the reports of parents interviewed, teachers routinely underestimated the retained children's feelings of failure, disappointment and confusion.

Three teachers expressed beliefs about retention that distinguished them from the others. The first was concerned about trying to understand the perspective of the pupil on retention.

> Of all the years to retain, kindergarten seems to be the safest, but I'm sure there are going to be emotional things. You know, it's really hard to say because a child doesn't verbalize that kind of emotional pain. The child seems to take it in stride, but who knows what's going on inside because they are not generally as willing to talk about it ... We need to talk with kids about how that feels.

The second teacher who stood out from the rest noted the complex interaction between the characteristics of the child and the beliefs and actions of the teacher as part of the child's environment:

> Many decisions that I make for children depend upon who they're going to have down the road. If they're going to a first grade classroom where the teacher understands development and can handle the differences in little children and not group kids into high, medium, and low groups, but take advantage of that heterogeneous grouping, then I don't worry about sending a kid on. On the other hand, if they're going to be put in a situation where, because they are young developmentally, and that teacher doesn't understand development, and doesn't know how to take advantage of the differences in little kids as far as instruction is concerned, then I worry about the child.

The third teacher distinguished herself by specifically acknowledging the responsibility of the teacher, curriculum, or school structure — as opposed to the characteristics of the pupil — for creating the conditions that lead to retention:

> I have a lot of trouble failing anyone. It means I haven't done my job. I feel it's my job to take all the kids who come in and teach them what they need even though they are behind in their development.

Practical vs. Propositional Knowledge

Teachers have beliefs and implicit theories of developing readiness for school that are explicable, internally consistent, and can be seen to reflect extant propositional theories in psychology. Furthermore, these beliefs predict (albeit imperfectly) teachers' retention practices. Beliefs about retention, however, fall into no clear pattern. Unlike their beliefs about development, teachers almost universally endorse retention. The following tentative explanations are proposed for the unanimity of practical knowledge and belief and its inconsistency with extant propositional knowledge.

Teachers Have Access to Misleading Data

The practical knowledge that teachers have about curricular choices, teaching practices, diagnosis and correction of immediate snags or setbacks in a pupil's learning is arguably superior to propositional knowledge in the professional literature. It is based on an on-going accumulation of experience with specific children and specific teaching and learning circumstances. There is immediate feedback to the teacher about the effect of particular interventions in context. It is concrete and immediate. In the case of a retention, however, the practical knowledge to which the teacher has access is incomplete and misleading. She sees that the child in his second year of a grade is more competent in the material already covered, and compared to his younger and less experienced classmates, is familiar with the routine and the work. Consequently, she concludes that retention is beneficial. What she lacks access to, however, is the information about what that child would have been like had he been promoted. Indeed, these unseen circumstances are hypothetical; they lack reality, and in fact, she may deny the possibility that with some acceptable level of 'struggling' the child would have succeeded in the subsequent grade and later on would be indistinguishable from his peers. The latter information is exactly what a control group study yields. Two groups start out alike, one gets the treatment — in this case retention — and the other group gets an alternative treatment or control condition. The control group shows the typical outcome that would have been observed if a retained child had been promoted. Since teachers lack this abstract information, they rely on their direct, but inadequate experience. Nor do teachers acquire feedback on what happens to retained children later in their school careers. A taller and quieter retained child may not seem too out of place in the early grades. But what about the fifth grade boy who can shave, the junior high student who can drive himself to school, the pubescent third grader, those who can vote or be drafted before finishing high school, the adult who no longer feels at home in a high school built for adolescents? This is the kind of information that is not available to the teacher's store of practical knowledge.

Retention as Logical Reaction to School Structure

The decision to retain is often rationalized as the protection of unready or incompetent children from the harsh realities of the higher grade. Kindergarten teachers are confronted with an external standard of performance — to make sure all children are ready to begin reading and figuring on the first day of first grade. The first grade teacher, in turn, is faced with the demand that all children be able readers by the end of first grade. In many districts and states, this common standard is reinforced by the administration and public reporting of accountability tests. To guarantee that promoted kindergartners are ready to read, they must go through a curriculum that achieves a measurable level of reading readiness skills; for example, letter-sound associations, consonant blends, listening and following directions, working independently or with their peers without bothering the teacher unduly, and worksheet skills such as printing their names on the proper line. This is too much for some pupils, who might be more appropriately educated in a kind of kindergarten based on learning through social interactions, natural language development, and guided exploratory play. The now predominant literacy-focused kindergarten curriculum, as described by Weber (1986), defines learning narrowly, assumes that the curricular content to achieve literacy and numeracy is known, can be broken down into small units, sequenced, taught directly, and assessed in standardized ways. The methods of teaching are assumed to be uniform for all pupils, and if a pupil fails to achieve, the same content and methods are repeated and intensified. If necessary, children are recycled through the whole package by retaining them for a second year in kindergarten.

Many teachers reject this view of schooling as inappropriate for young children, yet feel powerless to alter the structure of the school, the externally-imposed curriculum and accountability requirements placed on them. The only autonomy still available to them is the recommendation to retain a child who does not fit the structure. The rhetoric of teachers' beliefs about retention regularly places the problem of unreadiness or incompetence in the psychological make-up of the child rather than in the institutional characteristics of the school. The curriculum is left unexamined.

The Problem of Heterogeneity

The teacher is a self-interested theoretician. Though couched in the rhetoric of pupil benefits, her beliefs about retention are, unconsciously perhaps, conditioned by a wish for a more homogeneous and trouble-free class. The kindergarten teacher especially is confronted with a bewildering array of children of different chronological ages and backgrounds. Because some parents keep their children out of public school until they are 6 (to give them a competitive advantage), a range of ages over two years in a single class is not unusual. Some children come in with a rich background of family experiences and pre-schools, not to mention television shows such as *Sesame Street*. Others lack even the slightest degree of educational enrichment from home. Coupled with the standard, literacy-focused curriculum and parents' demands that children progress academically from wherever they are, this degree of heterogeneity overwhelms some teachers. In the study reported here, there were marked differences among teachers in their abilities to manage diversity in the classroom. For those whose only available tactic was to divide by abilities, seeking the solace of a more homogeneous group was a logical step. Such teachers support programs such as developmental kindergartens that siphon off the least mature, or urge parents to keep their children at home until they are more mature, or sort children into different educational tracks so that some do worksheets and pass to first grade and others play at the water table and then spend another year in kindergarten, or refer them for special education. Teachers also seek to reduce heterogeneity by supporting changes in age of legal school entry. These efforts may, however, largely be futile. There will always be a youngest child in a class, always be parents who try to beat the odds by keeping their children out for a year, and thus, great diversity within the kindergarten. Ample evidence exists in the literature on educational tracking and segregation that such practices actually create educational differences rather than solve them.

The study of teacher beliefs about retention opens a window on all the important issues of educational policy: who should be taught, how should schools be organized, how justice and equality might be attained and how teachers might be trained to deal with individual differences. This study has shown how teacher beliefs can be examined. With regard to retention, teacher beliefs have been shown to be constrained by the immediate context of the school structure and the broader context of what information is available to them and what kinds of decisions they can make. It remains to other researchers to design collaborative studies with teachers to examine these constraints and enable them to reflect more broadly on educational policies and practices.

References

FEIMAN-NEMSER, S. and FLODEN, R. E. (1986) 'The cultures of teaching', in WITTROCK, M. C. (Ed.) *Handbook of Research on Teaching*, 3rd edn., New York, Macmillan, pp. 505–26.
MILES, M. and HUBERMAN, A. (1984) *Qualitative Data Analysis*, Beverly Hills, CA, Sage.
SHEPARD, L. A. and SMITH, M. L. (1985) *Boulder Valley Kindergarten Study: Retention Practices and Retention Effects*, Boulder, CO, Boulder Valley Public Schools.
SMITH, M. L. and SHEPARD, L. A. (in press) 'Kindergarten readiness and retention: A qualitative study of teachers' beliefs and practices', *American Educational Research Journal*.
WEBER, E. (1986) *Ideas Influencing Early Childhood Education*, New York, Teachers College Press.

Chapter 8:
Ending Social Promotion in Waterford: Appearances and Reality[1]

Mary Catherine Ellwein and Gene V Glass

Editors' Introduction

Teacher beliefs about retention, investigated by Smith in chapter 7, might be considered to be informal or implicit policies that govern promotion decisions. In contrast, many school districts have implemented formal promotion-retention policies in response to the call for school reform. Chapter 8 is a case study of one such school district's efforts to raise standards.

Researchers Ellwein and Glass studied what happened in Waterford when a no-nonsense superintendent decided that students with inadequate skills would no longer be passed to the next grade. The identity of the district and principal players have been disguised. However, interview narratives and numerical data are authentic reports of what took place as the district implemented test-based promotion decisions. Professionals faced dilemmas about where to set passing scores on a test to allow for measurement error but maintain credibility with the public. What should be done with students in the gray area near the passing score? What if students passed the reading test but failed in math? What should be done with students who failed year after year?

In their analysis, Ellwein and Glass drew sharp contrasts between the initial rhetoric of the program and actual practice. Similarly, the intense and scrupulous early efforts to build a scientific test-based system were not mirrored by conscientious follow-on evaluation or data collection. Rather than attributing these findings to idiosyncracies of the case, the authors argue that this pattern is consistent across several cases where test-based passing rules were used symbolically to raise standards and satisfy the public.

Since 1983, the Waterford School District has administered locally-developed, criterion-referenced tests from kindergarten through to the eighth grade. Developed by a host of content specialists, school administrators and classroom teachers, these examinations cover grade-level material in reading, mathematics and, in some grades, writing. The tests are intended for use as 'progress indicators'. However, the tests bear a heavier burden for kindergarten, second-, fifth-, and seventh-grade pupils: scores on these tests are to be the primary criteria by which students are promoted or retained. Social promotion was to be ended in favor of a systematic and scientific set of procedures based on testing. Waterford's efforts to replace the traditional, but politically stigmatized, social promotion system with the new testing program are described in this chapter. We present a chronological description of the impetus, conceptualization, implementation and initial results of one district's response to the promotion-retention dilemma.

Background and Method

The study of Waterford's promotional gates program was one element of an in-depth study of competency testing and standard-setting (Ellwein and Glass, 1987). The purpose of this multi-site qualitative study was to examine a number of research questions:

(i)   For whom and for what purposes are test standards set?
(ii) How and by whom are standards established?
(iii) What consequences follow from the application of standards?

Each of five study sites, either a local or state education agency, administered competency tests and set standards by which decisions would be made about individual examinees (for example, grade promotion, high school graduation, college admission and teacher certification). On the basis of data generated by semi-structured interviews and agency documents, chronological narratives were produced for each site. Waterford's story was constructed from accounts given in ten interviews with eight district personnel and from seventeen documents. A draft of the chronology was circulated to the key informant and other district officials for confirmation of facts, clarification of ambiguities and general reactions. Although respondent validation was sought, considered and incorporated when deemed appropriate, no effort was made to secure official district approval of the interpretations drawn from the study.

Impetus for the Promotional Gates Policy

In the early 1980s, the Waterford School District (not its real name) hired a new Superintendent. Charismatic and competent, the new leader was viewed as the answer to many of the problems plaguing the district. There was a general feeling that the 'product' leaving the Waterford schools could be improved. In the words of the Deputy Superintendent,

> We met with a group of personnel people and they made allegations that [students] didn't know how to fill out application forms. The summary of many, many discussions was if the schools ensured that students reached their maximum academic potential, business could take over from there and train [students] to serve its purposes.

Superintendent Williams had a vision, an inspiring and invigorating vision that students could reach their maximum academic potential; and so he began to search for means to make it real. Social promotion was viewed as a major obstacle to this goal, and following a number of months of deliberations and discussion, the Superintendent announced that social promotion would no longer be condoned or practiced. Instead, quantifiable measures of progress would be used in making promotion decisions in Waterford. The Superintendent's announcement was formally incorporated into the district's five-year plan:

> Addressing the needs of students who are not achieving up to expectations is an important component of the mission of the Waterford School District. The following commitments will be made as the school district proceeds to develop policies and procedures for intervention and for promotion or retention of students ... Test data will be used as primary information to be considered in decisions about promotion or retention.

The Deputy Superintendent echoed the commitment in the district's five-year plan:

> The Board [of Education] had made a statement that the district was not going to promote students socially. We needed some measures as checkpoints to assure that students wouldn't slip through the cracks.

To this end, a committee was formed to make recommendations about achievement standards, promotional gates and student interventions. This committee was made up of over forty individuals from teaching, administration, curriculum and other special programs. After meeting for nine months, the group produced a number of recommendations which would serve as the blueprint for district retention policies and procedures.

Blueprint for Excellence

Recommendations from this district-wide committee dealt with a wide range of issues including achievement standards, promotional gates, curriculum interventions, retention policies, parent notice and due process, implementation timelines, position responsibilities, staff development, evaluation and budget estimates. A few of the recommendations will be discussed here, recommendations that would set the stage for the actual determination of test standards.

Criterion-referenced tests had been developed in reading and mathematics for grades K-9, with tests of writing in four of these grades (3, 5, 7 and 9). Instead of basing promotion decisions on test performance at every grade, the committee selected four grades to serve as the promotional gates. According to the committee's report:

> In order to provide students the experiences that accommodate the readiness of five year olds, the first promotional gate is at kindergarten. Here the focus is not so much upon achievement as it is upon readiness for school learning. Some students need additional experiences and/or maturing time before going on to first grade; that is, they need opportunities to build readiness. The gates at grades 2, 5 and 7 organizationally occur at about the middle of the K-3, 4-6 and the 7-8 schools. There is still enough time before the passage to the next school for necessary skill acquisition. The gate placed one year ahead of the normal 'end point' for that level of schooling allows for reassessment of the impact of the interventions during the repeated grade year with an additional year to monitor progress and support achievement gains of the students before leaving the environment of the primary, intermediate, or junior high settings.

In addition to recommending the grades at which the promotional gates would be placed, the committee identified the means by which test standards would be determined:

> Standards of performance for the tests will be established

centrally. The process to be used correlates test results with teacher-determined criteria of performance.

Instead of having one test score to separate students into pass or fail, two scores would be determined for each promotional gate test. According to the committee's report:

> Test scores that are closest to the standard that separates proficiency from non-proficiency may not accurately reflect performance due to error of measurement present in all tests ... Because those errors exist, scores from each test will be divided into three bands: satisfactory, questionable and unsatisfactory.

In describing the rationale behind the questionable (gray) area, the math consultant echoed the concerns of the city-wide committee:

> I think people have all seen situations where a child's test performance is not in agreement with their performance apart from the test. People didn't want to have an inflexible situation, one that nobody could work with.

The committee went on to recommend procedures by which promotion decisions would be made. Since examinees would score in one of three areas — satisfactory, questionable, or unsatisfactory — on each of two (or three) sub-tests, many different score combinations were possible for the entire promotional gate test. In the words of a committee member who prepared the committee's final report:

> One of the issues we dealt with was what would happen if a kid fails one test and passes the other(s). We came up with some decision rules and we fought and argued over those damn things, too. In the back of the whole argument were those people who were basically against retaining anybody and I think those people would argue that you should only retain those kids who fail all of the subtests. [Others would argue,] 'We have a superintendent who says kids won't pass if they fail a promotional gate, so how can you go ahead and promote a kid who has failed even one of the subtests?'.

After considerable debate, the committee finally agreed on a set of decision rules and approved a flow chart by which promotion decisions would be made in the Waterford schools. According to the Committee's final report:

> At kindergarten, there is one benchmark test which assesses

reading and mathematics readiness. Students who have scores in the satisfactory range generally will be recommended for promotion. Questionable scores will lead to a review of total performance to determine promotion or retention. Unsatisfactory scores will generally lead to retention.

The decision rules for second, fifth and seventh grade test performance were decidedly more complex. Depending on sub-test performance, students would be classified into one of three categories: promotion, review, or retention. Table 1 shows the possible patterns of sub-test performance for each category. As can be seen in the table, there are six possible combinations of performance on the two sub-tests in grade 2. For example, two of these performance patterns slot students into the promotion category: 1) pass both sub-tests [S, S]; or 2) pass one sub-test and score in the gray area on the second [S, Q]. In grades 5 and 7 there are ten possible patterns used to determine placement in the decision categories. For example, promotion would be recommended for students with one of the following performance patterns: 1) pass all three sub-tests [S, S, S]; 2) pass two sub-tests and score in the gray area on the third [S, S, Q]; or 3) pass two sub-tests and fail the third [S, S, U].

Students recommended for 'review' would have their fate decided

Table 1: Patterns of Sub-test Performance for Promotion Decisions

	Grade 2 Pattern on two sub-tests		Grade 5 and 7 Pattern on three sub-tests		
Promotion recommendation					
P1[¹]	S	S	S	S	S
P2	S	Q	S	S	Q
P3	—	—	S	S	U
Review recommendation					
P4	S	U	S	Q	Q
P5	Q	Q	S	U	U
P6	—	—	S	Q	U
P7	—	—	Q	Q	Q
Retention recommendation					
P8	Q	U	Q	Q	U
P9	U	U	Q	U	U
P10	—	—	U	U	U

Note: Where S = satisfactory sub-test performance
Q = questionable sub-test performance
U = unsatisfactory sub-test performance
[¹]Possible patterns of sub-test performance

by a group of district educators. As described in the committee's report:

> Students recommended for a review of total performance will have their scores examined by a review team consisting of the principal, the classroom teacher plus at least one other staff member (for example, social worker, counselor, reading or math specialist, or intervention teacher). A review of additional objective data, in addition to staff judgments, will lead to either a case conference, a retention recommendation or a promotion.

A case conference would be called when there had been no prior intervention or parent notice. Staff and parents would meet at the conference to determine whether the student would be promoted or retained. Although a consensual decision was seen as most desirable, the final decision to promote or retain a child would be made by the building principal.

An addendum to the committee's recommendations made fleeting reference to some non-test considerations in promotion decisions:

> A student should be retained for no more than one year at any single grade level. The next consideration for a repeated retention would normally occur at the next promotional gate. Any student recommended for more than one retention, excluding kindergarten, can be retained only after a case conference.

This set of recommendations addressed the inevitable questions of how to deal with multiple retentions during the course of a student's time in elementary school. Not only did the committee speak against repeated retention in a single grade, but they also indicated that retention should generally occur *only* at the promotional gates of 2, 5 and 7.

A committee member instrumental in the writing of the final report described the decision rules, flow chart and multiple retention policies as means for gaining cooperation from those members who expressed concerns about the promotional gates program:

> We were screaming about [these issues] and we finally came up with a flow chart which said here's how we'll handle promotion-retention decisions. The checks and balances built into the chart, like the opportunity for review, finally sold those folks who were against the whole concept from the beginning.

Three other relevant policies are noted:

1 All regular education students are expected to take promotional gates tests. The Individual Education Program (IEP) for special education students must specify which tests, if any, the students will take.
2 Retesting is allowed only after a special request by the teacher has been submitted.
3 Students who fail the promotional gate tests and are retained are eligible to receive retention services. Kindergarten retention services are delivered in a K-1 transition curriculum. Other grades offer pull-out programs skills work during the retained year.

Thus, plans were carefully laid for implementation of the four promotional gates. Tests would be piloted along a staggered schedule, standards would be set on the city-wide pilot data and students would be held to those standards in the year following the pilot. By spring 1986 the four promotional gates would be in place and guarded.

Setting Standards: Where Reason Prevails

With the standard-setting method selected and approved by the district committee, the testing office was given the responsibility for implementing the procedure. This office, in conjunction with the curriculum department, had been in the throes of objective writing, test development, bias reviews and was ready to begin piloting the first test (kindergarten) in Spring, 1983. Except for the particular people involved and the number of sub-tests for which standards had to be set, the standard-setting procedure described below was similar for all of the promotional gate tests. Before the tests were piloted, the district testing office sent letters to teachers asking them to judge each of their students as a 'master' or 'non-master' of the skills measured on the test. The following definition was provided to help teachers differentiate between the two types of student:

A master is defined as a student who knows enough of the basic skills in this area that if you had to make a decision about promotion or retention solely on this skill level as it will be measured by this test at this time, you would elect to promote the student. A non-master is defined as a student whose reading [math or writing] skills are such that if you only had two choices — to promote or to retain — you would elect to retain the student at this time.

Teachers were urged to draw upon any and all of the information they had about each student: classroom performance, other test scores and intuitive assessment of how the student would perform in the areas measured by the test. After teacher judgments had been obtained the tests were administered to a city-wide sample of kindergarten students. The district testing office then collected, organized and merged the two data sets and displayed them in tables like that shown in table 2.

The first column in table 2 shows the range of raw scores (five to forty-one) on the pilot administration of the kindergarten test. The next three columns display the numbers of students rated as masters and non-masters as well as the total number who earned the corresponding raw score. Column 5 is the ratio of students identified as masters to the total number of students earning a particular raw score. The last column only displays information at the middle of the frequency distribution: each entry is the percent of all students who scored at or below the corresponding raw score. For example, 25.4 per cent of the kindergarten students scored at or below twenty-seven on the pilot administration of the test.

For each sub-test at each promotional gate, similar frequency tables were constructed by the testing office for use by members of the standard-setting committees. Each committee was composed of ten to fifteen members including district teachers and principals, as well as individuals from the curriculum and testing offices. For each promotional gate sub-test, the committee would inspect the data shown in the frequency tables and apply the Contrasting Groups method to determine the test standards. Using this method, standard-setters would inspect the distribution of test performance, looking for the score obtained by equal numbers of masters and non-masters. For example, among the number of students who scored a twenty-four on the kindergarten test (n = 43), 51 per cent were labeled as masters. If the Contrasting Groups method was applied in the strictest interpretation, a score of twenty-four would be selected as the standard.

However, frequency tables like that in table 2 were not the only sets of information available to the standard-setting committees. The testing office also prepared a table for each of the recommended cut-scores which displayed test performance by ethnic group and sex of mainstream students, as well as breakdowns by other student groups:

M. C. Ellwein and G. V. Glass

Table 2: Kindergarten Master/Non-master Distributions for 2380 Pupils in Waterford School District (Spring 1983)

Raw score	# master	# non-master	# total	% master of total	% of all students scoring at or below
41	38	0	38	100	
40	74	0	74	100	
39	148	0	148	100	
38	156	2	158	99	
37	214	1	215	99+	
36	183	3	186	98	
35	173	2	175	99	
34	147	11	158	93	
33	110	12	122	90	
32	98	11	109	90	
31	102	24	126	81	
30	94	18	112	84	37.9
29	83	13	96	86	32.9
28	63	24	87	72	29.1
27	55	20	75	73	25.4
26	50	21	71	70	22.1
25	20	18	38	53	19.3
24	22	21	43	51	17.3
23	17	24	41	41	15.3
22	13	22	35	37	13.4
21	17	25	42	40	11.8
20	13	20	33	39	9.9
19	7	22	29	24	
18	4	20	24	17	
17	3	13	16	19	
16	2	20	22	9	
15	1	15	16	6	
14	4	10	14	29	
13	2	10	12	17	
12	3	15	18	17	
11	1	11	12	8	
10	0	5	5	0	
9	0	13	13	0	
8	0	7	7	0	
7	0	7	7	0	
6	0	2	2	0	
5	0	1	1	0	
n	1,917	463	2,380		

special education and limited English proficiency. Another table was prepared to indicate the percent of students (by ethnic group and sex) who would be sorted into one of three recommendation categories: promotion, review, or retention.

In addition to the normative data, a number of considerations were brought to bear on the committee's deliberations, considerations that may be grouped into three categories: technical issues, practical realities and appearances of the standards.

Technical Issues

The Director of Testing held firm notions of how the standard-setting should be done and what it should produce.

> As long as the committee members didn't violate what I thought was the intent of the Contrasting Groups method, then I basically took a position that they knew more about the curriculum and expectations to set a reasonable standard. To me, a violation would be if they set the standard where 80 per cent of the kids were rated as masters — any extreme [percentage] would be a violation of the method.

The committee acknowledged that there was no absolute standard. The math consultant, who served on a number of the standard-setting committees, described the prevailing attitude:

> Any standard-setting is arbitrary. I mean, the bottom line is that kids above the cut-score pass; kids below the cut-score do not. And the reaction is that the standard-setting is going to be arbitrary, but not arbitrarily arbitrary. You don't just go and draw a line. The Contrasting Groups method seemed to be a good enough process. You could move the cut-score up or down a few points and I don't know that doing so would make that much difference. When you get down to it, the kids who are marginal — a few points higher or lower than the cut-score — are going to get into some kind of [intervention] program anyway.

The Director of Testing echoed the math consultant's view:

> The committees worked very well ... It was like 'We have a job to do, so let's do what we think is the most rational and reasonable thing to do ... If I'm holding out [on group consensus] and my preferred cut-score is a point different, I'm not going to argue it'. Let's face it, the cut-score is not perfect. There's no magic point.

Practical Issues

Committee members were aware of practical concerns as well in the standard-setting process. The Director of Testing addressed concerns about particular cut-scores and their corresponding fail rates:

> And we weren't entirely dumb about what the district could afford. We never went and asked [central administration], but we knew what the common sense approach was.

When asked if potential costs influenced the recommendations given to the standard-setting committees, he replied: 'Sure. I'm not supposed to say that, but it was. I wasn't going to recommend a standard that would produce a 50 per cent fail rate'.

The Deputy Superintendent lent a slightly different perspective:

> When you consider that all of the people working on the tests and standards were seasoned teachers, their experience would tell them that a standard that identifies only a small percent of students is utopic. That's not a reality — it's not what teachers face in the classroom. The same thing is true if a standard failed 60 per cent of the students. Kids are doing much better than that. There's a certain amount of intuitiveness to a standard.

A language arts teacher on the committee spoke of the multiple interests that had to be accommodated by the group.

> Different people had different agendas when they set the standards. I think that when statisticians look at the data, they see the numbers in the distributions and rely on [those numbers] to pick out the high risk kids. And then someone from a curriculum viewpoint looks and says, 'Oh my god. What are we going to do? This is an 80 per cent minority group and there are all these kids, all in different places. How are we going to design a curriculum that is going to help these kids?' And then there's the administrative viewpoint: 'We don't have any classrooms. How are we going to schedule these kids? What are we going to do with them? Who is going to want to teach them when we put them all together — a lot of them are going to be behavior problems'.

Appearance of the Standards

A third set of considerations dealt with the appearance of the standards. In the words of the math consultant:

> The idea is that the passing score has to be high enough and the number of students failing low enough ... If you take a look, the cutoff scores range between 60 per cent and 76 per cent correct. I think our feeling was that if the cut-score is lower than 60 per cent, it is pretty low for a competency test.

Despite the various and often competing considerations, each of the four standard-setting committees was able to agree on performance standards. According to informants, the kindergarten cut-score (twenty-six) was easier to derive than those for the other promotional gate tests. Whereas the breaks between the master and non-master distributions were said to be distinct in the kindergarten data, the data for the higher grades were murkier and cut-scores could have been set in any number of places. In those instances, the committee relied on information about the failure rates to discern among candidate cut-scores.

Once the committees had set the test standards, the Director of Testing circulated the cut-scores among members of the Superintendent's cabinet for approval. According to the Deputy Superintendent:

> We would share the figures with the cabinet and our superintendent. They raised a lot of questions because they would have to answer to the Board of Education and the public. [Some of the concerns included] the different standards in terms of percent of correct items; the projected fail rates for each grade level; and the per cent of minority students who would fail. Their concern was something like this: 'I accept this standard, but what are we going to do about it? How can we make a difference so that the children who fail this year are not the ones who fail next year?'

The final step in the standard-setting process involved securing Board of Education approval. Every recommended standard was approved without modification. According to the math consultant,

> If we had come up with a standard by which 50 per cent of the kids would fail, I am sure the cabinet would have told us to go back to the drawing board. But, I think the standards weren't changed because as we were setting them, we were looking at the political realities.

Consequences of the Promotional Gates Program

Table 3 is a summary of the passing rates for each promotional gate test since piloting began in Spring 1983. These data were provided by the Director of Testing.

Passing rates on the promotional gate sub-tests fail to convey the whole picture for grades 2, 5 and 7. Rather, the per cent classified in each of the three recommendation categories (pass, review, retain) provides a much clearer picture of the impact of the tests on the pupils. Table 4 shows the per cent classified in each category by grade and year.

As can be seen in table 4, anywhere from 14 to 16 per cent of the students were slated for retention or performance review after the test standards were first applied. These percentages were lower than those observed in the pilot years in which 19 to 22 per cent of the students were not eligible for automatic promotion. When asked whether the fail rates on the promotional gate test were seen as reasonable by the district's constituency, the Director of Testing responded: 'The education community and community in general buy it. It seems rational.'

The metropolitan newspapers published test results each spring, and ranked individual schools by passing rates. Nevertheless, district officials felt that the reporting was generally even-handed. The Deputy Superintendent commented on the fairness of the publicity and, while not admitting to political motives, nonetheless was quick to analyze what took place in political terms.

Table 3: Promotional Gates Passing Rates in Waterford 1983–86

Grade and subject	Year			
	1983	1984	1985	1986
Kindergarten	81%[a]	89%	87%	86%[b]
Grade 2				
Reading	n/a	78%[a]	81%	87%[b]
Mathematics	n/a	85%[a]	90%	90%[b]
Grade 5				
Reading	n/a	n/a	80%[a]	87%
Mathematics	n/a	n/a	76%[a]	82%
Writing	n/a	n/a	74%[a]	87%
Grade 7				
Reading	n/a	n/a	83%[a]	84%
Mathematics	n/a	n/a	78%[a]	84%
Writing	n/a	n/a	70%[a]	82%

[a] projected passing rates from pilot test data
[b] passing rates from parallel form B

Table 4: Percent of Students (Grades 2, 5, and 7) Classified in Pass, Review and Retain Categories

Grade	Recommendation category	Year 1984	1985	1986
2nd	Pass	81[a]	86	85[b]
	Review	10[a]	9	7[b]
	Retain	9[a]	5	7[b]
5th	Pass	—	75[a]	81
	Review	—	13[a]	9
	Retain	—	13[a]	7
7th	Pass	—	78[a]	74
	Review	—	11[a]	9
	Retain	—	11[a]	7

Note: Figures do not add to 100% in the last column because of missing sub-test scores for a number of students
[a] derived from pilot test data
[b] based on parallel form

In retrospect, I think the media was very fair. We spent a lot of time going over the test results and I think the reporters sensed the seriousness of an error in reporting the results. And so, they were not alarmists. They didn't have control over their headline, so the headliner would tend to shock people with percentage of failures and percentage of minority students. It didn't seem to be detrimental; in fact, it was helpful. If what we were doing was for a political motivation, it would have been a good strategy because the common response was 'It's good to see a school district insist the kids learn and it's not fair to kids to pass them if they don't know what they should'.

What actually happened to students once they took the promotional gate tests? At the conclusion of this study (January 1987), the available information was scant. Although the Office of Testing could cite how many students passed and failed the *tests*, the department did not know how many students had been retained. The task of matching test performance and promotion-retention decisions was not the responsibility of the Office of Testing. Neither did the responsibility rest with the Office of Research and Evaluation. Although this department was responsible for evaluating the *services* delivered to students retained in grades K and 2 (and eventually grades 5 and 7), it was not responsible for matching and tracking test performance and subsequent promotion decisions. The task was said to be the responsibility of someone in data processing, but informants from the central administration had no idea as to the task's status nor the specific people responsible for its execution. The absence of actual counts notwithstanding, a few observations can be drawn about the link between test performance and promotion-retention decisions in Waterford. These observations are based on an integration of two sets of data; one set came from the Office of Testing and the other from the Office of Research and Evaluation. Bear in mind that the following observations are investigator inferences based on reconstructions of available data. They were not drawn nor offered by Waterford officials.

Table 5 is a display of the available information about the 1984/85 Kindergarten class. The columns indicate the numbers who passed and failed the 1985 promotional gate. The rows indicate the actual decisions made about these students: promoted to first grade or retained (with or without retention services) in kindergarten.

In Spring 1985, 89 per cent (n = 3123) of the kindergarten students took the kindergarten promotional gate test. As shown earlier in table 3, 87 per cent of these regular education students (n = 2717) scored at or above the cut-score, thereby passing the exam. The remaining 13 per cent (n = 406) scored in either the gray (n = 219) or unsatisfactory (n = 187) area, thereby placing them into the review or retain categories, respectively. Of retained kindergarten students receiving transition services in 1985/86, 278 scored in the gray (n = 109) or unsatisfactory (n = 169) areas of the 1985 promotional gate test. An additional eleven students who failed the test were retained but did not

Table 5: Kindergarten Test Performance and Actual Promotion Decisions (1985)

Decision	Promotional gate performance		
	Passed	Failed[a]	Total
Promoted	(2709)	(117)	(2926)
Retained			
retention services	1	278	279
no retention service	7	11	18
	2717	406	3123

Note: Numbers in parentheses inferred from other table cells.
[a] Includes those who scored below the passing score of 26

receive transition services and at least eight children were retained even though they passed (one of whom also received transition services designed for those who failed the test). In sum, approximately 117 students (29 per cent) of the 406 who failed the 1985 promotional gate were not found in 1985/86 kindergarten classrooms. It is likely that these students were promoted to first grade. This conclusion is borne out by the evaluation report released in Fall 1986, which indicated that more than 300 kindergarten students who failed or barely passed the 1985 promotional gate were promoted to the first grade.

Among the 2813 second graders, 90 per cent (n = 2521) of the regular education students took the 1985 promotional gate tests. As indicated in table 3, approximately 86 per cent (n = 2171) would be recommended for promotion to third grade and 14 per cent (n = 350) would be recommended for retention (n = 125) or review (n = 225). According to the evaluation report, only 162 of the eligible 350 students were retained and received retention services. It appears that over 50 per cent of the children eligible for retention were nevertheless promoted. Indeed, the district evaluators estimated that 400 students were promoted to third grade when their test performance indicated they should not have been.

Apparently, test information was used asymmetrically in making promotion and retention decisions in grades K and 2. With a few exceptions, students who passed the promotional gate tests were promoted. The link between performance and retention decisions was weaker. Although a number of students didn't clear the gates at each grade, many were nevertheless promoted. Rumors of this asymmetry circulated among district personnel and one informant commented on it:

> Kids are passed or retained on a larger agenda, and yet, I don't dare say that very loudly. We don't have the statistics to confirm anything, but I know there is a different number of kids in retention compared to those who were eligible for retention. What we don't know is what happened to those kids who weren't retained, nor why that happened.

If students were retained on a 'larger agenda', what non-test criteria were considered in the decision-making process? Again, there were no data to answer the question directly because the question was never officially asked by the district. Nevertheless, a few insights were gained by inspecting the two sets of data previously mentioned. It is possible that among those who failed the promotional gates, information about their ethnicity and gender may have influenced subsequent decisions to be retained. For example, minorities accounted for 59 per cent of the students who failed the 1985 kindergarten test. However, 69 per cent of the students who were retained and received transition services were minorities. Moreover, 56 per cent of those failing the kindergarten test were male, but they accounted for 65 per cent of the retained students who received transition services.

A similar pattern for ethnicity was observed at grade 2. Of those failing the reading and math sub-tests, minorities accounted for 61 per cent and 62 per cent, respectively. Of those receiving retention services, minorities accounted for 70 per cent — disproportionate to the per cent failing either. Because the district did not produce figures on the entire promotional gate (sub-tests combined) by ethnicity and sex, conclusions about either's influence on the decision-making process remain speculative.

The district informant last quoted provided yet another view of the link between district promotion policy and practice. According to this informant, elementary building principals had agreed to an unofficial modification of existing policy. Recall that policy held that students were (a) to be retained only at promotion gate grades; and (b) once retained, they should not be held back again within the promotion band (for example, grades 1-3, 4-6, and 7-8). Reportedly, the elementary principals modified the policy to correspond to their own notions of retention:

> There are some schools who prefer to retain after grade 1, because they feel that the sooner the retention, the better. So if a student is retained in first grade and then fails the grade 2 promotional gate, he or she will not be retained again.

Indeed, if this modification was widely practiced, the principals' discretion in making retention decisions would be broadened at the expense of the central policy.

At the time of this study, the district appeared uninterested as evidenced by its lack of systematic monitoring or reporting on this issue. Although officials neglected to examine the link between test performance and retention (or policy and practice), they did evaluate a number of aspects related to the services delivered to retained students. Several merit comment here. Both the kindergarten and grade 2 evaluations emphasized (i) description of the type and amount of services delivered; (ii) characteristics of enrolled students; (iii) teacher and parent opinions about the services; and (iv) teacher ratings of student progress and achievement. In general teachers perceived a positive impact on retained students' achievement and achievement-related behaviors (for example, time on task). In addition, district evaluators attempted to compare retained students' achievement with that of promoted (mainstream) students. To this end, the evaluators identified those students (kindergarten and second graders) who had scored low on the 1985 tests. All of the identified students had scored at or below the district's 30th percentile in 1985. Tables 6 and 7 show the per cents of students scoring below the same point on the 1986 tests for kindergarten and grade 2 respectively.

As can be seen in tables 6 and 7, students were not tested on a common metric. Although retained and promoted students had taken the same promotional gate test in 1985 (the 'pre-test'), they took different tests in 1986. Retained students retook the promotional gate test and promoted students were tested on the first grade criterion-referenced test. Nevertheless, evaluators compared performance distributions and remarked that greater proportions of promoted students scored in the lower portions of the distributions. However, unaddressed issues of unmatched samples, different test metrics, statistical

Table 6: 1986 Performance of Low-scoring 1985 Kindergarten Students

Status of 1985 Kindergarten students	% scoring below 30th percentile on 1986 test		
	K	1st Math	Rdg
Retained			
transition services	28	n/a	n/a
no transition services	23	n/a	n/a
Promoted	n/a	78	92

Table 7: 1986 Performances of Low-scoring 1985 Second Grade Students

Status of 1985 grade 2 students	% scoring below 30th percentile on 1986 test			
	2nd		3rd	
	Math	Rdg	Math	Rdg
Retained				
transition services	25	46	—	—
no transition services	NR	NR	—	—
Promoted	—	—	87	83

regression and difficulties with same-grade comparisons sabotage any conclusions about comparative achievement gains.

At the time of the multi-site study, Superintendent Williams was pleased with the promotional gates program. Two informants indicated that the Superintendent had yet to hear parental complaints about the program. When asked to comment on the status of the promotional gates program, the Director of Testing remarked enthusiastically:

> The program is in great shape. I would never in my fondest expectations have thought that it would be in as good a shape as it has been. The program has been well done.

Reflections on Waterford

Clearly, the events chronicled in this chapter reveal steady and thorough efforts to resolve the promotion-retention dilemma in Waterford. The traditional practice of peer promotion came under heavy attack and a rationalization of the promotion process was seen as an urgent need of the district. To this end, the district's best were brought together to plan and implement a program that would supplant heretofore irrational and haphazard practices. District personnel spoke of pupil readiness and skill acquisitions and after careful thought, testing technology was employed to assess these constructs. Teacher insight and knowledge were consulted in the setting of test standards as were pilot data of pass-fail rates. In acknowledgement of test error, 'gray areas' were created by the setting of a second standard on each promotional gate sub-test and decision rules were formulated to accommodate professional discretion. Finally, the tests were administered with care, painstakingly analyzed, and duly reported to the district's constituents. Indeed, the promotional gates program had been designed and implemented in an exemplary manner. Waterford had erected hurdles for its students and the consequences were made public — many had passed, but not all. Non-masters were identified and their fate was clear. Or so it was said. Recall the statement issued in the district's five-year plan:

> Test data will be used as primary information to be considered in decisions about promotion or retention.

Has this policy been practiced in Waterford? Has the district prevented students from slipping through the institutional cracks

Ending Social Promotion in Waterford

created by social promotion? At the time of this study, Waterford could not supply answers to questions such as these and so we are left with inferences drawn from an inspection of the available data.

On the basis of these inferences, we concluded that test performance and promotion decisions were related asymmetrically. Students who passed the tests were generally promoted, but the fate of those who failed was much less consistent with policy dictates. Some students were retained, many were not. Student ethnicity and gender may have influenced subsequent retention decisions, but we can only speculate at this point. We do not know how, or if, the review process was employed. Moreover, informal modifications like the one formulated by district principals may have influenced the decision-making process as well. The point is that no one really knew what happened in Waterford.

One might argue that it takes time to study the policy-practice connection. Events in Waterford were still unfolding at the conclusion of the study and perhaps officials may someday be able to portray the link between test performance and promotion-retention decisions. Time notwithstanding, we must not overlook the absence of means that would permit an analysis of the performance-promotion connection. Despite the efforts expended in formulating a rationalized promotion policy, the district had not included a mechanism to evaluate the actual practices and effects. When obviously relevant data are missing, one can generally infer an unwillingness to look at them — not oversight, but looking the other way. Why weren't the data collected to check on whether promotion in Waterford schools was still social or whether it had become scientific?

Predictably, some would argue that idiosyncracies of the Waterford program developers account for the absence of examination. From our vantage point, such an explanation is superficial and shallow. Systematic observations and analyses of the four other programs in the multi-site case study led us to conclude that Waterford's experiences were common and not idiographic. Rather we believe that the absence of examination may reflect on the motives that created and sustain the promotional gates program (and others like it). Therein may lie one larger lesson to be drawn from Waterford's story.

Much has been written of loose coupling in educational organizations (Glassman, 1973; Weick, 1976). Meyer and Rowan (1978) interpreted loose coupling as a detachment of technical activity from structure and effects from activity. According to their premise, schools exert strong control over the 'ritual classification of their curriculum, students, and teachers'; yet avoid controlling their 'instructional activities or outputs despite periodic shifts toward accountability' (p. 72). In Waterford, we witnessed tight control over ritual classifications of students. Rules defined students as 'masters' or 'non-masters'; other rules dictated their performance as 'satisfactory', 'questionable', or 'unsatisfactory'; and still others prescribed their fate: 'promote', 'review', or 'retain'. Meyer and Rowan concluded that although clear classifications such as these are routinely made by schools, there are few organizational mechanisms that oversee actual assignments to classifications. Indeed, Waterford had no visible plans by which the district could ensure that students were promoted or retained on the basis of test performance. Just as structure was loosely coupled with activity so too was activity decoupled from its effects. Almost as an afterthought, the district evaluation addressed achievement differences between promoted and retained students, but did so in a limited and convoluted way. In the end, any comparison of achievement gains was rendered meaningless.

Meyer and Rowan contended that the creation and control of ritual classifications, as well as the lack of control over outcomes, serve important functions. The creation of classifications legitimates schools and enables them to mobilize resources. Waterford's promotional gates program was a sign to the public that the schools were raising standards and 'scientizing' promotion practices. No longer would unscientific or social promotion be allowed. Students would be held accountable for their skills and denied promotion should their test performance warrant. As a result, the school district would earn the increased respect and confidence of the community. The image projected by the central administration is preserved by the principals in the buildings and the teachers in the classrooms provided they are given the latitude to exercise a good deal of discretion on who is promoted and who is retained, test performance notwithstanding.

Note

1 The work reported here was conducted under Grant # OERI-G00869003 from the Office of Educational Research and Improvement, US Department of Education, to the Center for Research on Evaluation, Standards, and Student Testing (CRESST), University of California, Los Angeles.

References

ELLWEIN, M. C. and GLASS, G. V (1987) *Standards of Competence: A Multi-site Case Study of Educational Reform*, technical report to OERI, Center for Research on Evaluation, Standards and Student Testing, University of California, Los Angeles.

GLASSMAN, R. B. (1973) 'Persistence and loose coupling in living systems', *Behavioral Sciences*, 18, pp. 83–93.

MEYER, J. W. and ROWAN, B. (1978) 'The structure of educational organizations' in MEYER, M. W. *et al.* (Eds). *Environment and Organizations*, San Francisco, CA, Jossey-Bass.

WEICK, K. (1976) 'Educational organizations as loosely coupled systems' *Administrative Science Quarterly*, 21, March, pp. 1–19.

Chapter 9:
Alternatives to Student Retention: New Images of the Learner, the Teacher and Classroom Learning

Penelope L. Peterson

Editors' Introduction

Penelope Peterson is Co-Director of the Institute for Research on Teaching and Professor of Educational Psychology and Teacher Education at Michigan State University. She is also editor of the Review of Educational Research *and Vice-President of the American Educational Research Association. Peterson is a distinguished researcher who has wedded research on how children learn with research on how teachers teach and ought to be trained as professionals. She was invited to consider the retention research and discuss alternatives.*

Peterson is also a leading authority regarding research on teacher thinking and teacher beliefs; she co-authored the chapter on 'Teacher Thought Processes' in the recent Handbook of Research on Teaching. *In this chapter Peterson uses findings from her own research to argue that teacher beliefs about the learner have powerful effects on educational practices, such as retention or non-retention of students. Although such belief systems are strongly held, teachers can change their beliefs when given access to new information. If teachers believe that children have a great deal of informal knowledge and ability, and see their task as arranging the learning environment to facilitate children's development of knowledge, then it is unlikely that teachers would elect to retain children as unready for learning.*

> Nothing influences learning so much as attitudes and beliefs about what produces it ... Achievement can be torpedoed by the idea that it is mostly a matter of luck, wealth, or native ability — an idea altogether too prevalent in American education today ...

When such hands-in-the-air resignation about achievement is reinforced by school administrators — who ought to know better — our national effort to provide equal intellectual opportunity to all our students is undermined. (William J. Bennett, (U.S. Secretary of Education) (1988) *American Education: Making It Work*, p. 34)

In the above quotation from his progress report on the status of the education reform movement in America, US Secretary of Education, William Bennett, argued persuasively that beliefs about the learner and learning may have profound effects not only on the educational opportunities and learning experiences provided to students in American classrooms, but also, ultimately, on these same students' achievement. Moreover, Bennett suggested that pervasive and deep-seated beliefs about the learner and about learning have seriously impeded the progress of educational reform in our country.

Bennett's statement provides a context within which to discuss the results of the present volume on retention practices in American education. Shepard, Smith and their colleagues have taken a sophisticated, multi-method approach to analyzing the effects of retention practices, the underlying processes that lead to retention or non-retention of students, and the processes that mediate the effects of retention practices on students. More specifically, the authors in this volume have analyzed and assessed evidence from multiple sources using a variety of methodologies to suggest that retention — holding back a child for another year in the same grade — does *not* improve subsequent achievement by that child. Moreover, the authors have provided evidence to suggest potential negative effects of grade retention on social-emotional behaviors, attitudes and self-concepts of the retained children.

Given these negative effects of retention, the researchers then undertook the important task of trying to understand the processes that underlie retention practices. Ellwein and Glass (chapter 8) and Smith (chapter 7) have gathered and analyzed data to address directly the question, 'What determines whether a student is retained or not retained in a grade?'

Understanding the Processes Underlying Retention Practice

Ellwein and Glass described the case of Waterford, a school district that attempted to 'replace the traditional, but politically stigmatized, social promotion system with a new testing program'. In the words of the Superintendent, the goal was to use test data 'as primary information to be considered in decisions about promotion or retention'. Ellwein and Glass examined the relationship between the district's new promotion policy and actual practice. At the end of the study, they concluded that 'test performance and promotion decisions were related asymmetrically. Students who passed the tests were generally promoted, but the fate of those who failed was much less consistent with policy dictates. Some students were retained, many were not ... The point is that no one really knew what happened in Waterford' (Ellwein and Glass, chapter 8).

One way of interpreting the findings of Ellwein and Glass is that all educational policies are mediated through the minds of the individuals who are charged with the responsibility of carrying out the policy. Thus, for example, all changes or reforms in classroom practice must, ultimately, be mediated through the minds of teachers. This perspective is consistent with the notion of reform in educational practice as a 'mind-changing' process as put forth recently by policy researchers. For example, McLaughlin (1987) has suggested that 'organizations don't innovate or implement change, individuals do' (p. 174). This perspective is also consonant with conclusions of researchers who have studied teachers, teaching and classroom practice, and have concluded that previous attempts at reform of curriculum and classroom practices may have failed because reformers attempted to prescribe programs of instruction without taking into account the beliefs and knowledge of the teachers implementing the program (Clark and Peterson, 1986; Romberg and Carpenter, 1986).

In our recent work we have found increasing evidence to suggest that teachers' beliefs and theories of children's learning and their perspectives on the mind of the learner may affect significantly teachers' classroom practice (Peterson, Fennema, Carpenter and Loef, 1988; Carpenter, Fennema, Peterson, Chiang and Loef, 1988; Peterson, Carpenter and Fennema, in press). Similarly, Smith (chapter 7) found that one of the most important variables in whether or not a kindergarten teacher retained a student was not the teacher's beliefs about the efficacy of retention, but rather the teacher's beliefs about learning and development.

Overview of This Chapter

In the discussion that follows, I will use our research to analyze some of the findings on retention practices in the present volume. The purpose of my analysis is four-fold. First, I argue that teachers' beliefs about the learner and about classroom learning have powerful effects not only on their specific classroom practices but also on their more general educational practices, such as retention or non-retention of students. Secondly, I suggest that teachers vary in their images of the learner and that their beliefs about the learner and learning may be strongly held. However, even though teachers' beliefs may be strongly held, teachers do change their beliefs. This leads to the third assertion: that one way for teachers' beliefs to change is as a result of being given access to new knowledge. For example, teachers may change their beliefs significantly by being given access to new research-based knowledge on children's learning even if this knowledge is based on a different image of the learner than they now have. Finally, I argue that what may be needed is a 'new' image of the teacher as knower, learner and thoughtful professional — a person who is able to use new research-based knowledge to inform and change her classroom practice. I conclude by suggesting that if research-based findings, such as those in this volume, are to affect practice, then teachers need to have access to findings, as well as time and opportunity to think through the meaning of research findings for their classroom practice. To provide a counterpoint for our subsequent discussion, I first recall Smith's findings on the relationship between kindergarten teachers' beliefs and their retention practices.

Kindergarten Teachers' Beliefs about Children's Learning

Smith found that what seemed to affect kindergarten teachers' retention practices was their beliefs about children's learning and development or their image of the learner. Based on interviews with forty teachers, she found that nearly all teachers tended to agree about the efficacy of retention. However, teachers differed in their frequency of retention of children. Subsequently, she classified teachers into groups of high-retaining teachers — those who retained 10 per cent or more of their kindergartners — and low-retaining teachers — those who retained fewer than 10 per cent of their kindergartners. When she did this, she found a significant relationship between teachers' beliefs about children's learning and teachers' retention practices. Sixteen of the nineteen high-retaining teachers were 'nativists' in their theories of development. According to these teachers' theories, the pupil's development proceeds according to an evolutionary, physiological unfolding of abilities. Nativist teachers viewed this unfolding process as largely outside the influence of teachers or parents. Thus, they probably held back or retained children in kindergarten because they perceived that these children were not physiologically ready for first grade. In contrast, only three of twenty-one low-retaining teachers were nativists. The remaining low-retaining teachers were non-nativists. These teachers were more likely to promote the child to the next grade, probably because they believed that the teacher in the next grade could influence the child's learning and development by remedial teaching, diagnosing and correcting the child's deficient skills, or by arranging the learning environment to adapt to the child's developmental level.

Old and New Images of the Learner

Although no systematic data exist on the prevalence of a 'nativist' theory among teachers in general, this conception of the learner may have long been part of the 'scientific knowledge base' that has been passed on to teachers. For example, I found such a view espoused a century ago in a book entitled *The Science of Education*, written in September 1887, by Dr Francis B. Palmer. At that time, Palmer was Principal of the State Normal School at Fredonia, New York and he designed his book 'as a text-book for teachers'. In the following quotation, Palmer described the mind of the learner:

> The notion attributed to some early philosophers that the mind possesses ideas as an inheritance or by virtue of its constitution must be regarded as satisfactorily disproved by Locke; but the notion which he substituted for it, that the untrained mind is like a piece of blank paper must certainly be rejected. There are no more ideas in the undeveloped mind than expressions of thought on a piece of white paper; but the ideas that may be developed in the mind are not subject so absolutely to the will of the teacher as the writing on paper is subject to the will of the writer. The teacher should first of all rise to the conception of the mind he seeks to develop as possessing an energy capable of developing only into certain fixed and definite forms of action, and in accordance with fixed laws, and should learn that to attempt to put other things there, or to develop the energy regardless of the mental laws is futile. Native Energy exists under certain well-defined Laws (Palmer, 1887, p. 45).

Alternatives to Student Retention

Palmer suggested nativist beliefs about the learner similar to the beliefs expressed by the kindergarten teachers that Smith interviewed. Palmer also discussed several laws reflecting a conception of the learning process that is also probably held by many teachers today. Palmer engaged in what might be called 'anticipatory plagiarism' of Benjamin Bloom and others' (1956) ideas by suggesting that cognitive learning proceeds from mastery of lower-order facts to higher-order reasoning and problem solving. As Palmer put it:

The mind must possess:
(1) Facts before principles and abstractions.
(2) Examples before precepts.
(3) Methods before reasons. (Palmer, 1887, p. 73)

According to this conception, the learner must first 'master' basic skills. Another prevalent conception that seems to abide side-by-side with the mastery-learning model is the belief that the mind of the learner is like an 'empty vessel'. Recently, I heard a Superintendent of Schools portray learners as 'empty vessels' into which the teacher 'pours' knowledge. He argued that differences between learners might be likened to differences in capacities between vessels with each capacity being more or less fixed and thus, outside the control of the teacher.

How might these conceptions of learning and the learner underlie the approach to standard-setting for retention or promotion that was taken in the Waterford school district (see Ellwein and Glass, chapter 8)? The Waterford school district sent letters to teachers asking them to judge each of their students as a 'master' or 'non-master' of the skills measured on the criterion-referenced test. The school district defined 'a master' as 'a student who knows enough of the basic skills in this area that if you [the teacher] had to make a decision about promotion or retention solely on this skill level as it will be measured by this test at this time, you [the teacher] would elect to promote the student' (p. 158). Retentions in Waterford were then accompanied by remedial skills programs.

It is unclear how the teachers in the Waterford study used the test information or their own knowledge of and beliefs about the learner to make the actual decisions about promotion or retention of their students. However, given the prevalence of 'nativist' conceptions of the learner, as well as 'basic skills' conceptions of learning, it is plausible that many teachers held these views and that these beliefs influenced their retention practices. The finding that disproportionate numbers of boys and minority children were held back, far in excess of the test-recommended proportions (p. 168), is consistent with the claim that these viewpoints mediated teachers' decisions.

In sum, certain dominant images of the learner and learning may be significantly related to teachers' retention practices. These include a 'nativist' conception of the learner such that teachers believe that they must hold the learner back until the learner has matured enough or is developmentally ready to go on. However, another idea is that the learner must acquire or learn 'basic facts' before the learner is able to go and master other skills and engage in 'higher-order' thinking and problem solving. Both these conceptions of the learner seem to be strongly related to the notion of holding the student back. In contrast, the research-based evidence in this volume suggests that retention or holding students back is *not* positively related to students' later learning and achievement. Thus, the question arises, 'What might be an alternative image of the learner based on recent research that would suggest alternatives to retention, particularly in kindergarten?' This view of the learner might also reflect an alternative view of children's learning and classroom practice that would involve changes in the kinds of learning and teaching prevalent in many elementary classrooms today. I turn now to a consideration of this question.

Alternative Images of the Learner and Learning

A new cognitive conception of the learner and learning is gaining increasing acceptance among researchers in cognition and instruction. This image is based on the idea that minds actively construct knowledge. This idea has an established basis in recent and current psychological research in cognition and instruction (see, for example, Glaser, 1984; Resnick, 1985).

A major lesson that might be extrapolated from recent theory and research on cognition and instruction has to do with learning and teaching the 'basics' in reading and mathematics. In the past, most teaching of the basics has rested on the assumption, derived primarily from task analyses and behavioral psychology, that students must learn the 'lower-order' facts and skills before being able to master 'higher-order' problem solving and application skills. A common metaphor is that the mind of the learner is like a tower of building blocks in which the foundation must be built before higher-level 'blocks' can be added. In contrast, recent theory and research from cognitive psychology suggest that a better metaphor is that knowledge is stored in the learner's head as a network of concepts or constructs and thus, the mind of the learner is like a 'tinker toy'. Learning involves the making of connections between the learner's existing network of knowledge and the new information to be learned. Instruction should facilitate these connections and the process of education might be defined as the construction of knowledge by the learner.

In a network theory of cognition and learning, the concepts of 'lower' and 'higher' order learning may not make sense. For example, computational skills may not exist as lower-order prerequisites for higher-order mathematical problem solving, but rather are learned in relation to, and as part of, the problem solving activity (see, for example, Resnick, 1985; Lampert, 1986). Similarly, as Resnick (1985) has pointed out, ample evidence exists that both 'top-down' and 'bottom-up' processes are involved in reading. The important point is that new information to be learned and taught needs to be related in a meaningful way to knowledge and information that the learner already knows. In a recent article, Ginsburg and Yamamoto (1986) summarized implications for classroom practice in mathematics education as follows:

> Much of mathematics education, particularly teaching the 'basics' usually takes a much different form, namely drilling students in calculational routines or number facts, or devising clever techniques, perhaps based on task analysis, to teach these topics. Teaching the basics usually deals in an isolated way with formal procedures and concepts separately, and ignores informational knowledge ... this is a misguided approach based on empty vessel theory that children know nothing of mathematics when they begin its formal study. But this is not true. Even before the onset of schooling, children possess abundant 'natural resources' in this area ... The educational paradox and dilemma are that children often fail to connect what they already know with what is taught in school. Hence, teaching the basics should involve tapping children's informal knowledge and encouraging its connection with various aspects of formal mathematics. We think that most children failing in school could succeed if only they were encouraged to use their natural 'intelligence' (i.e., their information knowledge) to deal with material that is, after all, not highly complex. (p. 364)

Although Ginsburg and Yamamoto applied the above argument to mathematics education, such an argument applies equally well to teaching the basics in reading (see, for example, Anderson *et al.*, 1985). Recent theory and research suggest that students benefit from instructional practices that relate new knowledge in a meaningful way to the knowledge that they have already developed. This means, for example, that reading should always be taught with a basis in meaning (for example, Anderson *et al.*, 1985; Applebee, Langer and Mullis, 1988) and that mathematics computation should be taught in the context of real-world problem solving (for example, Resnick, 1985; Carpenter, Fennema and Peterson, 1984).

In the following discussion, I use the case of learning and teaching of addition and subtraction in first-grade mathematics to illustrate the implications of this cognitive-constructivist conception of mathematics learning for thinking about children's learning and teachers' teaching of addition and subtraction in first-grade. This analysis may serve as a framework within which to think about kindergarten retention practices as described in this volume. For example, one might consider first, how this alternative conception of the first-grade child's learning of mathematics differs from the conception of the learner that seems to underlie the retention of a child in kindergarten because 'he or she is not ready to go on to learn first-grade mathematics'. Second, one might think about how this alternative conception of the learning-teaching process of first-grade mathematics might differ from the teaching of mathematics in the first-grade classrooms in schools that served as samples of kindergarten retention practices in this volume.

An Emerging Cognitive-Constructivist Conception of the Learner in Mathematics

In the early 1980s researchers in cognition and instruction and mathematics education discovered through interviewing young children that even before receiving formal instruction, most young children can successfully solve addition and subtraction word problems (see, for example, Carpenter and Moser, 1983; Riley, Greeno and Heller, 1983). For example, Starkey and Gelman (1982) showed that young 3-year old children who could count to five were able to solve a problem such as, 'Judy has two marbles. Her mommy gives her one more. How many marbles does Judy have now?' Even before kindergarten, when young children are given word problems or story problems, they use their informal knowledge to invent strategies for solving the addition and subtraction problem. These strategies have a clear relationship to the type of problem children are solving.

Children's Informal Knowledge of Mathematics

When young children first begin to solve addition and subtraction word problems, they are limited in their thinking about the problem to creating a direct concrete representation of the problem. For example, they use their fingers, physical objects, or counters to represent each quantity and the problem, and they can represent only the specific action or relationship described in the problem. For example, suppose a kindergarten child were given the following problem, 'Melissa has three cookies, how many more does she need to have six cookies altogether?' To solve this problem, the child might use counters to make a set of three objects, add more objects until she had a total of six objects, and then count the number of objects she had added. Through interviewing children and studying how they talk about problems, researchers found that children's problem solving strategies become increasingly abstract as they are able to engage in more abstract thinking and cognitions. Children begin to use more advanced counting strategies like 'counting on' or 'counting back'. For example, to solve the cookie problem above, the child might use a 'counting on' strategy if she recognized that it was not necessary to construct the first set of three objects. Thus, the child might simply count on from three to six by keeping track of the number of counts either on her fingers or with objects.

Children's Invented Mathematics Strategies

Eventually children memorize number facts that help them solve word problems or story problems. However, researchers have shown that children learn and memorize number facts over an extended period of time rather than all at once. Furthermore, children use number facts that they have memorized along with counting strategies when they do not have certain number facts memorized. Children learn some number facts earlier than others, such as doubles like $5 + 5 = 10$. Until they have memorized all the addition facts, many children use a small set of memorized facts to 'derive' other solutions for problems that have no other number combinations. The following protocol illustrates children's use of 'derived facts' to solve a word problem presented by the teacher:

Teacher: Six frogs were sitting on lily pads. Eight more frogs joined them. How many frogs are there then?
Rudy, Denise, Theo and Sandra each answer: '14' almost immediately.
Teacher: How do you know there were 14?
Rudy: Because 6 and 6 is 12, and 2 more is 14.
Denise: Eight and 8 is 16. But this is 8 and 6. That is 2 less, so it's 14.
Theo: Well, I took 1 from the 8 and gave it to the 6. That made 7 and 7, and that's 14.
Sandra: Eight and 2 more is 10, and 4 more is 14.

(From the *Cognitively Guided Instruction Project*, Carpenter, Fennema and Peterson, 1987).

Researchers have shown that most children, not just bright children, figure out that new facts can be derived from the memorized facts they have learned. These derived facts play an important part in children's thinking and cognitions as they solve addition and subtraction word problems.

In summary, researchers have documented that when children enter school, almost all children can solve simple addition and subtraction word problems by directly modeling the problem or by representing the problem. Many children are using more advanced strategies. Even without explicit instruction, children discover the basic strategies above, and even with instruction that emphasizes symbolic manipulation, children continue to rely directly on their strategies for representing the problem and on counting to solve problems. Children's strategies for solving addition and subtraction problems become increasingly abstract. Initially, children solve these problems by modeling them; but eventually they move on first to using more advanced counting strategies; then to deriving or inventing number facts from the facts they have memorized. And finally, children have number facts memorized up to $10 + 10 = 20$ and $19 - 10 = 9$.

Implications for Teaching First-grade Mathematics

One implication of the above findings is that children's informal knowledge might provide a basis for the child to develop mathematics concepts and computational skills and to learn mathematics with understanding. However, first-grade mathematics curriculum and traditional methods of teaching of addition and subtraction fail to build systematically on children's informal knowledge or support its development. Moreover, first-grade teachers may not have this awareness of children's knowledge and thinking in mathematics. Teachers' beliefs may not be consonant with the above cognitive-constructivist conception of the learner derived from recent theory and research; and teachers' teaching of addition and subtraction classroom practice may not reflect such a conception. With my colleagues Thomas Carpenter and Elizabeth Fennema, at the University of Wisconsin-Madison, I have been involved in a study in which we attempted to determine first, the extent to which first-grade teachers' knowledge and conceptions reflected those of the recent research and findings on children's learning of addition and subtraction described above, and second, whether giving teachers access to recent knowledge and research findings on children's mathematics learning of addition and subtraction would facilitate teachers' changing their knowledge and conceptions of children's mathematics learning.

A Cognitive-Constructivist Conception of the Learner and Classroom Learning

This new conception of the learner and classroom learning, and its possible relationship to classroom practice, can be represented by the following four assumptions in teaching elementary mathematics (see Peterson, Fennema, Carpenter and Loef, 1989):

1 Children construct their own mathematical knowledge.
2 Mathematics instruction should be organized to facilitate children's construction of knowledge.
3 Children's development of mathematical ideas should provide the basis for sequencing topics in instruction.
4 Mathematical skills, such as computation and memorization of number facts, should be taught in relation to understanding and problem solving in mathematics.

One's agreement or disagreement with each or any of the above statements implies not only a conception of the mind of the learner but also a related conception of classroom practice. For example, agreement with the first three assumptions would imply a view of the teacher and the learner as actively engaged with one another in constructing mathematical knowledge and understanding. A teacher who disagrees might believe instead that it is the teacher's role to organize and present mathematical knowledge; and it is the child's role to receive the mathematical knowledge presented by the teacher (Peterson et al., 1989).

The Prevalence of Cognitive-Constructivist Conceptions of the Learner among First-Grade Teachers

An important question becomes, 'How prevalent is a cognitive-constructivist conception of the learner among first-grade teachers who are now teaching compared to other more traditional conceptions of the learner?' Recently, we examined the extent to which forty first-grade teachers agreed with the cognitive-based perspective reflected in the above four assumptions. (For a complete description of this study, see Peterson et al., 1989.) Our results showed that the first-grade teachers in our small sample varied significantly in the extent to which they agreed with the above assumptions, with some teachers endorsing the cognitive-based perspective more than others. These differences in the extent to which teachers' beliefs corresponded to a cognitively-based perspective related to their knowledge of specific mathematics content, to their knowledge of individual children's thinking strategies, to the kind and the quality of the mathematics content and strategies that the teachers reported using, and to their goals for students' classroom learning in addition and subtraction. Thus, for example, more cognitively-based teachers emphasized problem solving as the highest priority in their teaching and classroom practice. They assumed that students' learning of computational skills and memorization of number facts would follow from the teaching of problem solving. In contrast, the less cognitively-based teachers emphasized number fact knowledge and computational skills, and assumed that they would teach problem solving only *after* their students had learned basic number facts in addition and subtraction. Further, teachers' underlying beliefs and conceptions of learning were related to their conceptions of the role of the teacher and the learner. For example, the more cognitively-based teachers saw the role of the learner as an active one, engaged with the teacher in the construction of knowledge. As one such teacher put it:

> ... like the teacher also has to be the learner. She has to pay attention to where the kids are, learn from where they are, and dictate what her next step is because there are a lot of different

learners and learners' styles. I guess learners must be actively involved in doing work and think about what they are doing and verbalizing what they are doing. (Peterson *et al.*, 1989 p. 31).

Relationship of Cognitive-Constructivist Conceptions to Student Achievement

One of the most significant findings from our initial study of teachers' beliefs was the finding that teachers' conceptions were related to their students' mathematics achievement. We assessed students' achievement using a test of twenty addition and subtraction computation items involving basic number facts and a problem solving test consisting of seventeen word problems in addition and subtraction. We found that teachers who were more cognitively-based in their beliefs tended to have children who were higher in word problem solving ability in addition and subtraction than did teachers who were less cognitively-based in their beliefs. However, teachers' beliefs were unrelated to their students' achievement of computational skills and knowledge of number facts in addition and subtraction. The differences in problem solving achievement seemed to be related to cognitively-based teachers' emphases on word problems as a basis for introducing addition and subtraction, and to their reported emphases on word problem solving throughout the year. Interestingly, when compared to less cognitively-based teachers, the cognitively-based teachers reported placing least emphasis on students' learning of addition and subtraction number facts and computation and relatively greater emphasis on students' word problem solving and understanding.

Although our findings for the relationship between teachers' beliefs and their students' achievement were only correlational, they suggested the possibility that students in cognitively-based teachers' classes were able to master computational skills and memorize number facts concurrently with their development of problem solving skills. Moreover, their students may have mastered number facts as well as the students in the less cognitively-based teachers' classes even though the latter teachers placed greater emphasis on mastery of computational skills. Thus, these findings suggested the possibility of a cause-effect relationship between teachers' cognitively-based conceptions of the learner, their classroom practice in teaching mathematics, and their students' problem solving and computational achievement in mathematics.

P. L. Peterson

An Experimental Study of Cognitive Conceptions of Learning and Classroom Practice

The possibility of a cause-effect relationship was addressed in an experimental study. Our purpose was to determine whether giving teachers access to research-based knowledge on children's mathematics learning would change teachers' conceptions of learning and make a difference in their classroom practices and subsequent student achievement.

Twenty teachers were assigned randomly to an experimental group — the Cognitively-Guided Instruction (CGI) group — and twenty to a control group. Experimental teachers participated in a four-week summer workshop where we gave them access to recent findings on children's learning, cognition, and problem solving in addition and subtraction. We did not train experimental teachers in specific techniques for altering their classroom instruction. Rather, we provided information and worked with them as 'thoughtful professionals', who construct their own knowledge and understanding. (For a complete description of this study see Carpenter, Fennema, Peterson, Chiang and Loef, 1988.)

As a result of the workshop, CGI teachers' measured knowledge was enhanced and their reported beliefs were more closely aligned with the four cognitive-constructivist assumptions above. In addition, data from systematic observations throughout the next school year indicated that CGI teachers changed their instructional practices and curricula in addition and subtraction. CGI teachers organized their instruction around word problems and often began the lesson by telling a story and posing word problems for the children to solve. Observational data showed that CGI teachers spent more time interacting with students on story problems and expected them to use multiple strategies. In contrast, control teachers had more of their interactions and student time engaged in number fact and computation learning.

The Iowa Test of Basic Skills (ITBS) and an experimenter-constructed word problem solving test were used to assess student learning, with appropriate statistical controls for any pre-test differences. Compared to students in control teachers' classes, students in CGI teachers' classes showed significantly greater ability to solve addition and subtraction word problems, particularly complex word problems. There was also a significant aptitude-treatment interaction (ATI) whereby CGI classrooms that were lowest on the pre-test showed the greatest advantage over controls. In addition, students in CGI classes were more confident of their ability to solve word problems and reported significantly greater understanding of mathematics than did control students. Finally, despite the observation that control teachers spent significantly *more time* on number facts, the students in CGI teachers' classes did as well as students in control teachers' classes on a computation test, and CGI students *actually did better* in their ability to recall number facts.

From our interview data we have evidence to suggest that teachers might have changed not only their conceptions of learning and expectations for children's mathematics achievement but also their conceptions of their own mathematics learning and abilities to teach mathematics with understanding. This hypothesis is supported by the words of one CGI teacher who, at the end of the study, was the second highest of the twenty teachers in having beliefs that were the most closely congruent with the cognitively-based perspective. Her beliefs at the beginning of the study provide a contrast to those she held at the end of the study.

Before the study began, teacher M was asked what kinds of word problems she had her children solve. In response to this question, she mentioned only one kind of problem — the kind that could be solved by answering the question, 'How many do you have altogether?' This kind of word problem is one of two types of problems that typically appear as story problems in first-grade mathematics textbooks. In order to solve this type of problem, teacher M said that she would teach her children to focus on the word 'altogether' and what the word means. Interestingly, mathematics educators as well as cognitive researchers have sharply criticized this 'key-word' approach because it focuses on a 'mindless' or rote approach to problem solving rather than on conceptional understanding of the problem (see, for example, Ginsburg and Yamamoto, 1986; Schoenfeld, 1982). When asked why she had children learn to solve that kind of word problem in addition and subtraction, teacher M replied:

> Because I didn't learn to solve them, and word problems are always hard for me. It was like, 'How do you even attack a problem like this?'

In contrast, a year later, at the end of the study, teacher M was again asked, 'Are there certain kinds of word problems that you deal with in addition and you believe all children should learn to solve?' In response she replied:

> They should learn how to solve all of them ... Um, you know, I would like all my kids to be able to, if I throw out any problems, say, 'Okay, I'm going to tackle it.' You know, not throw up their hands and say, 'I can't do it.'

In a follow-up question, teacher M was asked why she decided that these kinds of word problems were important for all children in her class to learn to solve. In a revealing statement she admitted:

> I think that going through the workshop last summer helped, because I had never done these kinds of problems in my life, and again, it was exposure and what kids could do with it.

Teacher M's words illustrate not only the interrelationship between teachers' beliefs and knowledge, and the effect of the workshop and the subsequent year of CGI teaching on a teacher's beliefs and knowledge, but also the empowering effects of access to knowledge and construction of knowledge by teachers.

The Interconnectedness of Teachers' Beliefs and Their Knowledge of Children's Abilities

We also found that CGI teachers' knowledge of their children's problem solving abilities was related to their beliefs and to their children's problem solving achievement. Why might this be the case? Perhaps CGI teachers who believed that students construct knowledge and that mathematics instruction should be organized to facilitate student's construction of knowledge also realized that they needed knowledge of students' problem solving abilities in order to plan and organize appropriate instructional activities for these students and to adapt instruction for them. Also, it might simply be the case that an important interconnection existed between teachers' knowledge and awareness of students' informal knowledge, the development of teachers' knowledge of children's problem solving abilities, and teachers' beliefs.

The following example is of a teacher who was the second most knowledgeable teacher in her ability to predict accurately individual students' knowledge and abilities to solve addition and subtraction word problems. Her words suggest an awareness that children have a lot of knowledge when they come into first-grade and that children actively construct knowledge in the process of learning addition and subtraction. When asked at the end of the year to 'describe the knowledge that the children in your classroom had about addition and subtraction when they started the school year', this teacher replied:

> It was all their own, basically. They had their own ideas of ways to solve the problems. They came from just a vast well. I think I counted 8 different ways that they solved the basic addition problem. It wasn't presented as a basic addition problem, but it was that. And they were generating their own concept of addition through their own past experiences.

When asked, 'Where do children get this knowledge?', the teacher continued:

> They come up with it, that's all. It's just something that we [teachers] have to be aware of and almost have to try to fit their whole thought patterns into our scheme of the way we teach, and the way that we are going to formulate some of the roles of the concrete that we expect. So, they [children] gain it from all the different experiences that they have prior to classroom experience.

This teacher's cognitive-constructivist view of the learner was also reflected in her response to the question, 'What do you think the role of the teacher should be in introducing addition to first graders?'

> I really hope that, initially, you're getting kids to find as many different ways to come up with an answer and be able to share that information without having all the modeling done for them initially. So that this whole idea of developing your own style and the way you go about solving a math problem is O.K.; and then building on the ways that children solve math problems. There are some real efficient ways; there are some ways to go about solving the problem by looking at relationships. They'll (the children) come up with them (those ways); and they'll generate those kinds of things so the teacher is facilitative more than a 'direct' teacher.

Using Research-Based Knowledge to Think about Retention Practices

Although we did not address directly the question of retention or promotion of kindergarten children in our study of first-grade mathematics teaching, I would like to speculate on how our findings might be relevant for the issues and questions addressed in this volume. We did not ask our CGI teachers whether any children who entered their classes at the beginning of the year should have been retained in kindergarten. However, if we *had* asked this question at the end of the year, I predict that most, if not all, CGI teachers would have replied that few or no children should have been retained in kindergarten. To put it another way, a typical CGI teacher probably would have stated that all children entered her class with the ability to learn mathematics with understanding. Indeed, CGI teachers came to believe that all children had a great deal of informal knowledge and abilities to solve word problems in addition and subtraction before these children entered first-grade and even before these children received any formal mathematics instruction. Our first-grade CGI teachers came to know and believe this because they had tested it out by asking their children individually and in groups to solve addition and subtraction word problems. These teachers found that, indeed, just as cognitive researchers had found, children *did* have a great amount of informal knowledge and abilities to solve word problems. As teacher M put it at the end of the year:

> Some first-graders don't need to be introduced to addition. I think teachers do kids injustice when they drill on things that children already know, because they (children) get bored. I found my kids a lot more exciting. I was more excited, and I tried to give things to them, and really listened to them. Before the holidays, one kid said '5 × 5 is 25 take away 20 is 5', and my mouth dropped open. And I said, 'Oh, they are ready for multiplication'. And not everybody was, but some kids were. So then it was my challenge to find out which kids were ready for it.

Thus, the challenge for the teacher became one of accessing and diagnosing the knowledge and abilities of the children to solve problems and then organizing and arranging the learning environment and learning activities to facilitate children's development of that knowledge. The teacher's goal was for students to learn mathematics with understanding and for the learning of mathematics facts and skills to be meaningfully related to the solving of mathematics problems. The findings from our study also highlight that the goal of learning mathematics with understanding is an important one that needs to be addressed. As teacher M put it:

It's embarrassing when people give you change. You know, I've gone to places, and these young teen-agers will give you change and have absolutely no idea if they are right or wrong. That's because they've learned math the wrong way. It's not that they have to be accurate 100 per cent of the time, but that they have a 'feel' that they are in the right ball park. There are certain concepts that kids should learn and feel good about ... Like if you add 0 to any number, that's going to give you the same number. [People should be able to say to themselves] 'Yes, I know this about numbers.' 'that this will happen to numbers'. and be able to build on what they know. I think some people don't have that confidence. I guess that's what I want to relate to my kids — that you know this now. You can build upon what you know.

Asking the Question: What Is Possible?

In addition to altering teachers' thinking about mathematics, teachers' goals for mathematics instruction, as well as teachers' knowledge and beliefs about the learner, the results of our study suggest that teachers went from asking the question, 'What is probable?' to asking, 'What is possible?' For example, I have reported on teacher M's reactions at the end of our study the first year. Teacher M continued the second year to use her cognitively-based approach to the teaching and learning of addition and subtraction in her first-grade classroom. In the course of the school year, she not only deepened her knowledge and understanding but also developed further her classroom teaching and instruction into a problem-based approach in which she truly allowed her students to construct their mathematics with understanding (see the case studies by Carpenter, Fennema and Loef, in preparation).

Although teacher M had a first-grade class with children who differed significantly in their entering abilities and knowledge of addition and subtraction at the beginning of the year, the types of problems that her children were able to solve during the year astonished not only herself, but others as well. For example, in April of the year, teacher M's first-graders solved the following problem:

There are fifty-five children on a school bus. Three-fifths of the children like chocolate chip cookies, and two-fifths of the children don't like chocolate chip cookies. How many children don't like chocolate chip cookies?

The children in teacher M's class solved this problem by constructing their own concrete representations (sets of objects) to solve the problem. The teacher and class did the problem together with the classroom discourse focusing on children's strategies for representing and solving the problem. A graduate assistant interviewed approximately half of the students in the class afterwards and found that approximately eleven of these twelve students were able to solve a similar problem readily. Those not familiar with the typical content of first-grade mathematics may not be surprised that first-graders in April of the school year were able to solve such a problem. These skeptics might be interested to know that the assistant later presented the same problem to a class of sixth-graders in the same school. The sixth-graders told the assistant that they didn't think they would be able to solve the problem because it was too hard. Subsequently, the sixth-grade students visited teacher M's classroom and worked with the first-graders to learn how to solve the problem.

Other Cognitive-Constructivist Approaches to Classroom Learning

Although I have focused on a specific study as an illustration of this new alternative conception of the learner and learning, such cognitive-constructivist approaches to classroom learning are currently the focus of study not only in mathematics, but in other subject areas as well, including reading (for example, Palincsar and Brown, in press), writing (for example, Florio-Ruane and Lensmire, in press; Scardamalia and Bereiter, 1986; Englert and Raphael, in press) and science (Anderson and Roth, in press). In mathematics, attainment of the curriculum goals set forth for students across grades K-12 by the National Council for Teachers of Mathematics seems to require serious consideration of recent cognitive theories of the learner and of mathematics teaching and learning (see, for example, Zarinnia, Lamon and Romberg, 1987). Moreover, other studies like our study are currently underway to examine the relationship between teachers' cognitive conceptions of mathematics learning and children's learning of mathematics with understanding.

Researchers are studying teachers' knowledge, beliefs and their related classroom practices and teachers' attempts to teach mathematics meaningfully and to facilitate students' active construction of mathematics with understanding (see, for example, Lampert, 1988; Cobb, Yackel and Wood, in press). Lampert (1987) has reported working with a group of teachers in a 'study group' in mathematics problem solving. In many of her vignettes of teachers, she reports changes in teachers' beliefs and knowledge about mathematics and the learning of mathematics and changes in teachers' own mathematics knowledge as well as in their children's knowledge of mathematics and children's construction of mathematical knowledge. The 'new' conceptions of Lampert's teachers showed some striking similarities to those of our CGI teachers. As the result of interacting with teachers in the solving of word problems, Lampert (1987) reported that teachers changed their ideas on the following: (i) what it means to know 'subtraction'; (ii) connecting teaching with the meaning of knowing; (iii) conceptualizing the standards for deciding whether students are learning what they are supposed to be learning away from a traditional belief that 'knowing mathematics' can be measured by whether students follow the rules for proceeding through the conventional arithmetic algorithm; (iv) a new conception of 'listening' to students' mathematics thinking; and (v) conceptualizing math as 'figuring things out' vs. math as 'getting things done'. These findings as well as those of others who have studied teachers' thinking and decision making (Clark and Peterson, 1986; Peterson, 1988b) suggest an emerging image of the teacher similar to the new image of the learner described above.

An Image of the Teacher as Knower, Learner and Thoughtful Professional

The new image of the teacher portrays the teacher as knower, learner, and thoughtful professional and thus highlights several important dimensions (Peterson, 1988b). First, the thoughtful teacher is engaged continuously in the process of learning and 'coming to know'. Because she is herself immersed in higher-level learning and thinking, she inspires and facilitates this kind of meaningful learning, thinking and construction of knowledge in her students. Second, this image of the teacher depicts the teacher in terms of the kind and quality of the thinking, learning, decision making and judgment in which she engages, not just in terms of her behavioral competencies. Third, this conception of the teacher suggests that teachers' thoughts, knowledge, beliefs and decisions will have a profound effect on teachers' classroom practices as well as on their students' classroom learning and achievement. Thus, teachers' knowledge, thinking, decision making, and beliefs become important determinants of classroom practice. Finally, such an image of the teacher assumes that for any changes in classroom practice to occur they must, ultimately, be mediated through the minds of teachers. Thus, reforms of classroom practice depend on teachers, educators, administrators, and policy makers taking seriously the centrality of teachers' professional knowledge, in attempting to implement education reform.

This view of the teacher as thoughtful professional also seems to underlie the vision of the teacher put forth in the Carnegie Commission's Task Force Report on Teaching as a Profession (1986) in which the Commission called for a focus on the teacher as a key to educational reform. As the Commission put it:

> Teachers must think for themselves if they are able to help others think for themselves, be able to act independently and collaborate with others, and render critical judgment. They must be people whose knowledge is wide-ranging and whose understanding runs deep ... they must be able to learn all the time ... teachers will not come to school knowing all that they have to know, but knowing how to figure out what they need to know, where to get it, and how to help others make meaning out of it (Carnegie Commission, 1986, p. 25).

These words suggest that for education reform to occur in classroom practice, teachers' 'minds' must be actively engaged in reform efforts and teachers' knowledge, beliefs, learning, and thinking must be considered.

Conclusion

In a recent paper, I argued that construction of knowledge and access to new knowledge may serve as foundations for a new reform both at the level of a classroom — in teaching and classroom practice — as well as at the level of the school (Peterson, 1988a). These ideas are derived not only from our CGI model and research, but also from the image of 'adventurous teaching' and approaches to classroom practice premised on construction of knowledge by the teacher and the learner (see, for example, Cohen, 1987a and 1987b). These ideas are also consistent with the notion of reform in educational practice as a 'mind-changing' process put forth recently by policy researchers such as McLaughlin (1987) and Elmore and McLaughlin (1988). Such a model implies an image of the teacher as knower, learner, and thoughtful professional.

Following from such a model, an interesting study would be to investigate exactly how teachers 'make sense' of the findings and interpretations presented in this volume. Possible questions include: What beliefs about learning, such as the building-block model, support retention practices? Why is retention-research counterintuitive? Is social promotion the only alternative to retention? What conditions must exist to support effective non-retention practices? Such a study follows from the model that we used in working with CGI teachers. The model was one of providing teachers with access to research findings and working with teachers in a collaborative mode as thoughtful professionals. Similar approaches are now being tried by others (for example, Clark, 1988).

A lively debate is now going on among teacher educators and researchers about the assumptions and processes of teacher education and the translation of research findings into educational practice by researchers working with teachers and teacher educators. The debate involves whether research should result in rules or prescriptions that are then given to teachers and teacher educators for implementation, or whether the translation of research findings into practice should involve thoughtful discussions and analyses of research findings between researchers and practitioners (see, for example, Berliner, 1987; Clark, 1988; Brophy, 1988). In discussing the relationship between educational research and educational practice, more and more educational researchers from a wide variety of perspectives including researchers on teaching, teacher education, and policy, seem to be concurring with the sentiments expressed by William James when he talked to teachers more than 100 years ago about the relationship between science and practice:

> You make a great, a very great mistake, if you think that psychology, being the science of mind's laws, is something from which you can deduce definite programmes and schemes and methods of instruction for immediate school-room use. Psychology is a science, and teaching is an art; and sciences never generate arts directly out of themselves. An intermediary inventive mind must make the application, by using its originality. (James, 1900, p. 15)

The present volume presents an important challenge for researchers who work with practitioners to study and determine how 'inventive minds' make the application of these findings on grade retention to educational practice. Such a study would inform our understanding of the relationship between research, policy, and practice not only on the specific topic of retention policies and practices discussed in the present

P. L. Peterson

volume but also on larger issues of education reform, currently being discussed at the state and local levels.

Notes

1   Work on this chapter was in part supported by the Center for Policy Research in Education (CPRE) which is funded by a grant from the US Department of Education, Office of Educational Research and Improvement (Grant No. OERI-G-008690011). The views expressed in this chapter are those of the individual author and are not necessarily shared by the US Department of Education, Rutgers University, Michigan State University, the University of Wisconsin-Madison or Stanford University. Some research reported in this chapter was supported by a grant from the National Science Foundation (Grant No. MDR-8550236) to Drs. Elizabeth Fennema, Thomas Carpenter and Penelope Peterson through the Wisconsin Center for Education Research at the University of Wisconsin-Madison. Opinions expressed in this chapter do not necessarily reflect those of the co-principal investigators or the National Science Foundation.

References

ANDERSON, A. and ROTH, K. (in press) 'Teaching for meaningful and self-regulated learning of science', in BROPHY, J. E. (Ed.) *Advances in Research on Teaching, Volume 1*, Greenwich, CT, JAI Press, Inc.

ANDERSON, R. C., HIEBERT, E. H., SCOTT, J. A. and WILKINSON, I. A. G. (1985) *Becoming a Nation of Readers: The Report of the Commission on Reading*, Washington, DC, National Institute of Education, US Department of Education.

APPLEBEE, A., LANGER, L. and MULLIS (1988) *Who Reads Best?* Princeton, NJ, Educational Testing Service.

BENNETT, W. J. (1988) *American Education: Making It Work*. Washington, D.C., US Department of Education.

BERLINER, D. C. (1987) 'Knowledge is power: A talk to teachers about a revolution in the teaching profession', in BERLINER, D. C. and ROSENSHINE, B. V. (Eds). *Talks to Teachers*, New York, Random House.

BLOOM, B., ENGLEHART, M., FURST, E., HILL, W. S. and KRATHWOHL, D. (1956) *Taxonomy of Educational Objectives: The Classification of Educational Goals, Handbook 1: Cognitive Domain*, New York, Longmans Green.

BROPHY, J. E. (in press) 'The uses and abuses of research on teacher effects', *Elementary School Journal*.

CARPENTER, T. C., FENNEMA, E. and LOEF, M. (in preparation) *Case studies of Cognitively-Guided Instruction*, Madison, WI, Wisconsin Center for Education Research.
CARPENTER, T. P., FENNEMA, E. and PETERSON, P. L. (1984) *Cognitively Guided Instruction: Studies of the Application of Cognitive and Instructional Science to Mathematics Curriculum* (proposal funded by the National Science Foundation, Washington, D.C.) Madison, WI, Wisconsin Center for Educational Research.
CARPENTER, T. P., FENNEMA, E., PETERSON, P. L., CHIANG, C. and LOEF, M. (1988) 'Using knowledge of childrens' mathematics thinking in classroom teaching: An experimental study', paper presented at the annual meeting of the American Educational Research Association, New Orleans, April.
CLARK, C. M. (1988) 'Asking the right questions about teacher preparation: Contributions of research on teacher thinking', *Educational Researcher*, 17, 2, pp. 5–12.
CLARK, C. M. and PETERSON, P. L. (1986) 'Teachers' thought processes' in WITTROCK, M. C. (Ed.) *Handbook of Research on Teaching* (3rd edn), New York, Macmillan, pp. 255–95.
COBB, P., YACKEL, E. and WOOD, T. (in press) 'A constructivist approach to mathematics education', in VON GLASERFELD, E. (Ed.) *Constructivism in Mathematics Education*, Holland, Reidel.
COHEN, D. K. (1987a) 'Teaching practice: Plus que ca change', unpublished manuscript, Michigan State University, College of Education.
COHEN, D. K. (1987b) 'Educational technology, policy, and practice', *Educational Evaluation and Policy Analysis*, 9, 2, pp. 153–70.
ELMORE, R. F. and MCLAUGHLIN, M. W. (1988) *Steady Work: Policy, Practice, and the Reform of American Education*, Santa Monica, CA, Rand Corporation.
ENGLERT, C. S. and RAPHAEL, T. (in press) 'Developing successful writers through cognitive strategy instruction', in BROPHY, J. E. (Ed.) *Advances in Research on Teaching, Volume 1*, Greenwich, CT, JAI Press, Inc.
FENNEMA, E., CARPENTER, T. P. and PETERSON, P. L. (1987). *Studies of the Application of Cognitive and Instructional Science to Mathematics Instruction* (Technical Progress report, 1 August 1986 to 31 July 1987), Madison, WI, Wisconsin Center for Educational Research.
FENNEMA, E., CARPENTER, T. P. and PETERSON, P. L. (in press) 'Learning mathematics with understanding', in BROPHY, J. E. (Ed.) *Advances in Research on Teaching, Volume 1*, Greenwich, CT, JAI Press, Inc.
FLORIO-RUANE, S. and LENSMIRE, T. (in press) 'The role of instruction in learning to write', in BROPHY, J. E. (Ed.) *Advances in Research in Teaching, Volume 1*, Greenwich, CT, JAI Press, Inc.
GINSBURG, H. P. and YAMAMOTO, T. (1986) 'Understanding, motivation, and teaching: Comment on Lampert's "knowing, doing, and teaching multiplication"', *Cognition and Instruction*, 3, 4, pp. 357–70.
GLASER, R. (1984) 'Education and thinking: The role of knowledge', *American Psychologist*, 39, pp. 93–104.
JAMES, W. (1900) *Talks to Teachers and Students*, New York, Holt.

LAMPERT, M. (1986) 'Knowing, doing, and teaching mathematics', *Cognition and Instruction*, 3,4, pp. 305–42.

LAMPERT, M. (1987) *Reinterpreting Mathematics: An Experiment in Teacher Education* (Report of the National Center for Research on Teacher Education) East Lansing, MI, Michigan State University.

LAMPERT, M. (1988) 'What is teaching mathematics for understanding in school classrooms?', paper presented at the Mathematics Education Research Conference, National Center for Research in Mathematical Sciences Education, University of Wisconsin-Madison, Wisconsin Center for Educational Research, May.

MCLAUGHLIN, M. (1987) 'Learning from experience: Lessons from policy implementation', *Educational Evaluation and Policy Analysis*, 9, 2, pp. 171–8.

PALINCSAR, A. and BROWN, A. (in press) 'Classroom dialogue to promote self-regulated composition', in BROPHY, J. E. (Ed.) *Advances in Research on Teaching, Volume 1*, Greenwich, CT, JAI Press, Inc.

PALMER, F. B. (1887) *The Science of Education*, Cincinnati, Ohio, Van Antwerp, Bragg and Co.

PETERSON, P. L. (1988a) 'New roles and classroom practice', paper presented at the annual meeting of the American Educational Research Association, New Orleans, April.

PETERSON, P. L. (1988b) 'Teachers' and students' cognitional knowledge for classroom learning and teaching', *Educational Researcher*, June–July.

PETERSON, P. L., FENNEMA, E., CARPENTER, T. P. and LOEF, M. (1988) 'Teachers' pedagogical content beliefs in mathematics', *Cognition and Instruction*, 5, 3.

RESNICK, L. B. (1985) 'Cognition and instruction: Recent theories of human competence', in HAMMONDS, B. L. (Ed.) *Master Lecture Series: Vol. 4 Psychology and Learning*, Washington, DC, American Psychological Association, pp. 123–86.

RILEY, M. S., GREENO, J. G. and HELLER, J. I. (1983) 'Development of children's problem-solving ability in arithmetic', in GINSBURG, H. (Ed.) *The Development of Mathematical Thinking*, New York, Academic Press, pp. 153–200.

ROMBERG, T. A. and CARPENTER, T. P. (1986) 'Research on teaching and learning mathematics: Two disciplines of scientific inquiry', in WITTROCK, M. C. (Ed.) *Handbook of Research on Teaching* (3rd edn), New York, Macmillan, pp. 850–73.

SCARDAMALIA, M. and BEREITER, C. (1986) 'Research on written composition', in WITTROCK, M. C. (Ed.) *Handbook of Research on Teaching* (3rd edn), New York, Macmillan, pp. 778–803.

SCHOENFELD, A. (1982) 'Measures of problem-solving performance and problem-solving instruction', *Journal for Research in Mathematics Education*, 13, pp. 31–49.

STARKEY, P. and GELMAN, R. (1982) 'The development of addition and subtraction abilities prior to formal schooling in arithmetic', in CARPENTER, T., MOSER, J. and ROMBERG, T. (Eds) *Addition and Subtraction: A Cognitive Perspective*, Hillsdale, NJ, Erlbaum.

ZARINNIA, E. A., LAMON, S. J. and ROMBERG, T. A. (1987) 'Epistemic teaching of school mathematics', in ROMBERG, T. A. and STEWART, D. M. (Eds) *The Monitoring of School Mathematics* (Vol. 3), Madison, WI, Wisconsin Center for Educational Research.

Chapter 10:
Policy Implications of Retention Research

Ernest R. House

Editors' Introduction

Ernie House is Director of the Laboratory for Policy Studies and Professor of Education at the University of Colorado-Boulder. He is internationally recognized as a scholar in educational evaluation and educational change. Because of his credentials as a policy researcher, House was invited to react to the chapters on retention research.

Professor House has first-hand knowledge of retention policy issues, having chaired the audit team called in to investigate the evaluation of New York City's Promotional Gates Program. Here he relates the New York experience and uses strong words to summarize the research findings in this volume. His analysis offers an explanation as to why beliefs about retention are unperturbed by negative evidence.

In 1981 New York City launched an ambitious new educational program to revamp and revitalize the city schools. That year the schools retained approximately 25,000 students in the fourth and seventh grades because of low test scores. A new chancellor decided that neither the teachers nor students were trying hard enough and that more pressure was needed to ensure that students learn what they should. Any student who was behind more than one grade level on the district reading test at the fourth grade or more than one-and-a-half years behind at the seventh grade would be held back. And with few exceptions they were. This included about one-quarter of the students at those grade levels.

The next step was to put the retained students into special classes of twenty or fewer students with specially trained teachers and special materials and programs, where the students would stay until they acquired the necessary skills to enable them to progress to the higher grades, that is until they had attained the appropriate test scores. The first year this program required about 1100 additional teachers and cost the city well in excess of $40m. New York City elementary classrooms at this time averaged about forty-three students, approximately 80 per cent of whom were from minority groups.

This retention program was called Promotional Gates, the idea being that deficient students would be checked at the designated 'gate' and not allowed to pass through until they had acquired the necessary skills to do well in the educational system. This checking would send a message to both students and teachers that social promotion was no longer allowable in New York City. The next year the program was expanded to include mathematics achievement and plans were to expand to other subject areas in later years. The Gates program received a great deal of publicity with the media generally supportive, although the 300,000 member parents' union was opposed.

Within the unusual arrangements of New York City government, the Mayor's office supplied most of the money for the new program and insisted that it be evaluated and that 'evaluation auditors' from outside be contracted to oversee the evaluation, which was conducted by the New York City Schools' Office of Evaluation. Two colleagues, Robert Linn and James Raths, and I, all at the University of Illinois at that time, undertook the auditing task. For the next two years the New York evaluators collected data, primarily test scores. When the scores were analyzed, there were no substantial achievement differences between the students who had been held back and those who in previous years had been promoted. That is, the students in the Gates program had progressed educationally about as well as had students in other special programs who had not been held back. The same results were also obtained the following year.

About this time the Chancellor was offered a job by David Rockefeller to head a New York City commission and left the schools. The program continued under successive chancellors but was increasingly deemphasized and assigned a less prominent place. This book of research on student retention explains in part both why this episode in New York City occurred and why it did not succeed as anticipated.

The practice of holding students back a year in school — 'flunking' them — is almost universal in the United States, endorsed by most educators and the public. Hundreds of thousands of students are retained at grade level every year; no one knows exactly how many. The formalized retention programs which employ standardized test scores and rigid cut-off points are recent innovations, but the basic practice has long been an integral feature of American schools. It is an extremely important educational practice because of its great cost — having a student repeat a grade obviously adds a year's cost — and because of the powerful negative effects upon the students retained.

This book demonstrates that the practice of retaining students in grade is absolutely contrary to the best research evidence. Few practices in education have such overwhelmingly negative research findings arrayed against them. Yet educational professionals and the public are almost universally in favor. This is an unusual situation: much of the time the best educational practice is far in advance of educational research. That is, the finest teachers are capable of classroom judgments that are sounder and more effective than educational research can prescribe or even understand. Yet in this case I find the research evidence to be sounder than professional judgment. Why is there such an enormous discrepancy between the practice and the research?

The Studies

First, there is the overwhelming evidence of the ill effects of this practice. The evidence is of several kinds, which enhances its credibility. Holmes' meta-analysis of the retention research literature demonstrates that most studies have found the practice to be either ineffective or harmful. When averaged across all studies, the group of students retained are a quarter of a standard deviation worse off than comparable students who were promoted. This negative effect is in fact larger in magnitude than the positive gains associated with normal remediation programs.

These negative effects are even stronger when one considers academic achievement alone. When children of the same age were compared, the retained group lost .45 standard deviation in achievement on average. And this negative difference increased each succeeding year. Only when the students were compared at different ages but the same grade, for example, students who were retained in first grade (and hence a year older) were compared to their peers when both had finished second grade, did the retained students show a positive advantage. And even this advantage disappeared by the end of third grade. The results on measures of personal adjustment are not as dramatic, but they too show negative effects for the students retained. Overall, these statistics present a stark picture of the negative consequences of flunking children.

Of the sixty-three studies included in Holmes' meta-analysis, only nine recent ones completed in the 1980s reported some positive effects of holding children back. These positive studies were alike in that the programs were all in suburban settings, included few if any black students, and retained students with average IQs who were reading and performing at or near the national norm. In fact, one wonders why these children were retained at all. The students were put into special classes with a low teacher/pupil ratio, given lots of extra help, and were mainstreamed part of the day. When compared to children who were passed but *did not receive any extra help* at the end of a particular grade, i.e. the retained children were a year older, the retained children showed positive effects. Hence, one cannot say that retention has negative effects for all students under all circumstances. But one might ask why none of these studies provided the truly critical comparison of *retention and remediation* compared to *promotion and remediation*.

Negative results were also found when investigating 'transition rooms' and other means of retaining children in kindergarten. If there is one age at which retention might be expected to have benefits, it is in kindergarten. Children enter with widely varying degrees of maturity and background and are less likely to be aware of the stigmatizing effects of being retained (one might suppose). Yet Shepard and Smith's chapter reports the results here are negative as well. In Shepard and Smith's controlled study teachers rated the retained students equal in achievement and maturity to comparable students who were passed on, even though the kindergarten students were then a whole year older. Furthermore, parents reported many emotional problems arising from the retention even when they were in favor of it.

Perhaps the most astounding negative evidence is provided by Grissom and Shepard, who found that failing a grade is strongly associated with dropping out of school in later years. The effect is as strong as the effects of achievement itself in determining whether the student drops out. In Austin, for example, the sole fact of repeating a grade increased the chances of a white female or an Hispanic male dropping out by 30 per cent — when all other factors such as achievement were controlled. Hence, we are faced with the incredible fact that a practice that is supposed to help students in school greatly increases the chances of their dropping out. It would be difficult to find a more pernicious practice. The research evidence is absolutely one-sided in finding negative effects from flunking students. I know of no educational practice in which the research is in such agreement.

Why Does This Occur?

What do the major participants in these events think about the retention? Byrnes has provided a partial answer in her survey of educators and parents in a large city. Fully 74 per cent of the principals, 65 per cent of the teachers and 59 per cent of the parents in this school district thought students should 'always' or 'usually' be retained if they qualified. 'Lack of basic skills' was the reason respondents most agreed upon as the basis for holding students back. More than half the principals and teachers thought that 'emotional immaturity' was also a good enough reason, but only 19 per cent of the parents thought so. Neither did parents believe that excessive absence was a sufficient reason, but most educators did.

The typical student held back in this district came from families with many children and had parents who were low-income and Spanish-speaking. Although 'lack of basic skills' was the reason most cited for retaining students, Shepard found retained students in some districts were eight months *above* the national norms in reading performance. One suspects that 'lack of basic skills' is quite a relative standard varying widely from district to district and classroom to classroom, and that the criteria for retention are not only variable but also arbitrary in many cases. One wonders how the classroom behavior of these students affects how educators view them.

The stigmatizing effects on the children of being retained are stunning. In Byrnes' interviews 57 per cent of the girls retained refused to identify themselves as having been held back, even though they could accurately name others who had been. In spite of euphemisms employed by both parents and teachers, these very young students called it 'flunking'. Not only did some students conceal the fact they had flunked, many others reported being teased and ridiculed by their peers. Fully 84 per cent reported feeling 'sad, bad, or upset'. Only 6 per cent reported any positive feelings, and even those feelings were mixed with negative ones.

These children said that their parents were 'mad' (48 per cent) and 'sad' (28 per cent), and half reported being punished. First graders: 'They spanked me and [I got] grounded'. 'Mad! Dad paddled me and kicked me out of the house'. Student interviews suggest no doubt about the immediate trauma of the event. Flunking evokes ridicule and punishment, shame and humiliation. If these students knew that being retained would also damage their academic performance in future years and cause many of them to drop out of school, thus significantly reducing their life chances, they would feel even worse. At this stage they were reassured by their protectors that this was for their own good. Being helpless, they probably believed it.

What about teacher reaction to all this trauma? Students were most likely to find out about their failure not from their teachers face to face but from their report card or from their parents. Tellingly, teachers avoided talking to the children about it. When they did, they employed euphemisms or gave untrue explanations as to why the students had failed. Sometimes they tried to lead the children to come to the conclusion themselves, which invariably meant inducing them to see the inadequacy of their own performance compared to other children. Most teachers said that by concealing the non-promotion and not discussing it, they were helping the student avoid stigmatization. Teachers did indeed worry about flunking students but reassured themselves that it would be to the children's advantage for them to stay in the same grade. Teachers feared ridicule from their own colleagues if they sent the students to the next grade improperly prepared.

When asked whether they thought that retaining their particular students was effective, an incredible 89 per cent of the teachers said that it was. In only 8 per cent of the cases did the teachers express some doubts. Nor did the teachers think that the students who were retained viewed the experience negatively, when in fact the students regarded it as punishment and as stigmatizing. This is a striking misreading of the students' reactions by the involved teachers. How could the teachers think this?

Smith has suggested part of the answer in her study. She found that teachers have deep-seated beliefs about the development of children. Half the teachers she interviewed held 'nativist' views about child development. They believed that children develop in a linear fashion, 'unfolding' through set stages when they are ready, and that this unfolding occurs largely outside the control or influence of teachers and parents. The teachers who believed this flunked large numbers — over 10 per cent — of their students in kindergarten. If the children had not 'unfolded' to the point of doing the work or behaving, teachers felt they might as well keep the children back a year until the proper development did occur.

Some schools with teachers of this nativist persuasion held back 30 per cent of the students, whereas teachers of other beliefs, such as the 'remediationists', held back less than 1 or 2 per cent. The remediationists, by contrast, believed that teachers could teach the necessary skills to all students. However, teachers of all persuasions endorsed retention, even though not all practiced it. Many teachers even expressed the belief that next year the retained child would move from the bottom of the class to the top. Retention would save the child from becoming frustrated and failing in the future, they thought, and many teachers claimed the children experienced no stigma from retention. Most teachers could not recall a single negative example of harmful repercussions, while reciting many stories about children who had been socially promoted and who had subsequently suffered in later years.

Parents did not want their own children retained, even though a majority of parents endorsed the practice in the abstract. Teachers blamed parents for fighting against the retention recommendations when the teachers thought it best for their children. Teachers routinely misjudged the children's feelings and the resistance of the parents, according to Smith. The teachers located the child's inability to perform or behave properly in the psychological make-up of the child rather than in any characteristics of the school.

What about the school administrators? In their case study of a large school district, Ellwein and Glass have provided a picture of how test-based retention programs are implemented in large cities. This particular school district had been criticized for the poor quality of its students. A new superintendent was hired who vowed to improve the quality of the schools by abolishing 'social promotion' and thereby toughening educational standards. The rhetoric used to promote his new 'Gates' program was tough — 'master, non-master', 'promote, review, retain' — a rhetoric to impress the public that something rigorous was being done. The emphasis was on public relations.

Committees of teachers, administrators and test experts established cut-off scores, and when all was said and done, between 60 and 70 per cent of the correct answers on the test was deemed passing, quite an arbitrary percentage. Most students who were 'non-masters' were minority students and male. Only a small number of students was eventually retained, although exactly how many was unclear because the students were never studied by the district to see what happened to them later. This program was declared a great success and highly publicized both locally and nationally. As in New York City, establishing a public image that the school district administration was 'getting tough' with both students and teachers was an important consideration.

Conclusions

This then is the picture that emerges from the studies in this book. Students are retained in rather arbitrary and inconsistent ways, and those flunked are more likely to be poor, males and minorities, although holding students back is practiced to some degree in rich and poor schools alike. The effects of flunking are immediately traumatic to the children and the retained children do worse academically in the future, with many of them dropping out of school altogether. Incredibly, being retained has as much to do with children dropping out as does their academic achievement. It would be difficult to find another educational practice on which the evidence is so unequivocally negative.

On the other hand, the practice is almost universal in the United States, with estimates that from one-quarter to one-third of American students are retained at one time or another. Teachers, administrators and the public are strongly in favor of this practice, with teachers and administrators claiming to see only positive results from retaining the students and no negative effects. School administrators in large cities and legislatures in a few states have recently implemented massive retention programs, often called 'promotional gates' programs, in response to pressures to raise educational standards. These programs employ standardized tests and cutting scores in an arbitrary manner.

What can be done? The most forthright action would be a mandate to cease retaining students in schools. But, of course, this is not possible. Quite the reverse is happening, particularly in cities and states with large minority populations. The belief in retention is deep-seated, held by teachers, administrators, and the public alike. It appears that we are in the grip of a tightly held ideology rather than a simple educational belief. Several signs point in that direction. First, retention is a practice that produces extremely negative effects, absolutely contrary to its claims, yet it is impervious to all evidence that it is wrong. Direct negative evidence is not even perceived by teachers and administrators. Better ways of dealing with low achieving students are ignored. Certain groups — males, the poor, and minorities — suffer disproportionately. That is, the interests of particular groups of people are served at the expense of other social groups. All this is legitimated by theories, arguments, and language that turn out to be spurious upon inspection. Retention has all the signs of an entrenched ideology rather than a simple educational belief which happens to be wrong.

Educational practitioners often ignore research, and much research is eminently ignorable. In this case, however, the evidence is extensive and unequivocal. It includes test scores, teacher ratings, parent ratings, interviews, surveys, personality and emotional adjustment measures, case studies — everything from elaborate statistical analyses to asking students how they feel. Almost everything points in the same direction — retention is an extremely harmful practice.

Furthermore, teachers act peculiarly towards the practice. They distance themselves by conveying their failing judgments through report cards rather than face to face. They perceive absolutely no negative effects upon students, even though all one has to do is ask or observe the students and parents. Teachers contend that students are not stigmatized while parents and students say that they are ridiculed by their friends and classmates. The schools themselves collect no data on these students, nor do they follow them to see how they fare down the road. All this adds up to educators protecting themselves from information that might indicate something is seriously wrong. Seeing no ill effects whatsoever is a clue that a protective ideological shield has been put into place.

As Smith and Shepard (1987) have noted, there are good reasons why the teachers' perspectives may be askew. Teachers do not see students farther down the line in the educational system. They see the students they have retained that year, who are now older and may be doing better temporarily than last year over the same instructional material. Teachers cannot compare the students' current progress with what the students might have done had they been passed on. They cannot observe these same students drop out of school ten years hence or see that they are significantly behind their peers who were passed on. The view that student development is a linear, staged process uninfluenced by learning experiences is supported by certain theories of child development which are questionable themselves.

Three other factors also suggest the ideological nature of this practice. First, other industrial countries seem to do without it quite well. Retention in Japan is unknown. Second, there is intense public pressure to institute such policies originating outside the educational organizations, although the practice has been accepted in American schools for decades. Legislators and governors see this practice as politically attractive, particularly in cities and states with large minority populations. Third, the practice differentially affects minority children, particularly poor males, thereby seriously damaging their educational chances and future job prospects. The public rhetoric is that these programs are instituted to help just such children, who will be brought up to educational standards by being retained. All this suggests not simply a case of collective ignorance but a case of ideological distortion.

I will not labor the point further other than to say that contemporary American beliefs assume that children will have approximately equal life chances and that this will be accomplished primarily though education that will provide knowledge and skills that will enable them to compete in the world. It is apparent that this equalization of life chances has not been successful for many, especially minority students. The blame is most often placed upon the students personally for not availing themselves of the educational opportunities rather than upon the social system itself. Retaining students appears to be a way of instilling the needed skills, though in reality it is a way of increasing the likelihood that students will eventually drop out of school. Blame is deflected away from society and onto the individual students and their families.

Because of the ideological nature of the retention practice, one can expect intense resistance to changing it. Stopping the practice requires publicity, education, and legal action. A first step would be to publicize the research findings, as this book attempts to do, though that will hardly suffice, given the ideological nature of the practice. Publicity is essential to attract the attention of educators, reduce the public pressure in favor of the practice, bolster the confidence of parents who wisely resist having their children retained, and secure the support of important policy-influencing organizations.

Second, pre-service and in-service training for teachers, with the disadvantages of retention as a theme, would be a modest step forward, although deep-seated belief makes this difficult as well. It is essential in reeducating teachers to present them with better remedies to the problems of underachieving and immature students, rather than simply telling them they have been wrong. The point is not that many students do not need extra help but rather that retaining them is not the way to provide it. It will take a strong reeducative program to counter the beliefs of teachers in this matter.

The most effective remedy in the long run would be for teachers to conduct action research of their own in their own schools, following their own students who have been retained, and examining the consequences. This would be the most persuasive evidence to teachers and would not require the educators to believe in advance that the practice was pernicious. But since there is little action research conducted by teachers in American schools on any topic, this seems an unlikely solution. It would also take a great deal of time.

Short of that, school districts should or should be required to follow and document the fortunes of those students they retain over a number of years. This is a reasonable demand and places the responsibility directly upon the school district where it belongs. If districts were required to study and provide special assistance to retained students for a number of years, they would be less arbitrary and casual in holding students back and in assuming good effects from doing so. They would be faced with strong evidence of the ill effects of retention which they have been so successful in ignoring.

Perhaps the most effective action that could be undertaken immediately is recourse to legal sanctions. The courts, though too often used, are sometimes an effective means of striking at pernicious practices that are ideologically based. A child advocacy or civil rights group might embrace this issue as a cause. Since the criteria for retaining a student are so arbitrary and the effects so pernicious and so disproportionally directed at minority groups, a well publicized court case might substantially reduce the frequency of the practice in American schools. The legal brief could be approached either as a violation of civil rights or as a harmful practice, like corporal punishment, that should cease. The one-sided nature of the research evidence suggests that such a case could be won.

There are also topics deserving further study. Most of the research literature deals with achievement results and personal adjustment measures. What are the stigmatic effects of being held back and exactly how does this lead to the student dropping out eventually? Is this a matter of shame carried forward throughout life? Of social alienation? Exactly what are the beliefs of teachers, administrators and parents that lead them to endorse this practice? How do they acquire and justify these beliefs? What are the legal and ethical implications of this practice, considering that it is primarily directed at males and minorities? Exactly to what extent are minorities, males and the lower social classes differentially affected? Are there indeed some students with special characteristics who can benefit from being retained under special circumstances?

Too much of the school agenda is controlled by legislation now, but it well may be that preventing retention requires legislative action. I endorse this reluctantly because of the usual excess of rules and regulations that comes with legislated programs. However, it is now the case that some state legislatures are already mandating retention policies. So it seems inevitable that state legislators must be informed about the ills of this practice to prevent them from fomenting unwise policies.

I expect the effort to abolish student retention in the United States to be long and hard. It is a practice, like bleeding patients, that exists with public approval because professionals don't know what else to do with certain students and because it serves important vested interests in the society as a whole. For example, in spite of their previous experience and failure with their retention program, the New York City schools have recently hired a new superintendent from Minneapolis who gained recognition for his 'Promotional Gates' program there. He is considering reinstituting such a program in New York City once again.

References

SMITH, M. L. and SHEPARD L. A. (1987) 'What doesn't work: Explaining policies of retention in the early grades', *Phi Delta Kappan*, 68, pp. 129–34.

Chapter 11:
Flunking Grades: A Recapitulation

Mary Lee Smith and Lorrie A. Shepard

In this volume we have presented a point of view about retention in grade. We were not always partisans. We formed this point of view as we assembled and critically appraised the theoretical and empirical work on this subject. Campbell and his colleagues (Brewer and Collins, 1981) described the building of social science knowledge as an evolving ratio of trust to doubt. Although an absolute truth about a slice of social life such as the practices and effects of grade retention cannot be attained, scholars can tip the balance, increase the ratio of trust to doubt by considering systematically the separate pieces of evidence. The typical errors and the inevitable biases of social research can be canceled out when the separate research studies have employed a variety of methods, construct operationalizations, and researcher perspectives. When the findings of these various pieces converge, the conclusions are robust. According to Campbell (1986), when such conclusions have been subjected to the critical review of the disputatious scholarly community, their capacity to affect beliefs is enhanced. The literature on retention and its effects meets the standards of multiple methods, operations, and perspectives and has been subjected to critical scrutiny — an ongoing process which this book extends. Thus our own point of view has evolved and we hope to affect the point of view of our readers.

We believe that the accumulated evidence about retention is sufficiently conclusive that policy-makers and practitioners must take notice. As House (chapter 10) noted, no other body of educational research is so one-sided as that relating to retention. In summary, the conclusions are these:

Retention in Grade Has No Benefits for Either School Achievement or Personal Adjustment

Meta-analysis of scores of studies reveals that at-risk students who are promoted achieve at the same or higher levels than comparable at-risk students who have been retained and spent two years rather than one year in a grade. The negative effect (the achievement of retained students being less than that of promoted students) ranged in magnitude from one-fifth to one-third standard deviation (an effect between a few months and a half-year in grade equivalent achievement units). Effects measured long-term were more strongly negative than those measured short-term. Well-controlled studies yielded as strong or more strongly negative findings than did poorly-controlled studies. In addition, retained children are no better off than initially comparable promoted children on measures of personal and psychological adjustment: self-concept, attitude toward school and attendance. The few studies in which retention seemed beneficial were either poorly controlled or employed populations of unusually bright pupils with questionable need for retention (chapter 2).

Retention Is Strongly Related to Later Dropping Out of School

Large-scale surveys of dropouts and graduates reveal that substantially more dropouts than graduates have at some time in their career been retained in grade. Although achievement explains part of the connection between retention and dropping out, retention increases the probability of eventually dropping out of school by 20 to 30 per cent, even with achievement, socioeconomic status and gender controlled (chapter 3).

Two Years in Kindergarten, Even When One Year Is Labeled 'Transition Program', Fail to Enhance Achievement or Solve the Problem of Inadequate School Readiness

Transition programs, which provide an extra year of school between kindergarten and first grade, are no different — in spite of their different philosophies — from simply retaining children for a second year in kindergarten. Although they are predicated on the idea that immature children should be given an extra year to grow or to repeat the pre-first grade experience, controlled studies show that children so treated do no better than their counterparts who are promoted directly into first grade. The findings of no difference or no benefit hold whether the children were selected for retention on the basis of immaturity or low achievement. Of the twenty-one studies reviewed, only one study favorable to two years in kindergarten was well-controlled, and it measured only short-term outcomes. Therefore it cannot be said that retention in kindergarten is more beneficial than retention in later grades. Our own study confirmed the results of extant literature: promoted children suffered no disadvantages compared to equivalent children who had two years of kindergarten (chapters 4 and 5).

From the Students' Perspective, Retention Is Conflict-laden and Hurtful

Clinical interviews with retained students show strong patterns of evidence that these children viewed their retention as 'flunking', as a punishment for some quality or action. They felt angry or sad and feared the reactions of their families and classmates (chapter 6). The majority of parents whose kindergartners were retained reported negative experiences such as being teased by neighbors as well as adjustment problems caused by not progressing along with one's classmates.

Discrepancies between Propositional and Personal Knowledge

The conclusions stated above contrast sharply with the abiding faith in the merits of retention held by many teachers, educational reformers, and many laypersons. The reform package of the 1980s, echoing the opinions of the public, features the mastery of grade-level skills as the basis for advancing from grade to grade and for attaining the credentialed status of high school graduate. Teachers, too, seem to reject the idea of social promotion, the system of progressing through grades with one's age-mates.

In addition to these popular opinions, teachers hold views about retention that are overwhelmingly sanguine. In clinical interviews, they expressed the personal beliefs that retentions, when handled properly by teachers and parents, almost invariably enhance achievement and personal adjustment. For example, they believe that the retained child will be one of the top students in the class he or she repeats. Immature, frustrated and troublesome in his or her original grade, the child will be happy, confident and a classroom leader the second time through. Teachers deny the possibility that the children might be bored or careless when they encounter the same worksheets and lessons they had worked through once before. Nor do teachers pay much attention to the problem of a child failed because of his ineptness in reading but whose math skills are acceptable. The child gets a second dose of the already known math, along with the identical fieldtrips, art projects, as well as the instruction in reading that may be needed.

Any emotional distress the children or their parents experience as a result of the retention is temporary or non-existent, according to teachers' beliefs. To say that these beliefs contradict the reported experiences of the children themselves is an understatement. Retained children, even those who acknowledge the rights of the school to make such a decision, report anger, sadness, teasing by other children, as well as related emotional reactions in their parents. Yet teachers who acknowledged that the child might feel bad blamed parents for the way the decision was treated. Teachers tended to retreat from interactions with the retained children, leaving it to parents or report cards to deliver the bad news. Those who involved themselves tried to make the children believe that the next year's work would be too difficult for them and that they were less adequate than their promoted classmates.

Whether or not kindergarten teachers in our study practiced retention, they endorsed its benefits (chapter 7). Their retention rates and how they decided whom to retain were influenced by their images of the learner and their personal beliefs about the nature of child development and what early childhood education should be. For example, teachers who believe that children develop readiness for learning according to a physiological and psychological unfolding (unrelated to what teachers and parents do) practiced retention and endorsed it as a tactic to give the child another year to mature. Following the extra year, which could be spent in the same grade, in a transition program, or at home, the child will have developed readiness for school and can meet the rigors of the next grade with confidence and ability to learn. According to this view, retention or its equivalent protects young children from inappropriately difficult curricula in the later grades. Other teachers endorsed retention as a way of correcting deficient learning skills. If kindergartners still have not mastered letter sounds in May, they need another dose of instruction before they can be taught the next skill in the sequence, such as word attack skills. According to this belief, retention for another year in grade is the conventional way to provide this extra dose of instruction. Teachers at all levels worry that, if they promote children who have not mastered grade-level skills, the next grade teachers will send the promoted but incompetent children back to them or otherwise vilify the socially promoting teachers.

Our reviewers added to our interpretations of the discrepancy between propositional knowledge and the personal knowledge and beliefs of teachers. Peterson (chapter 9) attributed teachers' beliefs about retention to their lack of access to propositional knowledge and the lack of opportunity for teachers to reflect on and make sense of this information and incorporate it into their personal knowledge systems. She argued that both types of belief about development and early learning are outmoded as psychological theories. Neither belief makes use of the cognitive-constructionist psychological theory that the child's mind actively constructs knowledge. It follows that instruction should be aimed at relating 'new knowledge in a meaningful way to the knowledge that they have already developed'. Such an image of learning and teaching challenges concepts and practices that predominate in contemporary schools: drill on building-block skills, mastery learning hierarchies, active teaching and passive learning, and the like. The cognitive-constructionist theory is only one of several competing views (those of Dewey, Vygotsky, sociolinguists, whole language specialists, and others) that challenge either skills-oriented or maturationist instructional practices.

Peterson's interpretation converges with our argument that teachers' beliefs about the efficacy of retention grow out of their personal knowledge that children do in fact make some progress when they repeat a grade and the lack of access to information about what progress these children *would have made* had they been promoted. This latter knowledge can only come from a contrived experiment, results of which are either not known to teachers or are rejected when they conflict with personal knowledge. When a bright, immature child is retained in kindergarten and subsequently shines in first grade, teachers tend to believe he is doing well *because* he repeated. Teachers fail to compare this child to equally bright, immature children who are sent directly to first grade and do well, a situation that (according to controlled studies) occurs just as often. When a low-achieving, immature child is promoted and struggles at the bottom of his class, teachers conclude that things would have been better if only he had been retained. When a low-achieving child is retained and still struggles, teachers tend to believe things would have been worse had he been promoted (or perhaps the child was handicapped and thus failed to benefit from retention). Teachers also have no access to knowledge about the long-term effects of retention; for example, the effects of retention on the probability of dropping out are not common knowledge.

House (chapter 10) interprets the discrepancy between propositional and the personal knowledge of teachers differently from Peterson. He suggests that teachers are gripped by an ideology that precludes a disinterested review of the research evidence on retention which (contrary to Peterson) is available but ignored. By ignoring contrary evidence and denying the deleterious consequences of retention, teachers satisfy the interests of public schools to appear to be accountable for achievement mastery but act against the true interests of students.

Consistent with House's point of view, we have argued that teachers are not disinterested theoreticians. No matter how altruistic their motives, they operate in organizational, political and historical contexts that shape in part their beliefs. These we have addressed in the following categories.

Homogeneity

Teachers frequently express the wish for more homogeneous groups and act in ways that they believe will restrict the range of abilities within their classrooms. Actions that fall in this category are tracking, special education placement and retention. In our study of kindergarten teachers and classrooms, for example, some teachers actively promoted parents' decisions to hold children out from school until they had attained the age of 6 (thus putting at risk those children whose parents could not afford day-care or preschool). Although couched in language of the benefit to the child, it was clear from the teachers' statements and actions that the younger, immature children proved troublesome in the classroom and detracted from their providing the instruction from which the majority of the pupils could profit. Teachers also supported a change in the legal age of school entry, supposing that an older group would contain fewer immature and disruptive pupils. Retentions, transition placements, and two-year kindergartens were all seen as ways of ensuring a more homogeneous set of entry-level skills among the kindergartners and first graders. Placement of children in transition classes restricted not only the range of abilities with which the teacher would have to cope, but also restricted the possibilities that children have of learning from other pupils. In addition, many of the teachers made use of within-class ability groups as the sole means of dealing with heterogeneous abilities and proficiencies.

Evidence suggests, however, that all such arrangements offer, at best, a temporary and, at worst, the contrary effect. Retaining a child in first grade means that the next year some first grade teacher will have pupils with a range of ages of well over two years, with corresponding variations in size, maturity and accomplishment. In any elementary grade the range of achievement spans several grades. If kindergarten retention is more often used with academically able but immature children or subscribed to by socioeconomically advantaged parents (chapters 4 and 5), then retention will exaggerate the range of individual differences in the classroom. Ability grouping benefits the most able group while restricting the amount and frequently the quality of instruction received by the least able group.

Many teachers fail to realize that, even with such tracking policies there will always be a child who is the youngest, the smallest, the least able and the least mature in any group of children. These extremes in a distribution attract the teachers' attention and tend to be labeled as deviant rather than different. In contrast, kindergarten teachers in our study who retained few children were apt to accept heterogeneity more readily and provide productive learning experiences for children of all sorts. They tended less often (compared to high retaining teachers) to seek solutions that used tracking and segregating. Teachers need help in learning how to cope with very heterogeneous classes by means short of rejecting pupils who cannot keep pace. The educational community has offered tracking as a panacea without providing alternatives.

The Place of the Grade in American Schools

As the basis for organizing pupils and learning opportunities within schools, the grade is neither universal nor historically inevitable, though we are apt to take it for granted as such. The age-grouped grade is a social invention. Labaree (1984) noted that American schools were once organized individually by merit, with pupils progressing on the basis of finishing a series of texts. But when the numbers of pupils to be educated increased, the structure of the schools changed.

> Grading was a response to two forms of pressure exerted on the new school systems, one organizational and the other cultural. Organizationally, the sharp rise in the number of students put the common schools under intense pressure to develop a system of instruction which was fiscally, socially and pedagogically efficient. The result was that they abandoned the inefficiency of traditional individualized instruction in favor of the economies of scale embodied in the simultaneous instruction of an entire class. Since, under this new technology, the whole class learned the same material at the same time, the students could then proceed on to more difficult material as a group. Individual craft production gave way to large-scale batch production, which in turn led to batch promotion — cohorts of students of similar age and, presumably similar ability, moving through a progression of educational stages.
>
> Culturally, the new schools were under pressure both to embody and to transmit meritocratic values — particularly the belief that in US society rewards are allocated according to individual ability and effort, and that they are earned, not given. To the extent that a student's rise to each higher stage came as a result of personal achievement, the school system was a hierarchy of merit. Thus, concerns about both efficiency and merit led to the grading of students. The resulting tension centered on promotion. The question was whether the primary unit of promotion was the age-cohort or the individual. The ideal case for educational efficiency has always been to move entire classes through the grade levels like an assembly line with no rejects. The meritocratic ideal has been to promote only those who have reached an acceptable level of achievement (Labatree 1984, pp. 68–9).

The reforms of the 1980s call for merit-based promotion. Yet the fiscal support of the public schools precludes abandoning 'batch processing' on anywhere near the scale suggested by, say, the promotional gates programs in the large urban centers. Rhetoric promising to detect and remediate deficiencies fails to acknowledge the sheer magnitude of the deficiencies measured in grade-level units (whatever the merits and problems of such scales as indicators of achievement). For example, some Chicago ninth-graders (chapter 3) entered high school with achievement scores at the third-grade level. Reformers seem to assume that low achievers are just slightly behind and will be positively motivated to avoid retention by just working harder. Yet the same reformers are rarely heard to recommend that young people who, like those in Chicago are five years' behind in achievement, should spend five years in eighth grade.

Since a true merit-based promotion system is economically impossible, retentions in practice are largely symbolic (Ellwein and Glass, chapter 8). Superintendents and policy-makers advocate promotion based on mastery of grade-level skills and, by so doing, project a tough public image and increase the support of a community worried about declines in achievement and loss of international economic superiority.

Viewed another way, from the perspective of social structures, retentions can be seen as mechanisms by which the school maintains its existing structure while warding off attacks from outside. Five to 10 per cent of the lowest achieving students in a grade are retained, and thus the school appears to be meritocratic. To be genuinely meritocratic, however, would require a return to an organization based on individual, rather than group, instruction, too costly and radical a change for the schools to accomplish. The more efficient, age-cohort organization is therefore maintained. The cost is borne by the student (who pays with psychological hurt and an unproductive year) rather than by the school or the teacher. Imagine an alternative structure wherein the teachers would bear the cost of being demoted or furloughed when their pupils failed to learn. This analysis is similar to that of Coles's (1978) analysis of the category of learning disabilities. He argued that the schools hide their failure to teach effectively by categorizing certain pupils as learning disabled, deflecting what should be the school's responsibility to the defective brains of a minority of pupils. In both cases, retention for low achievement or immaturity on the one hand and categorization as learning disabled on the other, the structure of the schools is maintained by labeling and otherwise singling out some children as failures.

A different perspective on graded education is suggested by what has been done in recent decades with precocious children, those functioning one or more years beyond grade level standards. Skipping grades is a practice, akin to retention, intended to align children with grade-level instruction targeted for the class average. Because skipping grades has recently been viewed as causing poor social adjustment, the practice is less prevalent than it once was. In addition, double promotions did not solve instructional problems because individual differences in achievement often exceeded the one-year correction in grade placement. Nor is a child's precocity uniform in all subject areas. Today's teachers are expected to adapt instruction to accommodate the needs of more able students and provide enrichment while keeping gifted children with their agemates. All the arguments against skipping parallel the rationale for social promotion with one exception: failure to skip students achieving above grade level does not have to be justified to the public as a failure to respect meritocratic principles.

The Factory Model of Schools and the Accountability Culture

Consistent with Wise's (1979) prediction, schools have become more bureaucratic than they once were. The more like factories they become, the more retention becomes a desirable mechanism for teachers and administrators. According to Katz (1975), the model of schools as factories comprises the following characteristics:

(i) Highly centralized administration. There is a strict hierarchy of authority from board and superintendent to central administrators to principals to teachers, with power and responsibility concentrated at the top.

(ii) Standardized curriculum. What is offered to pupils, even pupils in widely different circumstances and locations, is standard. For example, textbooks, instructional programs, school organizations and discipline programs are determined by the central administration for all separate schools. This crystallizes the notion that there is such a thing as a grade-level curriculum, the curriculum that must be offered at a given grade, and lessens the ability to adapt to individual differences.

(iii) Diminished teacher autonomy. Consistent with the first two characteristics, teachers have little power (other than advisory) to alter or set curriculum, school organization, or even instructional techniques. Teachers are viewed less as professionals than as operatives. They lack the authority to alter arrangements for children who do not fit the grade-level mold.

(iv) Grade isolation. A factory clearly differentiates the functions that must be performed in each of its divisions. A grade level can be thought of as one of these divisions. For third-grade teachers to cover the material prescribed by the district curriculum guide, the pupils who come into their classrooms in the fall must have mastered the material prescribed by the second grade guide. This is tantamount to the raw material that comes into the manufacturing division of a factory. And like the quality control function in a factory, the third-grade teacher is held responsible for the outputs, namely, mastery of third-grade material. Knowing these responsibilities in advance the third-grade teachers may reject the raw material, send it back to second grade, lest they themselves fail the accountability test nine months later.

Testing for grade-level mastery is a growing trend, and such testing almost inevitably implies paper-and-pencil measures of building block skills. Scores on these tests are becoming the primary standard for demonstrating that schools and teachers are performing responsibly. This trend reaches its nadir in promotional gates programs wherein large numbers of children are retained based on their competency test performance. Although promotional gates are plausible on the surface and appeal to the public, experience shows that, contrary to lifting the overall level of pupil achievement, they can have adverse consequences. First, the standard for passing may be set so high that large numbers of children fail and must be remediated. Remediation usually involves teaching to the test rather than pursuing any broader educational goal. Testing experts understand that repeated testing increases test performance, even if the person has learned nothing in between tests. Those who fail the retakes are retained, with all the negative consequences described in this book. Contrary to common sense, the threat of failure is a poor motivator, especially for disadvantaged and minority pupils (Levin, 1987). Second, the standards are routinely compromised, teachers' judgments substitute for test scores in the actual promotion decision, thus making the test an expensive and redundant public relations device. Alternatively, the promotional gates test may be made so simple that virtually everyone passes it on the first or second administration.

Retentions are a way of recycling pupils through material that administrators demand be mastered and certified at a given grade level. Thus retentions represent a response to the accountability culture and the factory model of schools. Yet, as this volume has made clear, the accountability function is largely symbolic, as no real gains in achievement are made by the pupil who is so recycled.

Our own research contributes to the factory metaphor of schools presented by Katz. First, the curriculum of high-retaining schools focuses on literacy, narrowly defined. In these schools, the purpose of education is seen as instilling skills in reading and mathematics. The curriculum is seen as linear, one block resting on a previously learned block (Peterson, chapter 9) so that a child who failed to master grade-level skills must be recycled before he or she can go on to the next block. Retention is a logical consequence. Second, we saw that this narrow, literacy-defined curriculum is pushed downward into kindergartens. Instead of being a time for socialization and acquiring good work habits and good feelings about school, kindergartners are put through a regimen of preparation for first grade, pushed to master sounds, letters, elementary math and the like, in a fast-paced academic program. If mastery is not attained by all, then the first grade teachers cannot begin the teaching of reading at the beginning of first grade, so the children have to be retained. Third, we noted that schools that retain also practice other means of segregation — tracking and special education placements — at a higher rate than low-retaining schools.

There are many alternative views of schools that compete with the factory model of organizations (Morgan, 1986). In them, teachers can be viewed as collaborative decision-makers who are responsive to local circumstances. Pupils contribute to their own education, make their own meanings, respond as feeling individuals rather than as raw material shaped by manufacturers or empty vessels into which knowledge and skills are poured. High expectations are set by encouraging each student and recognizing each accomplishment rather than by rejecting those who do not measure up to classroom standards. In the low retaining schools we studied, teachers and pupils were apt to be viewed and to view themselves in this way. Grade-level standards were neither strict nor standardized, and retentions were not used to enhance the school's image of accountability. In terms of long-range achievement trends, these schools were no better nor worse than the others.

Can Anything Be Done about Retention?

The usual response we have received from teachers about retention has so far been to ask what else they can do when they have a pupil who has not met grade-level expectations. Many feel helpless to change the curriculum or challenge the structure of their schools. They worry about promoting low achieving pupils to the harsher climate of the next grade. They press us for solutions.

The literature offers few models. Lieberman (1980), after reviewing the negative evidence on retention, suggested that educators ought to institute a diagnostic and consultative decision-making process to determine whether children should be retained in grade. This staffing process would resemble that used in special education placement. The reasoning behind such a recommendation is this. Although the effects are *negative on the average*, retention must benefit *some* pupils. Therefore we should identify in advance *which* pupils will likely benefit and retain them. Assessment specialists, teachers, administrators and parents would meet and discuss the child's characteristics, including his or her age, sex, achievement, and likely response to the retention. Then a decision would be made.

We categorically reject this approach. Evidence clearly shows that educators are not able to predict which children will benefit from retention (Rose, Medway, Cantrell and Marus, 1983).[1] Nor does the staffing model result in fair or valid placements, as our research on staffing of learning disabled children showed (Shepard, Smith and Vojir, 1983). Fewer than half the children who were identified as learning disabled in the Colorado population exhibited the characteristics listed in official and professional definitions of the condition, in spite of their having gone through the same staffing and decision-making process recommended by Lieberman. Ethnographic accounts of the decision-making process (Smith, 1982) have shown that it is rarely collaborative and usually governed by the sentiments of the teachers and assessment specialists. We regard this staffing process as a way the school attempts to appear rational, scientific, and fair in the process, while the outcome of the decision is anything but valid or beneficial.

Following the same logic as Lieberman, Light (1981) developed a rating instrument to help educators decide whom to retain. Items from this scale include sex, age within grade, physical size, English language fluency, current grade level, deprived experiential background, parents' school participation, previous retentions and intelligence. Several reviewers have faulted Light's scale for lack of evidence of validity to make retention decisions (Hannifan, 1983; Sandoval, 1982; Watson, 1979).

Including a characteristic such as physical size is inherently invalid and discriminatory, because no evidence exists to establish reliably a correlation between size (within broad limits) and school success. Perhaps Light reasoned that children who are small for their age are less likely to experience stigma from retention. However, children do not infer the meaning of retention by making size comparisons (chapters 5 and 6). Instead they know directly that they failed and are teased by other children who know. Correlations of successful retention with chronological age, gender, or size are larger in teachers' minds than they are in the results of careful empirical research.

Alternatives

Dissemination and Action Research

Following Peterson (chapter 9), we advocate programs in which teachers are given access to the evidence on the effects of retention. They should have time to consider the implications of this research in their own settings. In those places where the factory model does not govern schools and where teachers have some power to alter curriculum and school organization, teachers may be open to knowledge that is both new and contrary to their common sense. For example, our findings were presented to a group of teachers in a school district. They were persuaded by the results and formed study groups and eventually worked toward a new school organization that would allow for alternatives to retention. Action research, conducted by teachers in collaboration with researchers, is the next logical step.

Legislative and Judicial Action

Following House (chapter 10), we advocate political activity to counter the ideology and vested interests that exist in some districts and states. For example, action groups should petition legislatures to delay standardized testing for accountability at least to the intermediate grades and to eliminate promotional gates. Legislators and other policy makers should be encouraged to see accountability in broader terms than paper-and-pencil tests.

Because gender and size are invalid indicators and because the burden of retention falls disproportionately on the poor and ethnic minorities, corrective action against high retaining districts should be sought through the courts. A National Academy of Sciences panel studying special education placements argued that any treatment must unambiguously benefit the child to warrant a decision that separates the child from his or her peers (Heller, Holtzman and Messick, 1982). Clearly retention has not met that test and invites legal action.

Parental Action

In our study, high-retaining teachers attempted to persuade parents as soon as their children became candidates for retention. Teachers promised that the children would move from the bottom of their class to the top. Teachers warned that if these children were not retained now, they would certainly fail later or otherwise come to grief. Teachers intimidated recalcitrant parents by demanding that they sign a statement that promotion was against the recommendation of the staff, which would bear no responsibility for the child's future welfare. Many parents were convinced by the evidence or frightened into compliance. But a significant minority walked away. In many cases, they removed their children from that school into another public school or enrolled them in a private school. Some actually changed residences so that their children could be promoted with their class. Others braved the decision, keeping their children in the same school, but in the next grade, watching closely for any retaliation. These cases illustrate that parents can have an active and informed voice in the decision. However, not all children have parents who get involved. Once again, poor and minority parents are likely to have fewer options in finding another school or in combating the pressure from school personnel.

Well-informed parents may help to solve the problem of retention in another way: by restraining themselves and others from the decision to withhold from kindergarten their children (usually boys) of legal school age. Known as academic redshirting, this practice is rationalized as follows. The child has attained the age that will allow him legally to enter kindergarten, but only by a month or so. For example, his birthday is 1 August and the entry birthday is 30 September. His parents worry that he will be among the youngest and smallest in his class. They worry that he is 'immature' and the school staff reinforces their concern. They want him to have a competitive advantage, so they decide to wait a year, in the interim he goes to pre-school, private kindergarten or stays home with his mother. The next fall he enrolls in public kindergarten at the age of 6. Looking around at the 5-year-old boys in his class, his parents feel justified in their decision. Many of their friends in high socioeconomic neighborhoods are coming to the same conclusion.

Research shows that in any class of first graders, there will be a difference of 7 or 8 percentile ranks in reading achievement between the oldest and youngest (Shepard and Smith, 1987). So the parents' decision seems justified, if they look only at the interests of their own son. By the end of the third grade, however, the advantage of the oldest has disappeared, and they are indistinguishable from the rest. There is no lasting *academic* advantage to the practice of holding children out of school until they are older and more mature. The only possible lasting advantage might be to the boys' atheletic careers, for interscholastic sports are tied to grade levels rather than to age or ability levels.

In exchange for these temporary, individualistic and perhaps dubious values (further advantaging the already advantaged) the children whose parents lack the ability to hold them out an extra year suffer. They are consigned to the role of youngest, smallest and least mature in a relative distribution that has been arbitrarily and unfairly shifted upward.

This alone would not be problematic if the teacher is capable of dealing effectively with so great a range of characteristics. The teacher must now offer a program that accommodates multiple levels of academic and social curriculum and organization. However, it is sometimes the case that teachers shift their own conceptions of what constitutes 'normal' grade level characteristics, with the result that the legal school-aged child becomes the deviant, 'too immature for kindergarten instruction' because he cannot learn the same material at the same rate as the boy a year or more older. The teacher may respond to the parents' demands that the material covered be more rigorous and advanced. Meanwhile, the youngest, smallest (likely also to be of disadvantaged or minority status) becomes the likely candidate for retention by virtue of his position in a distribution trending upward and by expectations and curriculum that are no longer appropriate for 5-year-olds.

In this country we are apt to think of public school generally and each grade within it as a race with equal starting points and equal chances to succeed. A more appropriate metaphor might be the tournament (Rosenbaum, 1976) in which the participants are further disadvantaged at each stage by their prior poor performances. Thus, the youngest and lower class child starts out behind his older grade cohort, performs poorly in comparison, then is retained or tracked into the less able group. He begins to think of himself as a failure, starting each subsequent grade farther and farther behind, impoverished of opportunity to compete for life's advantages: perhaps part of an academic underclass in the making. Thus when parents must make a decision about holding legal-aged children out of school, they should be asked to consider not only the welfare of their own children but the consequences to the group as a whole.

District Policy Changes

In our original policy study (Shepard and Smith 1985), we recommended to the district only that they counteract the statements made by teachers that retention is beneficial. For a variety of reasons, some of them economic, the district administrators went beyond our recommendations to eliminate two-year kindergartens and discourage retentions. To the best of our knowledge, this policy change resulted in no negative effects on overall achievement, though the staff with intellectual commitments to the affected programs were distressed at their demise.

Although retentions for immaturity are more easily corrected than retentions for low achievement, this action illustrates how district administrators may make changes by fiat. Officially disallowing retentions, however, fails to change the structure of the schools which give rise to the practice. In a district that is organized on the factory model, employing narrow literacy-focused curriculum and demanding accountability by test scores, simply disallowing retention misses the point. The likely result will be something like increased referrals to special education. Or, it is also possible that if a principal disallows retention without providing alternatives, a few teachers may withdraw learning opportunities within their classes from pupils they perceive ought to have been retained. The policy change must be collaborative and accompanied by support for teachers and pupils.

Promotion plus Remediation

For children whose achievement is substantially below some broadly defined grade-level average, the most effective remedy is not retention but promotion accompanied by remediation. Tutoring, summer school, pull-out or within-class individualized instruction have all been shown to be more effective and less costly than retention (with or without special assistance). This solution overcomes teachers' legitimate concerns that the next grade may be too demanding for the unsupported but promoted student. One district we know of has eliminated the pejorative term 'social promotion' and requires the promotion of at-risk pupils be accomplished with a plan that specifies the remediation that each child will receive.

Flunking Grades: A Recapitulation

Postponement of Literacy Demands

The evidence on the effects of early teaching of reading is controversial; nevertheless it has had substantial impact on educational practice, particularly for the disadvantaged. The theory goes that, since disadvantaged children have not had educational support or stimulation at home, the public school must intervene to provide a rigorous regimen of instruction in basic learning skills as well as broad cultural exposure; the earlier, more intensive, and repetitive, the better. The opposing philosophy holds that children bring to school great resources of curiosity and communicative competence that can be used as a basis for a more fulfilling and complete education. This is true for all social classes and ethnic groups. However, building such a program for children (sometimes referred to as whole language education, experiential learning, language experience, and the like) precludes drilling on basic building block skills in early grades. These learning theorists have as their primary goal that the children become readers and writers. Mastery of basic skills such as identifying medial sounds are seen by current psychological theorists as acquired not prior to, but as a result of, interaction in meaningful ways with written texts. Because acquisition of skills comes later, accountability testing for basic skills also needs to be postponed or replaced by assessment of the children's comprehension and appreciation of texts of others and their own. The skills-oriented approach to early learning is consonant with basic skills and mastery testing. But failures at competency tests of narrow skills are inevitable, as children progress at dramatically different rates in the early years. Failures on tests also occur because the teachers have failed to engage the pupils' interests or capabilities, particularly if the only way the teacher knows to individualize is to vary the pace of instruction or form a new ability group.

In one of the low-retaining schools we studied, one teacher explained why she never considered retention. She said that none of the staff became concerned if a particular child still could not read by the end of second grade, so long as he or she was engaged in learning and pursuing particular interests. The second-grade teacher was able to provide an environment that encouraged pursuit of individual learning and interaction with texts. Rarely did such a child fail to learn to read before the end of the third grade. Meanwhile, that child was not made to feel like a failure merely because of failure to master tested skills. It must be noted that, in this particular district, there was no state-wide or district-mandated mastery testing of competencies, so that the teachers

231

were not pressured to produce high average scores or year-to-year growth on achievement tests. Teachers had the luxury of allowing individual paces for learning.

Broadening the Scope and Conception of Accountability

So long as there are narrow tests of competence as the sole arbiter of accountability, there will be retentions. Standardized and other competency tests are frequently used for accountability purposes when their original purpose was to survey typical performance at a grade-level. The public believes naively in tests, which are sometimes poorly written, invalid and discriminatory. As a basis of accountability, tests put emphasis on narrow aspects of the curriculum and ignore broader educational aims. The district that publishes rankings of schools by achievement test scores encourages teachers and principals to neglect parts of the curriculum not covered by the test and even to teach to the test. Research has shown (Cannell, 1987; Koretz, 1988) that *test results* can go up even when real achievement does not, simply because of familiarity with and teaching to the test, selectivity of tests and decisions about who will be tested, and the technical features of standardizing the tests themselves. For these reasons, tests are poor bases for deciding whom to promote or retain.

A broader conception of accountability that involves descriptions of what goes on in classes, teacher judgments about accomplishments of pupils, portfolios of students' work, interviews with students after significant learning events, and the like will provide more authentic accountability to the public for the schools' performance and will lessen the need to show toughness by retaining pupils who perform poorly on poor tests. In addition, teachers will have less interest in rejecting 'factory inputs' because of fear for the year-end test results if they can show by other means that effective education has occurred and progress has been made.

Reconceptualizing School Organization

Because of the salience of the concepts of grade and grade-level instruction, some schools exhibit rigid grade segregation: third graders do third-grade work, and anyone in grade 3 doing second-grade work is deviant and troublesome. We have seen other schools that worked to case grade segregation. For example, one school developed mechanisms for moving children from one grade to another for specific instruction. Third-graders behind in reading but average in other subjects would have reading in a second-grade class and remain with their age-cohorts for the rest of the day. Some had a double dose of reading this way as well. There were as many upward shifts as downward shifts so that no one was stigmatized for moving around. Ungraded primary organizations may serve the same function, unless the decision to retain is merely postponed so that children end up with five years of school before fourth grade. In another school, teachers initiated a program in which the pupil who was a candidate for retention was promoted. But the teacher into whose class the child was promoted signed a statement that he or she would individualize instruction and provide an appropriate educational experience for that child. Groups of teachers then monitored the subsequent progress of the promoted child.

Acceleration

In school systems where retention is used, there must be developed equivalent mechanisms for accelerating pupils retained at an earlier stage in their careers. This recommendation comes from the widely shared experience that retained children are bigger and older than their classmates, and are bored by an instructional experience designed for younger children. Observation of sixth-grade classes, particularly in disadvantaged schools, poignantly reveals these pupils, some of whom are recruited by the teacher as teacher aides, runners or enforcers. In some cases, whatever characteristic led to the decision to retain, it has been overcome, and the children are socially and psychologically ready to rejoin their age cohorts. But then the staff argues that the child has not had the specific instruction in the grade into which he or she could be accelerated, so no action is taken. Special intensive individual or small group instruction could be offered at that point.

Levin (1987) described such a program for disadvantaged pupils. He noted that schools responded to the failure (low achievement and retention) of disadvantaged pupils by relegating them to impoverished rather than enriched educational experiences. What these schools mean by remediation is described this way:

> By deliberately slowing the pace of instruction to a crawl, the existing intervention model emphasizes endless repetition of

material through drill-and-practice. The result is that the school experience of disadvantaged youths lacks vitality, and their slow rate of progress reinforces our low expectations. The programs omit interesting applications and assignments in favor of drudgery. The premise is that students must learn fundamentals before they can be offered anything more challenging. As a result, both language and mathematics skills are virtually without substance, emphasizing mechanics over content. Such a joyless educational experience diminishes the possibility that the child will view school positively ... The achievement gap between advantaged and disadvantaged students will grow. (p. 20).

Although Levin did not specifically mention retention as part of the typical remedial program for low-achieving disadvantaged pupils, we believe that his analysis applies. Indeed, his characterization of existing intervention models may even explain the connection between retention and subsequent dropping out. Levin proposes a transition school, one that aims to close the achievement gap within a specified time so that the child will re-enter the mainstream prior to secondary school. The program within this school is characterized by 'high expectations, deadlines by which they will be performing at grade level, stimulating instructional programs, planning by the educational staff who will offer the program, and the use of all available parental and community resources' (p. 20). The instruction is fast-paced, developed to flow from the interests of the children, meaningful rather than mechanical, using cooperative learning and peer-tutoring, and oriented around ordinary problems and events. Because the program is outside the structure of the schools, participation in it by both pupils and staff confers high rather than low status. Parental involvement is strongly encouraged.

Conclusion

The alternative courses of action described here confront, elude or soften the ordinary structure of the public schools. The age-cohort grade, grade segregation, competency testing as the basis of promotion and accountability demand contribute to the practice of retention. To some, retention is a way of demonstrating rigorous standards. To children, retention is flunking, an indication that they themselves are deficient. For the system of public schools, retention functions as a way to preserve the structure of efficient, grade-level production while enhancing the meritocratic image. But because retentions do nothing to promote the achievement of the affected individuals or the average of the group as a whole, and because the disadvantaged and minority children are most apt to be affected, retention should best be thought of as educational waste and a denial of life chances to those who most need the benefits of education. Retention has high cost and virtually no value, save the public relations advantages for the schools. Those children who are retained or otherwise failed by public schools are thereby deprived of rightful learning opportunities and, more important, opportunities to succeed in life beyond school.

Note

1   One study cited to the contrary was reported by Sandoval and Hughes (1982). They identified three groups of retained first graders: (i) those moderately 'successful' on achievement but not adjustment; (ii) those successful on both; and (iii) those failing on both. Through multiple regression and other correlational methods, the researchers were able to 'predict' which children had successful retentions, although no cross-validation or confirmation was attempted. Correlates of successful retention included relatively high achievement and high self-concept, perhaps implying that the most successful retainees are those who need the treatment the least. The most damning finding from this study, however, was that even the most successful retainees were no better than promoted controls on a variety of outcome measures taken at the end of first grade. Therefore we feel justified in our statement that prediction of which children will benefit from retention is currently beyond the ability of educators.

References

BREWER, M. B. and COLLINS, B. E. (Eds) (1981) *Scientific Inquiry and the Social Sciences*, San Francisco, CA, Jossey-Bass.

CAMPBELL, D. T. (1986) 'Science's social system of validity-enhancing collective belief changes and the problems of the social sciences', in FISKE, D. W. and SHWEDER, R. A. (Eds) *Metatheory in Social Science*, Chicago, IL, University of Chicago Press.

CANNELL, J. J. (1987) *Nationally Normed Elementary Achievement Testing in America's Public Schools: How All Fifty States are above the National Average*, Daniels, WV, Friends for Education.

COLES, G. S. (1978) 'The learning disabilities test battery: Empirical and social issues', *Harvard Educational Review*, 48, pp. 313–40.

HANNIFIN, M. J. (1983) *Review of Light's Retention Scale*, Accession Number An-09062160, Buros Institute Database (Search label MMYD), Bibliographic Retrieval Services Inc. (DRS).
HELLER, K. A., HOLTZMAN, W. H. and MESSICK, S. (Eds) (1982) *Placing Children in Special Education: A Strategy for Equity*, Washington, DC, National Academy Press.
KATZ, M. B. (1975) *Class, Bureaucracy and the Schools*, New York, Praeger.
KORETZ, D. (1988) 'Arriving in Lake Wobegon: Are standardized tests exaggerating achievement and distorting instruction?', *American Educator*, 12, pp. 8–15.
LABAREE, D. F. (1984) 'Setting the standard, Alternative policies for student promotion', *Harvard Educational Review*, 54, pp. 67–87.
LEVIN, H. M. (1987) 'Accelerated schools for disadvantaged students', *Educational Leadership*, 45, pp. 19–21.
LIEBERMAN, L. M. (1980) 'A decision-making model for in-grade retention (non-promotion)', *Journal of Learning Disabilities*, 13, pp. 268–72.
LIGHT, H. W. (1981) *Light's Retention Scale — Revised Edition*, Novato, CA, Academic Therapy.
MORGAN, G. (1986) *Images of Organization*, Beverly Hills, CA, Sage.
ROSE, J. S., MEDWAY, F. J., CANTRELL, V. L. and MARUS, S. H. (1983) 'A fresh look at the retention-promotion controversy', *Journal of School Psychology*, 21, pp. 201–11.
ROSENBAUM, J. (1976) *Making Inequality: The Hidden Curriculum of High School Tracking*, New York, John Wiley.
SANDOVAL, J. (1982) 'Light's Retention Scale does not predict success in first-grade retainees', *Psychology in the Schools*, 19, pp. 310–14.
SANDOVAL, J. and HUGHES, G. P. (1982) 'Outcomes of first grade non-promotion', paper presented at the annual convention of the American Psychological Association, Washington, DC, August.
SHEPARD, L. A. and SMITH, M. L. (1985) *Boulder Valley Kindergarten Study: Retention Practices and Retention Effects*, Boulder, CO, Boulder Valley Public Schools.
SHEPARD, L. A. and SMITH, M. L. (1986) 'Synthesis of research on school readiness and kindergarten retention', *Educational Leadership*, 44, pp. 78–86.
SHEPARD, L. A., SMITH, M. L. and VOJIR, C. (1983) 'Characteristics of pupils identified as learning disabled', *American Educational Research Journal*, 20, pp. 309–32.
SMITH, M. L. (1982) *How Educators Decide Who Is Learning Disabled*, Springfield, IL, Charles C. Thomas Press.
WATSON, D. (1979) 'The relative efficiency of Light's Retention Scale in identifying children for retention', paper presented at the annual convention of the National Association of School Psychologists, San Diego, March.
WISE, A. E. (1979) *Legislated Learning*, Berkeley, CA, University of California Press.

Index

ability grouping, 5, 220
acceleration, 233–4
accountability, 223–5, 227, 232
achievement
  and dropping out, *see* dropping out
administrators
  see also principals
  and retention, 208, 209
Arizona
  retention in, 8–9
Austin Independent School District
  dropping out in, 37–8, 43, 45–52
  retention and dropping out in, 43, 45–52, 205
  Office of Research and Evaluation in, 46

back-to-basics, 1
basic skills, 3–4
Bennett, William, 175
Bloomington (Minn.)
  dropping out in, 36
Brevard County public schools, 70
Byrnes, D., 11, 108–31, 206

California Achievement Test (CAT), 35
Carnegie Commission
  Task Force Report on Teaching as a Profession, 196
causal modeling, 34, 35, 43–58
  limitations of, 57–8
CGI
  see Cognitively Guided Instruction

Chicago
  dropping out in, 39–43, 52–4
  school entrance age in, 52–3
Chicago Public Schools
  dropping out and retention in, 52–4
child development
  teachers' beliefs about, 12, 136–9, 207–8, 210, 217
cognitive-constructivist approach
  to learning, 180–98, 218
cognitive dissonance theory, 103–4
Cognitively-Guided Instruction
  (CGI) group, 188–90, 192, 195, 196–7
Colorado
  kindergarten retention in, 79–107
competency testing, 1, 2–3, 6, 12, 151–73, 224, 231, 232
Comprehensive Test of Basic Skills, (CTBS), 81, 88, 89–91, 94, 105
CTBS
  see Comprehensive Test of Basic Skills
Current Index to Journals in Education, 18
curriculum
  as linear, 225
  and standardization, 223

Dade County (Fla.)
  dropping out in, 35
developmental kindergarten, 64, 65
  see also kindergarten retention
Dissertation Abstracts International, 18

237

Index

double retentions, 8–9, 74–5, 157–8, 168
  see also retention
dropping out
  and absenteeism, 45
  and achievement, 39–43, 44, 46, 49, 53, 58
  and causal modeling, 34, 35, 43–58
  characteristics of students, 36
  and discipline, 45
  and ethnicity, 43–4, 46, 49, 51–2
  and gender, 43, 49, 51–2
  reasons given for, 58–60, 61
  and retention, 10, 34–63
  and socioeconomic status, 43–4, 46
  and student attitudes, 45

education
  and economic crisis, 1
Education Index, 18
educational excellence movement, 1
educational reform, 1, 12, 151–73, 174–201, 208
  in 1980s, 1
  and public opinion, 172, 208
  standards in, 151–73
  and teacher beliefs, 174–201
  teachers and, 196–8
Ellwein, M.C. and Glass, G.V., 12, 151–73, 175–6, 179, 208
ethnicity
  and dropping out, 43–4, 46, 49, 51–2
  and retention, 6–7, 168, 171, 180, 209, 210–211, 227

Florida
  retention rates in, 9
flunking
  see also retention
  definition of, 1

Gallup surveys, 4
gender
  and dropping out, 43, 49, 51–2
  and retention, 6–7, 168, 171, 180, 227
Gesell Developmental Test, 68–9
Gesell tests, 68–9, 72, 91
Glass, G.V.
  see Ellwein and Glass
graded education, 4–5, 220–3
  history of, 4–5
graduation tests, 2–3
Gredler, G.R., 66–7, 75, 80, 104
Greensville (Va)
  promotion system in, 3
Grissom, J.B. and Shepard, L.A., 10, 34–63, 205–6

Handbook of Research in Teaching, 174
High School and Beyond survey, 45, 59
Holmes, C.T., 10, 16–33, 34, 65, 66, 204, 205
Holmes, C.T. and Matthews, K.M., 10, 16, 17, 18, 23, 28
House, E.R., 12, 202–13, 219, 227

Individual Education Program (IEP), 158
Iowa Test of Basic Skills (ITBS), 46, 49, 50, 51, 188
ITBS
  see Iowa Test of Basic Skills

Jackson, 10
James, William, 197
Japan
  lack of retention in, 210

Katz, M.B. 224–5
kindergarten retention, 4, 10–11, 64–78, 79–107, 132–50, 154, 155–6, 158, 159, 160, 163, 166–7, 169, 177–8, 182, 205, 215–16, 220, 225
  see also retention
  academic effects of, 79–107
  and academic readiness, 72, 75–6, 105, 216
  affective outcomes of, 106–7
  and age, 91–2

238

aims of, 72, 105
and conceptions of learning, 182
effects of, 10–11, 64–67, 94–104
emotional effects of, 79–107
and immaturity, 72, 75–6, 91, 105, 216
internal and external validity of research on, 92–4
increases in, 65
methodological issues in research on, 71–5, 80, 92–4
negative effects of, 11, 70–1, 75–6, 80, 92–3, 96–107, 205
no difference results regarding, 67–9, 89–91, 92–3, 105, 106–7
and outcome measures, 11, 79, 87–8
parent ratings in research on, 94–104
and personality characteristics, 91, 106
positive effects of, 69–70, 89–90, 91, 92–3, 96–104
and promotional gates program, 154, 155–6, 158, 159, 160, 163, 166–7, 169
reasons for, 65
review of research on, 66–76
sample used in Colorado research on, 81–7
and self-concept, 106–7
and subsequent retentions, 74; see also double retentions
and teachers' beliefs, 132–50, 177–8
teacher ratings and, 88–92
test score results and, 88–92
Kirkwood School District, 69

learners
images of, 217
learning
and cognitive conceptions, 180–4
cognitive-constructivist conception of, 182–95
and 'empty vessels' model, 179
and mastery-learning model, 179
network theory of, 180–1
skills-based approaches to, 231
legal sanctions
against retention, 12, 212–13, 227
Levin, H.M., 233–4
Light, H.W., 226
Linn, Robert, 203
loose coupling
in educational organizations, 171–2
Los Angeles
dropping out in, 36

Master's Thesis in Education, 18
mathematics
and children's construction of knowledge, 185, 192–5
children's informal knowledge of, 183, 192
children's invented strategies in, 183–4, 193–4
and cognitive-constructivist theories, 184–96
and learning theories, 181–95
teaching of, 184–96
Matthews, K.M.
see Holmes and Matthews
Maxwell, W.H., 17
meta-analysis, 16–33
definition of, 18–19
Metropolitan Readiness Tests, 71
minorities
see ethnicity
Mississippi
retention and dropping out in, 34

Nation at Risk, A, 1
National Academy of Education, 2–3
National Council for Teachers of Mathematics, 194
National Longitudinal Survey, 59
New York City
promotional gates programs in, 3, 12, 202–13

Index

overage
    and retention, 47–8
    and dropping out, 34–63

Palmer, F.B., 178–9
parents
    and attitudes to retention, 11, 79–80, 88, 94–104, 105, 106–7, 108, 110–14, 117–18, 126–7, 130, 206–7, 208, 228–9
    and withholding children from kindergarten, 228–9
Pasco School District (Wash.)
    dropping out in, 36–7
Peter W. v. San Francisco Unified School District, 2
Peterson, P.L., 12, 174–201, 218, 219, 225, 227
pre-kindergarten, 65
    see also kindergarten retention
principals
    and attitudes to retention, 108, 109, 110–14, 130, 206
promotion
    at district level, 12, 151–73
    setting of standards for, 154–63
        and appearance of standards, 162–3
        and practical issues, 161–2
        and technical issues, 161
promotional gates programs, 3, 12, 151–73, 176, 179, 202–13, 221, 224
    consequences of, 164–70
    disadvantages of, 224
    evaluation of, 168–70, 171–2
    origins in one district of, 153–8; see also New York City, promotional gates programs in
    and promotion-retention decisions, 165–72, 176, 179

Raths, James, 203
readiness rooms, 65
    see also kindergarten retention
reading
    inability, 2

remediation
    see retention, and remediation
Research in Education, 18
retention
    see also double retentions; kindergarten retention and academic achievement, 17, 20–2, 24, 25, 26, 27, 39–43, 44, 75, 109, 180, 204–5, 215, 230
    and acceleration, 233–4
    and accountability, 224–5, 232
    administrators and, 208, 209; see also principals
    and age, 74–5
    aims of, 234–5
    alternatives to, 12, 112, 113–14, 174–201, 209–13, 225–35
    attitudes to, 11, 108–31
    characteristics of students selected for, 44, 112, 113, 121–5, 130, 206
    cost of, 109, 203, 204
    dissemination of research results on, 227
    district level policy on, 12, 151–73, 212, 230
    and dropping out, 10, 34–63, 205–6, 211, 215, 219; see also dropping out
    and effect size, 18–19
    and emotional problems, 205
    and ethnicity, 6–7, 168, 171, 180, 209, 210–11, 227
    and gender, 6–7, 168, 171, 180, 227
    and ideology, 209–11, 219
    and immaturity, 109, 230
    in kindergarten, see kindergarten retention
    legal sanctions against, 12, 212–13, 227
    methodological issues in research on, 71–5, 80, 92–4, 134–6
    misleading data on, 147–8
    negative effects of, 10, 19–24, 26–8, 70–1, 130, 145–7, 175, 203, 204–6, 209, 210, 215,

216–17, 226–7, 235; *see also* kindergarten retention, negative effects of
in nineteenth century, 5
no difference effect of, 67–9
notification of students selected for, 118, 126, 207, 217
and overage students, 47–8
and parental action, 228–9; *see also* parents
parents' attitudes to, 11, 79–80, 88, 94–104, 105, 106–7, 108, 110–14, 126–7, 130, 206
and personal adjustment, 22–3, 27
policy implications of research on, 12, 202–13
popular opinions of, 4, 113, 216–17
positive effects of, 23–6, 27–8, 69–70, 140–3, 205; *see also* kindergarten retention, positive effects of
possible action against, 211–13
principals' attitudes to, 108, 109, 110–14, 130, 206
prior to first grade, *see* kindergarten retention
and promotional gates program, *see* promotional gates programs
and propositional knowledge, 147–50
public opinion on, 4, 11, 113, 109, 216–17
and public relations, 222, 235
rates of, 6–9
and rating scales, 226
reasons for, 111, 113, 118–19, 121–5, 127–8, 130, 147–50, 171, 175–6, 178, 206, 207–8
and remediation, 25–6, 28, 66–7, 205, 230, 233–4
responsibility for decisions on, 111–12, 113, 157
reviews of research on, 10, 16–33, 34–63
and school organization, 148–9, 232–3

and school structure, 148–9, 232–3
and self-concept, 10, 11, 23, 76, 215
and self-esteem, 10, 112
and social structure, 222
and socioeconomic status, 109
and staffing model, 226
statistics on, 6–9, 18–28, 35–61
students attitudes to, 108, 114–25, 129–30, 216
and student motivation, 109
surveys of views on, 110–30
teachers' attitudes to, 108, 110–14, 125–30, 168–9, 206
and teachers beliefs, 11–13, 132–50, 174–201, 216–25
and teachers' knowledge, 191–5
Review of Educational Research, 10, 16, 174

St Louis
dropping out in, 38–9
Santa Clara Inventory, 82, 83, 84, 86–7
school districts
and retention, 12, 151–73, 212, 230
school organization
reconceptualization of, 232–3
schools
as bureaucratic, 223–5
and centralized administration, 223
curriculum in, 223
and dropping out, 10, 34,–63
enrollment data for, 6
factory model of, 223–5, 230
and grade retention, 223–4
meritocracy in, 222–3, 235
and retention, *passim*
Science of Education, The, 178
SES
see socioeconomic staus
sex
see gender
Shepard, L.A., 10–11, 64–78, 206
see also Grissom and Shepard; Smith and Shepard

241

Index

Shepard, L.A. and Smith, M.L., 1–15, 79–107, 205
Smith, M.L., 12, 132–50, 175, 176, 177–8, 179, 207–8
 see also Shepard and Smith
Smith, M.L. and Shepard, L.A., 214–36
social promotion
 end of, 1–4, 12, 151–73, 203, 208, 216, 230
 in twentieth century, 5
socioeconomic status
 and dropping out, 43–4, 46
State Normal School, Fredonia (N.Y.), 178–9
students
 and achievement in mathematics, 187
 and attitudes to retention, 108, 114–25, 129–30
 characteristics of those selected for retention, 112, 113, 121–5, 130, 206
 classification as 'masters' and 'non-masters', 158–60. 172, 179–80, 208
 and denial of retention, 115–16, 206
 and negative experiences of retention, 120–1
 and notification of retention decisions, 118, 126, 207, 217
 and parents' reactions about retention, 117–18, 206–7; *see also* parents
 as precocious, 222–3
 and retention, *passim*
 teacher images of, 178–84
 and teachers' beliefs concerning learning, 174–201

TAP
 see Tests of Achievement and Proficiency
teacher training, 211
teachers
 and action research, 211, 227
 and attitudes to retention, 108, 110–14, 125–30, 168–9, 206, 207, 210
 and autonomy, 223
 and belief, 218
 and beliefs and knowledge of students' abilities, 190–5
 and beliefs about learning, 12, 174–201
 and beliefs about retention, 11–13, 139–47, 174–201, 216–25
 and changes in conceptions of learning, 188–95
 and child development, 12, 136–9, 207–8, 210, 217
 and classification of students as 'master' and 'non-master', 158–60, 172, 179–80, 208
 and classroom practices, 186–91, 195–6
 clinical interviews with, 133–50
 and cognitive-constructivist conceptions of learning, 184–95, 218
 and conditional benefits of retention, 142–3
 and diagnostic-prescriptive approach, 137–8
 and heterogeneity, 149–50
 and homogeneous classes, 149–50, 219–20
 images of, 195–8
 and images of learners, 178–84, 217
 as interactionists, 138
 and interactions with parents of retained children, 144–5
 as knowers, learners and thoughtful professionals, 195–6
 and knowledge, 218
 and long-term effects of retention, 218–19
 and misleading data on retention, 147–8
 as 'nativists', 136–7, 139, 140, 142, 144, 177–8, 179–80, 207–8

242

and negative effects of retention, 145–7
as 'non-nativists', 137–9, 178
and positive attitudes to retention, 128–9, 140–2, 147–50, 207, 208, 210, 216–17
and practical knowledge, 133, 147–50
as remediationists, 137, 138, 208
and research results, 196–8, 227
and retention practices and beliefs about development, 139
and school structure, 148–9
and student achievement, 187
and treatment of retained children, 127

Tests of Achievement and Proficiency (TAP), 46, 50
Texas
  see also Austin Independent School District
  school entrance age in, 47–8
transition programs, 64, 65, 66–7, 68–73, 75–6, 86, 104–5, 205, 215–16, 219–30
  see also kindergarten retention

USA Today, 34

Waterford School District (pseudonym), 151–73, 175–6, 179–80